MEDIUM COOL

A candid of Mrs. Bates, the watchful hostess of the Bates Motel, in Alfred Hitchcock's *Psycho*. The 1960s have begun.

MEDIUM COOL

The Movies of the 1960s

ETHAN MORDDEN

 ALFRED A. KNOPF • NEW YORK • 1990

THIS IS A BORZOI BOOK
PUBLISHED BY ALFRED A. KNOPF, INC.

Copyright © 1990 by Ethan Mordden
All rights reserved under International and Pan-American Copyright
Conventions. Published in the United States by Alfred A. Knopf, Inc., New York,
and simultaneously in Canada by Random House of Canada Limited, Toronto.
Distributed by Random House, Inc., New York.

Library of Congress Cataloging-in-Publication Data
Mordden, Ethan, [date]
Medium cool : the movies of the 1960s / Ethan Mordden. — 1st ed.
p.   cm.
ISBN 0-394-57157-6
1. Motion pictures—United States—History.   I. Title.
PN1993.5.U6M655   1990
791.43'0973'09046—dc20   90-53105   CIP

Manufactured in the United States of America
First Edition

To

Robert Gottlieb,

with thanks

The author wishes to acknowledge the aid and comfort of his Union Jill agent, Joan Brandt; of copyeditor Mildred Maynard, as deft and comprehensive as ever; of Karen Mugler, the Annie Oakley of the production editorial department, spang on target; of Antoinette White, liaison between the orders of the house and the delirious vanities of the outside world; and of editor Vicky Wilson, in respect and fondness and keen camaraderie.

CONTENTS

MEDIUM COOL

Mrs. Bates Is
Watching You

The camera pans the city skyline, objective, remote, lipping the office towers as a non-smoker demonstrates the ingestion of cigarette smoke. Touch me not. Hollywood's establishing shots traditionally treated the American urban landscape with *feeling*: as in the stimulating melee of personal and economic ambitions that Warner Brothers gives us in its Broadway backstagers; or in the penthouse dazzle of Metro-Goldwyn-Mayer's Joan Crawford rags-to-riches sagas; or in the facetious chic of a Paramount society comedy, wherein Dizzy Dame Mary Boland is selfish but amusing and Depression Debutante Claudette Colbert has irony. Those were the days. We knew where we stood: because Hollywood knew.

But *this* camera has no feeling, and this city, so far, lacks meaning. There is no point of view, no information guiding our perception. We get an American town, a somewhere, so plain and big and empty that even in black and white we know we're not missing any of its colors. This is a place of boredom and money where people can't have what they want. "Phoenix, Arizona," a title tells us, flashed over the view. "Friday, December the eleventh. Two forty-three P.M." The year, by the way, is 1960.

As the camera continues its apparently aimless survey of Phoenix, it moves closer to the architecture, pulling down to approach a nondescript building and enter a window under partly drawn blinds. Inside, a shirtless man is wiping his chest with a towel. A woman is on the bed, in bra and slip. From their dialogue we gather that both are unmarried (he is divorced), that they are lovers with no immediate hope of marriage (his debts stand in their way), and that this is the middle of a working day and the two have slipped into a hot-sheets hotel for a quickie.

The complete lack of moral scrutiny in the way this material is presented is shocking for a Hollywood film, American in its bluntness but European in its tolerance. One thing Americans knew how to do by this time was to delimit the use of sex in their cinema, especially regarding when and where one was allowed to have it, most especially if one wasn't married to one's partner. After 1933, when the halfhearted Production Code was revitalized and absolutely applied to Hollywood's product, sex in American film was something that occurred offscreen, only at night, and involved a couple married to each other, preferably Greer Garson or someone equally adept at keeping urges in their place. Yes, in 1953 there was *From Here to Eternity*'s ecstatic celebration of adultery on the beach, with Burt Lancaster and Deborah Kerr, but that was an operatic excursion, sex, soaring surf, daredevil passion, scenic Hawaii, and mad sad wonder *a grande orchestra*. It was exceptional, defiant—not merely another hour in another day of an American city, as we get in Phoenix. It is as if Hollywood no longer needs to defy, no longer regards the breaking of taboo as exceptional.

Furthermore, the utter lack of guilt we find in this hotel room ignores the protocols of hypocrisy that Hollywood traditionally observed. It is a brazen realism: two people doing what comes naturally without first consulting the Production Code to see what has been declared plausible. Have they no shame?

True, that opening voyage past the window blinds suggests an invasion of secret—perhaps seedy—territory. But is this not *our* reading, conditioned by what we know Hollywood allowed? The tone of the scene itself is quite uninflected. What we do sense, and fairly, in the passage through the window, is an unprecedented frankness: a looking into human affairs with an honesty that will no longer tolerate restrictions. The film, by the way, is *Psycho*.

In the summer of 1960, when it was new, *Psycho* was celebrated for among other things its novelty of killing off its star* Janet Leigh relatively early in the story—not for her premarital sensuality, nor even for embezzling money so she and John Gavin can get married and stop trysting in nondescript buildings (or anywhere) in Phoenix, but simply because Leigh runs into bad luck. In fact, she changes her mind in midflight, and is planning to return to Phoenix with the stolen money at the time of her murder. Anyway, Alfred Hitchcock was never an adherent of Production Code mentality—never had to be, because his forte was narration through impression and atmosphere, too speculative for Code honchos to grasp. Hitchcock eludes. Those who come back to *Psycho* after a long absence are often amazed at the extraordinarily suspenseful feeling of the first forty minutes—all the more so because the action is so ordinary. Yes, Leigh does drive off with a purloined fortune, but in manners and dialogue the first third of *Psycho* gives us nothing we couldn't encounter anywhere in America—a vain, deluded office colleague (daughter Pat Hitchcock, as it happens; had the Master no loyalty, no tenderness? None), a dully prudent boss, a vulgar millionaire, a suspicious patrolman, a wiggy hotelier . . . ah, *there's* the rub. The host of the dangerous place, Anthony Perkins, is, from the first and very unmistakably, way over the top, fidgety, hesitant, ambivalent—do I, don't I? Traditional Hitchcock villains (or whatever they are: the troublesome people) are indistinguishable from the populace. This makes the false guiltiness of the traditional Hitchcock innocent (Robert Donat in *The Thirty-nine Steps,* Robert Cummings in *Saboteur,* Cary Grant in *North by Northwest,* Jon Finch in *Frenzy*) all the more disturbing. Nothing is what it seems. But then Hitchcock had long been a maker of disturbing art, art that challenges rather than exalts its public. Hitchcock concedes us happy endings—alleviative resolutions, anyway. But he doesn't believe in happy as a rule, not in the way that such directors as D. W. Griffith, Frank Capra, and George Cukor did. Hitchcock had predecessors in John Ford, King Vidor, John Cromwell, and Josef von Sternberg. He is not the first ironist in Hollywood history. But he is perhaps its first absurdist, the one who tells us that there is no safe place, that we can encounter the murderously bizarre anywhere in Amer-

---

*Technically, Anthony Perkins, Vera Miles, and John Gavin are the top-billed names, to brusquely shifting graphics and Bernard Herrmann's shrieking *sinfonia.* Still, Leigh was the best-known member of the cast. We get a hint of the unique nature of her role in her credit: "and Janet Leigh as Marion Crane."

ica, even at a quiet motel on our way from Phoenix to self-discovery. Especially at a quiet motel.

Hollywood had been proclaiming the United States as the ultimate safe place from Day One: a land of community, vision, love. Frank Capra showed us that if we but repress Edward Arnold, yea, we would know paradise, or something more practical: democracy. Now, in *Psycho,* Hitchcock shows us—far more profoundly than in any earlier film—that there can be no safe place, because the world does not consist of the good, the wise, and the generous taking on the wicked, the unreasonable, and the selfish. The world consists of dense psychologies of desire, fear, and resentment in a state of constant explosion. The world is not safe, because people are dangerous. Not only crooks and loonies but all people. A mother can be dangerous. *Psycho*'s mother, Mrs. Bates, is a ferociously self-righteous monster who "protects" son Anthony Perkins from Janet Leigh by stabbing her into messes in the famous shower scene—famous as much for the shock of the violence (in 1960) as for the realization (later in the decade, in the context of the extremely graphic violence that *Psycho* helped unleash in film) that it is surprise and razor-keen editing that give the scene its terror, not slasher technology. We never even see the knife touch Leigh. No, we do see it. It just wasn't filmed.

Granted, this mother figure turns out to be Perkins himself in an act of split personality. The real Mrs. Bates rests in peace, stuffed. But what kind of mother must she have been when quick, to have engendered such terrifying impersonation? What kind of people are there in the world? The Hollywood of the 1920s, '30s, '40s, and '50s prescribes rather than reflects, as if trying to inspire or even bully its public into changing into beings that moviemakers can admire. Griffith demands tolerance of you, Raoul Walsh guts, Howard Hawks loyalty and wit. If you can't be Clark Gable or Marlene Dietrich, can't you at least achieve Jimmy Stewart, Myrna Loy? A shopgirl can be a princess—Joan Crawford made it, didn't she?

In the 1960s, however, writers, actors, and directors suddenly retire the traditional character models. They begin to observe rather than idealize the world. To put it roughly, for the first fifty years the movies are about romance. Nothing happens in the 1950s. Then, from 1960 on, the movies are about reality.

Alfred Hitchcock seems to have been the one to realize and implement this, the director who first saw that the 1960s had begun. Certainly, *Psycho* is a breakaway event in his career. Aesthetically, the film signals no departure for Hitchcock: its elements of masquerade, deception, and paranoia are familiar Hitchcockian elements. Its ability to generate a menace of insecurity even without any clear evidence of danger, as in the half hour or so that leads up to Leigh's murder, is typical Hitchcock. There are the droll double meanings, eloquent only on second viewing, as in Perkins's "Mother . . . what's the word? . . . isn't quite herself today," and, "She just goes a little mad sometimes."

But as a cultural symbol *Psycho* stands out from all that has preceded it in Hitchcock's oeuvre. Simply the initiating act of the Master thrusting up the hotel blinds on real life startles beyond his subtlest earlier probings. Hitchcock before *Psycho* might be essentialized in a single shot in *The Thirty-nine Steps,* after Mr. Memory's final performance, when the police close in on his murderer and, enough shown, Hitchcock holds on a long shot of the stage as the curtains lyrically fall together. This is Hitchcock the director of *theatre,* the storyteller of all the world's a stage. His villains are performers, his heroes people who suddenly find themselves trapped in culprits' roles, cast as murderers, spies, saboteurs. But the Hitchcock of *Psycho* raises his curtain on a back-street sex break in a shabby hotel room, and Perkins's Norman Bates, for all the flamboyance of his impersonations (of his mother and of himself), is no thespian but a demented nerd. He just goes a little mad sometimes.

The 1960s had begun. Overnight, everywhere one looks in American film, creators are turning against received notions of moviemaking. Like Hitchcock in *Psycho,* they *break* away, force the issue, rebel—against the Fascism of studio heads, the oppression of the Production Code, the dreary gleam of the generation of stars chosen to succeed Gable and Crawford and Davis, the routine of genre. Perhaps the enforced conformity of the American 1950s, combined with the collapse of the studio structures, energized the rebellion. Is it a coincidence that Senator Joseph McCarthy and MGM's Mrs. Bates, L. B. Mayer, both died in 1957?

Bosses like Mayer saw themselves as archons of a patriarchal, racist, sexist, virtually tribal America, their vision enforced by their control of ninety percent of the nation's theatres. The moguls not only ran the business as authoritarians but took on America's authoritarian world-view—collaborating, for instance, in the Production Code censorship set up in 1934 and in the House Committee on Un-American Activities' purge of leftists and independents. Hollywood must uphold American values. In hard times it must strengthen morale. In good times it must warn against the danger of losing one's hardness, of tolerating or even accommodating anti-American values.

Of course, "American values" is a variable term, as producer Samuel Goldwyn learned in making *The Best Years of Our Lives* (1946), a saga of servicemen's return and reacclimatization. The title is not meant ironically. We are supposed to believe, by the end, that the postwar era, now and here in the United States, will be a golden age. Yet the film does not stint on certain tense realities, such as the terrifyingly aggrieved look on the face of a mother as she greets her son, a paratrooper who has lost both his hands; or the veteran's difficulty in finding work; or banks' reluctance to grubstake propertyless vets. Perhaps this was a Communist plot to demoralize the nation, this determination to reveal and confront. *The Best Years of Our Lives* was not only controversial; it was, to its makers' surprise, dangerous. On the radio, its director William Wyler actually expressed doubt that any more such movies would—as he put it—"be allowed."

Be allowed. One must understand life in the American 1950s in order to understand film in the 1960s—though anyone who did not live through America's postwar years would have trouble picturing its expanse and depth of repression, not only the libel campaigns and blacklisting but the heedlessly enthusiastic assaults on libraries as hotbeds of insidious propaganda. Tolstoy! Steinbeck! Robin Hood! "He robbed the rich and gave to the poor," said the pouncing Mrs. Thomas J. White, of the Indiana State Textbook Commission. "That's the Communist line. It's just a smearing of law and order." American life had erected a kind of Stalinism, in which any independent thinking, on any subject, led to charges of treason. Americans were being turned into an overwhelmingly consistent people with, supposedly, one great set of likes and dislikes— something the community of Hollywood should have found easy, then, to address and hold. One size of film would fit all.

But just as there really is no one American people, the community of Hollywood was a myth and always has been. For decades, a chance gathering of Jewish moguls and Irish directors, oiks and intellectuals, liberal writers and conservative directors, Shakespearean Brits and Bible Belt peasants, the gifted and the opportunistic, and the amazed and the hungry all shared at least some sense of mission despite their differences, perhaps because the movies really were subversive—at first. Forcing open a closed and sectionalized culture, Hollywood marshaled a continent into the great American movie audience, diverse in origin yet monolithically motivated, like Hollywood itself. However, as the movies became acculturated, a national habit, the business began to grow conservative. HUAC's attack utterly rent Hollywood as a community, while the rise of television and the dismantling of the studios' theatre empires (because of a 1948 Supreme Court antitrust ruling) threatened Hollywood as an industry. Look at it as a western: Frank Capra and John Ford shoot it out on the Main Street of Andy Hardy's Carvel, Idaho, on a steadily diminishing budget.

The center broke, all the center of Hollywood, all the lying and hoping and arranging and feuding that kept the business solid in the Studio Age. The movie business shattered. The big studios tottered and contracted, and surviving stars and directors set up independent production companies and found themselves, overnight, their own moguls. No longer need they accommodate anyone else's idea of what was appropriate, seemly, healthy in subject matter and its treatment, in characterization and casting, in what was heard and what was seen. Stars and directors had run the movies back in the days of Old Hollywood, when Little Mary and Doug, Gloria Swanson, Charlie Chaplin, Cecil B. DeMille, and Saint D.W. made all their own decisions, business and artistic. Producers always had business power, but by 1929, and the disruption caused by the transition into sound, the producers had seized artistic power as well, virtually driving out all who stood in their way. (Note that of the above list of Old Hollywood leaders, only DeMille survived into the talkie era on an energy level and of a reputation comparable to those of his silent years.) Now, in the 1950s, in another great disruption, with the old moguls dead, replaced, or in jeopardy and their theatre monopolies broken up to allow independent production to share the nation's screens, the stars and directors reclaimed the power once held by Little Mary and Chaplin.

Some of them, no doubt, had always wanted to take charge of their careers, and would have done so long before had the producers not so thoroughly entrenched themselves. Some others may have been inspired to go independent in horror at the way Hollywood caved in to—even welcomed—McCarthyism. Repression disheartens; it also radicalizes. Some simply wanted a bigger share of the profits on their films. Some, in league with the bold young writers spoiled by the freedoms of television, sought to bolster their careers with unusual projects unthinkable under the rule of the iron moguls.

Whatever their motivation, the stars, directors, and writers who spent the 1950s reordering Hollywood into a network of small self-starting units were true revolutionaries. They did not cause the convulsion that overturned the system. The Supreme Court did. Television did. McCarthyism did. Hollywood itself did, in the fat-cat smugness of the unprecedently lucrative war years, which led the moguls to believe they could have business as usual forever—the six or seven years following the end of World War II must be, technologically and aesthetically, the least creative in the history of the movies.

But the revolutionaries of the 1950s did reinvent the system by which movies were made. We must remember, however, that this was at first strictly an artistic revolution, not a political one. "The 1960s" is our 1848, our 1917, buzzword, myth, and article of faith at once. Yet the films that establish the arrival of the New Age are almost never political in content. Like *Psycho,* they explore a vast new liberty, but only for the sake of more original or naturalistic or unique storytelling. Do not look for a sixties social scan in sixties movies until much later in the decade.

One element of our sixties social legend is very much a part of our sixties cinema from the start: rebellious youth. The lore of the Kids may be the most potent invention of the 1960s, still fascinating in, say, *The Big Chill* (1983), when we seniors examine the survivors almost autobiographically, balancing their nostalgia with ours; and when our juniors measure history in the intelligent camaraderie of these extinguished firebrands. Surely the Kids did affect the culture. The 1960s was their day. I leave it to others to chart the Kids' contributions in politics, sex, and fashion, but in one area at least the nation's youth unquestionably changed the nation: music. In 1960, American pop music was Tin Pan Alley, especially the great Broadway masters. By 1970, American pop music was rock.

The Kids push into sixties cinema in their combat with the presiding generation. Of course, this is a trope of the 1950s, partly derived from increasing hostility between the young and the authorities and partly, one surmises, as an available vessel for liberal moviemakers' expressions of antibourgeois criticism. One thinks of James Dean's tortured scream of "You're tearing me apart!" to his feckless parents in *Rebel Without a Cause* (1955), of Marlon Brando's lawless biker gang in *The Wild One* (1954). "What are you rebelling against?" he is asked, and answers, in one of the decade's best remembered facetiae, "Whadaya got?"

Even uncelebrated programmers of the day support the rebellion. *I Was a Teenage Frankenstein* (1957), a low-budget howler, might have been made by teenagers from a teenager's *Weltanschauung* as "father" Whit Bissell bullies and blackmails his monster "son" Gary Conway. And note that Bissell's lab assistant, Robert Burton, is a spineless schmengie and Bissell's fiancée, Phyllis Coates, is a cliché finagler, intent on the size of her engagement diamond and on prying into secrets. When she learns too much, Bissell orders the helpless Conway to murder her, and seems to regard the collapse of his love life with no more than a tinge of regret that the bourgeois protocols will miss their observance. All grown-ups are rotten.

Generational war is one of the few transitional certainties connecting the end of the Studio Era to the 1960s. Most adults, especially parents, are perceived as Fascists, however well-intentioned they hope to be. Their hobby is screaming at kids, and their religion is conformism. They trust no one under thirty. "Why don't you listen just once, Mother?" Patty McCormack asks in Buzz Kulik's *The Explosive Generation* (1961), and asks it calmly, as if kids have to be understanding with these idiot parents, who are so systematically intolerant. They want teacher William Shatner fired for giving his students a "sex questionnaire." Of course, it's always the handsome, stimulating, patient, and even vaguely hip teachers who get into these troubles—but then who ever needed to fire a mediocrity? It's the individuals who threaten us. Denying the individual in ourselves and keeping other individuals down was the central energy of the American 1950s. And the kids of that day went along with it—this was, semi-officially, the "silent generation." Now it's the 1960s, and the new crop of kids is explosive, not irresponsibly difficult but effectively militant, particularly on the McCarthyesque issue of the firing of a teacher. The lines are drawn and the kids are right: they are sick of the 1950s, though student Billy Gray (Bud Anderson of *Father Knows Best,* imposing credentials) unnerves us with a spraying of "cool" and "sick" in leftover beat style.

The kids are right even when they're wrong. *The Explosive Generation* upholds freedom of education, but particularly the freedom *to educate*: it's William Shatner's liberty, really, that's on trial. John Frankenheimer's *The Young Savages* (1961) also uses a nonconformist adult as a link between society and the kids, though Frankenheimer's kids are not suburban sweeties but the hoods of the inner city. This will be tricky. How can we empathize with a generation whose representatives are in fact savages, the same people who menace us on the streets? In a typical fifties look at juvenile delinquency, Richard Brooks's *The Blackboard Jungle* (1955), the solution is to isolate the truly evil punks from the merely misguided punks, especially when Sidney Poitier is one of the latter. By the 1960s, the problem becomes less one of good kids and bad kids and more of blinding inequities in the social structure. Frankenheimer's Sympathetic Grown-up, Burt Lancaster, learns that these young savages, New York City gang members, are victims as well as culprits. An assistant District Attorney trying a murder case, Lancaster has to sacrifice the respect of his colleagues and a political future when he lets considerations of education, economics, and racial hostility inform his sense of justice.

The Broadway adaptation *West Side Story* (1961), goes even further, romanticizing the same scene with dance, ecstatic song, and soap-opera casting. Everyone's so *pretty*—is this New York or a beach-blanket movie? Frankenheimer's hooligans look like real hooligans; he hired some of them right on the New York streets while on location. But *West Side Story* is Jerome Robbins dance opera, and its Jets and Sharks hail from the Broadway of Sardi's and Shubert Alley, not that of the bodegas and schoolyards farther uptown. Still, how else could this singular Broadway musical have been filmed but with the kind of people who perform Broadway musicals? Certainly the city itself looks as authentic as Frankenheimer's, even when the gangs break into ballet, though Natalie Wood's Hispanic toilette strains credibility somewhat. What is most interesting about *West Side Story* is that here the kids are totally on their own, cut off from any possible adult advocate. The original show's playbill emphasized this, posting the dramatis personae by group—first the Jets and their girls, then the Sharks and theirs, and last the Adults, including an obnoxious policeman, an antagonistic detective, and a hand-wringing candy-store owner, who plays the Friar Laurence figure in this updating of *Romeo and Juliet*. Granted, *West Side Story*, as a composition, is a product of the 1950s, not the 1960s. Yet the work did not become a classic till it was filmed; the stage show was admired but somewhat unappreciated when it was new. Perhaps its ecumenical sympathies were too advanced for the 1950s, though its finale, in which the two gangs join forces in a cortège for the slain hero as the adults look on, useless, is too pat, too benevolently wistful, for the hard-edged 1960s.

What *is* the sixties view of the generation war that began in the

1950s? The answer lies in the post-McCarthy attitude of sixties movie-makers, the feeling of having killed off an atrocious father, a Mr. Bates. In the 1950s, Americans must cooperate with authority—if only stylis-tically, apparently, in public—just as moviemakers had to cooperate with the old moguls. In the 1960s, a less regimented environment allows a more self-motivated behavior, just as less regimented moviemakers enjoy a greater latitude in what they may film.

So fifties generation-war films tend to view conformist pressure (at a mild level) as a healthy social antidote to the disorder of rebellion: sur-render to the Wild Ones yields a dissolution of society. Sixties generation-war films tend to view conformist pressure (at *any* level) as destructive: surrender to Mrs. Bates turns you psycho.

This lesson is epitomized in the greatest of the early-sixties kids-versus-parents film, Elia Kazan's *Splendor in the Grass* (1961). No picture could be less political, yet Kazan and writer William Inge articulate the salient fear of the decade: that authority is corrupt and stupid and mur-derous. Is this not a *political* fear, especially when expressed by artists who survived the "egghead"-baiting American 1950s?*

Splendor takes us to Kansas in the 1920s, a quiet place, even a safe one. Inge's teenagers enjoy an idyll of school and recreation and romance. Inge drew his title from a line in Wordsworth's "Ode on Intimations of Immortality from Recollections of Early Childhood," which opens:

> *There was a time when meadow, grove, and stream,*
> *The earth and every common sight,*
> *To me did seem*
> *Appareled in celestial light,*
> *The glory and the freshness of a dream.*

So it began. Yet

> *It is not now as it hath been of yore;—*
> *Turn wheresoe'er I may,*

*Kazan survived it at first hand, facing a red-white-and-blue Central Com-mittee for his liberal activist past, when he more or less denounced the viciously repressive American Communist Party. What would have happened to him if he hadn't so acted? Strangled by the left, strangled by the right.

By night or day,
The things which I have seen I now can see no more.

What goes awry in Inge's paradise is parental interference in the love of
Warren Beatty and Natalie Wood. They are ideal high-schoolers: mature
for their age, respectful of conventions and appearances and other people's
feelings, anything but young savages. This is the kind of children parents
should be glad to produce. But Beatty's and Wood's parents are obtuse,
selfish fools, especially Beatty's father, Pat Hingle.

There is something very central about Hingle's role and performance.
A Kazan protégé on Broadway in Tennessee Williams's *Cat on a Hot Tin
Roof,* Inge's own *The Dark at the Top of the Stairs,* and Archibald MacLeish's
J.B., Hingle had become an exponential figure, the mildly oafish mid-
American petty-bourgeois family man, envious and grasping in Williams,
sympathetic in Inge, innocently martyred (in a part modeled on Job) in
MacLeish. Hingle was an average husband, then, a typical father. For
Inge and Kazan to make this basically nice guy the archvillain of the
piece is to tell us, most painfully, that not all the evil in the world is
done by those we identify as the enemy. And Hingle is indeed a most
painful sight, pushing and grabbing at Beatty in a show of familial
"affection," inveighing, advising, and decreeing like a Topekan Pope, and
destroying Beatty and Wood's romance with a do-gooder reasonableness
that borders on insanity. "He isn't a very good listener, really, is he?"
says Beatty's dean at Yale.

This study in parental aggression is all the more telling for its depth
of perspective, its subtlety of gesture, its overwhelming believability. "The
first play especially written for the screen by William Inge," the posters
boasted—note "play" rather than "screenplay," as if *Splendor in the Grass*
were meant to stand directly in line with Inge's four Broadway smashes
of the 1950s, *Come Back, Little Sheba, Picnic, Bus Stop,* and *The Dark at
the Top of the Stairs.* Yet of course writing for the screen gave Inge a chance
to open up his one-set, fifteen-character playscripts into an intimate panorama of what he knew best, small-town Midwestern life. Just the immediate Beatty and Wood family circles comprise an absorbing diversity
of person, for Beatty's sister Barbara Loden is Beatty's opposite, so defiant
of Hingle's regime that she is halfway to Town Tramp; and Wood's father
is a pleasant, passably tolerant fellow. Wood's mother, Audrey Christie,
however, bears all the marks of the provincial beldame. "That's what

happens to girls who go wild and boy-crazy," she warns Wood. *What's what happens?* They get impregnated and have to risk their lives in a druggist's back room to redeem the family honor. Christie heard the gossip at a DAR meeting from a woman who lives across the street from the girl's family and "knows everything that goes on in their house!"

We, too, know everything that goes on in these houses, even in the bathtub, where Wood is put through an operatic mad scene that shows, as rarely, that she could act when she got the chance and the coaching of a Kazan. (It didn't hurt that Wood was enjoying an affair with Beatty at the time, under Kazan's sage encouragement. Sexual tension, above all, drives this movie's plot.) Building on Inge's writing, Kazan conjures up an extraordinarily persuasive township, the world in little. A minute, in Kazan, is a real minute. Lines are not necessarily spoken in responsive alternation but interlocked and even doubled up in duel, to bring out the rigidity and intensity in the clash of generational will. And the most quotidian moments are exhibition pieces—a family photograph session, a swimming date—even the moment when stalwart Beatty tries to stop sister Loden from making a spectacle of herself at a country-club dance. Kazan brings out all that moment's torments and ambiguities: Beatty as authority though himself authority's victim, Loden as natural enemy of all *except* Beatty, both of them as mutual supporter and critic at once. It is easy to observe that a film this open about adolescent sexuality and parental intolerance was culturally impossible before 1960—Kazan in 1951 had had to agree to a bowdlerizing and a slight remoralization of *A Streetcar Named Desire,* on a theme much less threatening: the dreamer versus the realist. Something poetic there, not revolutionary. *Splendor* is about reason versus power. *That's* revolutionary. And more; if even an edited *Splendor* script had been shot in the 1950s, would it have enjoyed such depth of execution? Isn't the fastidious naturalism that Kazan conjures up in *Splendor*—the *almost* self-regarding brilliance of narrative presentation—a product of the post-1950s shift toward moviemaking honesty?

We have only to examine Kazan's own *East of Eden* (1955) to agree, for it is notably similar to *Splendor in the Grass.* Like William Inge, the scenarist Paul Osborn (drawing on John Steinbeck's novel) was a Broadway veteran. Again we get the period small-town setting, a generation-war theme, and a mixture of stage and screen people in the casting, especially in the triangular romance of Julie Harris (theatre person), Dick Davalos

Wild Kids. Above, they're menacing the solid citizenry (hipsters Peter Brown, Ann-Margret, and James Ward with clean-cut John Forsythe; note Ward's threatening razor) in *Kitten with a Whip*. Below, they're going weird because of thwarted romance in *Splendor in the Grass* (Natalie Wood, Gary Lockwood). "Deeny, come back here!" Lockwood cries. "Where're you goin'?" To hell in a nervous breakdown.

(movie person), and James Dean (bizarre person). Yet for starters *East of Eden* cannot stand up to *Splendor* on technical grounds, with its over-wrought sound track, its mélange of location work and studio mock-ups (most risible when we cut from a real bean field to a phoney street scene), its too literary script, the odd moment or two of awkward post-dubbing, and the occasionally stagey performances, particularly from Heavy Father Raymond Massey. True, put Julie Harris and James Dean together for a heart-to-heart in a daisy field and you'll get something better than any-thing in *Splendor,* scene for scene. But too much of *East of Eden* is unbal-anced, its vitality sapped by sentimental punctuations, its realism undermined by Hollywood "effects," its Jo Van Fleet showing up the undisciplined fireworks of James Dean. Van Fleet, as a bordello madam, is Dean's unacknowledged mother, and their big scene together shows how much more character she can present with no-nonsense stand-and-deliver than he can with all the Method in the world. She speaks up; he swallows words. (Yes, I know, it's lifelike, but I'm missing text.) She looks you in the eye; he gazes at nothing. She plays one thing at a time; he plays ten things all at once throughout the scene. That's about six or seven too many. And she won a Best Supporting Oscar, which, unlike the Best Actor or Actress, usually denotes *real* talent at work.*

At that, *East of Eden* was outstanding in its day for the lyricism of its three youthful leads, which reminds us how unadventurous—conform-ist, no?—so much of fifties movie acting was. *Splendor in the Grass,* on the other hand, was outstanding in the 1960s as a "best of kind," not a special film in a time of ordinary films but a special film in a time increasingly devoted to the extraordinary.

---

*Typical Best Actor and Actress Awards: Wallace Beery for *The Champ,* Norma Shearer for *The Divorcee,* Bing Crosby for *Going My Way,* Loretta Young for *The Farmer's Daughter,* Grace Kelly for *The Country Girl,* Charlton Heston for *Ben-Hur,* Elizabeth Taylor for *Butterfield 8,* John Wayne for *True Grit.* Typical Supporting Awards: Hattie McDaniel for *Gone With the Wind,* Jane Darwell for *The Grapes of Wrath,* Donald Crisp for *How Green Was My Valley,* Walter Huston for *The Treasure of the Sierra Madre,* Anthony Quinn for *Lust for Life,* Wendy Hiller for *Separate Tables,* Rita Moreno for *West Side Story,* Lila Kedrova for *Zorba the Greek,* Peter Ustinov for *Topkapi,* Estelle Parsons for *Bonnie and Clyde,* Robert De Niro for *The Godfather II,* Tatum O'Neal for *Paper Moon,* Vanessa Redgrave for *Julia,* Linda Hunt for *The Year of Living Dangerously.* Typical awards, I say; and there's a lot more color in the second list. By the way, Dean was nominated as Best Actor for *East of Eden*; he lost to Ernest Borgnine for *Marty.*

Ironically, the 1960s were devoted as well to a form that had been regarded for decades as uneventful, prosaic, even stupid: the B movie. Thin, cheap, and quick to make, the B of the Studio Age was strictly a genre piece—a western, a campus musical, *Tarzan* rip-offs, monster horror, skating fun with icy, tactful Vera Hruba Ralston. Another genre became popular in the 1950s, science fiction. This arena produced such cold-war classics as *The Day the Earth Stood Still* (1951) and *Invasion of the Body Snatchers* (1956), the one a plea for disarmament and the other a parable on the growth of McCarthyism (though it works as well as a stylization of Communist infiltration).

The B film remained a second feature and the staple of the children's matinée till the early 1960s, when maverick filmmakers exploited its potential for low-risk experimentation. Given the number of the nation's screens (especially those catering to the undiscriminating drive-in audience), a movie with a *very low budget* and a brief but *very wide first release* (known as a "saturation booking") cannot fail to make *some* profit. Build your business entirely on B's and the profits will accumulate. It almost doesn't matter what you turn out—in fact, as we'll see, the more grotesque, idiotic, and (of course) sexy and violent the B's became, the more attention they garnered. What fascinates about this underworld of "exploitation" pictures, combining ancient genre practices with new topics to create biker westerns, sci-fi gangster melodramas, teen beach musicals, camp Guignol, drug weepies, and so on, is its amount of, once again, sheer nonconformist defiance.

These films are smarter than they act, often ridiculing the conventions as they observe them. Interestingly, the king of the sixties B, the producer-director Roger Corman, began making films in the dead center of the 1950s, when mavericks felt most repressed, thus most defiant. Corman opened shop with the simplest and most uninflected of B types— *Five Guns West* (1955), *The Day the World Ended* (1956), *The Undead* (1957), *Attack of the Crab Monsters* (1957), *Rock All Night* (1957), *Machine-Gun Kelly* (1958), *I, Mobster* (1959). Suddenly, in *The Little Shop of Horrors* (1960), Corman greatly deviates from the protocols of the programmer. *Little Shop* is an alien-invasion picture; the alien is a man-eating flower. This is a gimmick, no more. What is innovative about the film is its setting, a grungy flower shop on New York's Lower East Side. The people who work in and frequent the shop are utterly unlike anyone encountered in a movie before, a troop of nerds and schmudls, mostly Jewish and all unattractive.

Till now, B-movie actors tended to be inadequate replicas of major-studio star types, the same only less so: wooden or shapeless heroes, dim heroines, boring sidekicks, colorless villains. They were never deliberate violations of the casting codes. But in *Little Shop* Corman *flourishes* the baseness of his characters. Where else can we find people so vile yet so boring? The film takes some color momentarily in a cameo by the very young Jack Nicholson as a masochist reveling in a dentist appointment, but in the main the movie entertains on a kind of sixties premise of doing the undoable, of testing the borders of what would be allowed now that the 1950s are over. Technically, *Little Shop* looks primitive in an almost greasy black-and-white and truly perfunctory decor, a demented modesty of production. The monster plant on which all depends is something less than a special effect. Yet given Corman's rashly dowdy place and people, the ultra-B presentation seems apt, even revolutionarily persuasive. It is nonconformist, therefore virtuous—for in its little horror way it helps recall us to lost strains of diversity and independence.

Another possibility for the B was to stop accepting its role as Hollywood's offal and try to promote its artistry even within the tight budget. This, too, expresses a vital rejection of the practice of establishment Hollywood, as the B had long been not only the cheapest of movies, but the most unworthy, the place where the least able directors, writers, techies, and actors worked. Nor were Hollywood's B units a training ground for new talent. If anything, they were a dump for has-beens and washouts. And so the producers liked it. They didn't want anything ingenious or experimental from their B's—ingenious costs money and experiments disrupt routine. If it works, don't fix it: work it.

So the idea of using the B as an entrée for young talent is as transubstantiating as is giving the B personality and flair. Yet it became routine in the 1960s. Corman himself would introduce Francis Ford Coppola, Peter Bogdanovich, Monte Hellman, Jonathan Demme, Robert Towne, and Martin Scorsese, among others; and he introduced them to all aspects of moviemaking, for everyone pitched in over at Corman's. This, too, is an act of self-renewal, for in the Studio Age one was supposed to do one thing well. It was only in the pioneer days of Old Hollywood that directors wrote scenarios and stars produced. By 1929, one specialized, admitting such exceptions as producer-director (and narrator) Cecil B. DeMille, director-cinematographer Josef von Sternberg, or writer-director John Huston. Since it was the producers who mistrusted the versatile, however, versatility—like so much else that contradicted Studio Age dictums—became attractive in the 1960s. This, too, improves the B movie. A sharp director retools dull sets; game actors improvise to enliven a dead script. The B develops a quality it had never had before: vitality.

Thus we are often struck by a film that in subject matter, casting, and budget appears to be a B but has the quality of a very inexpensive A. *Studs Lonigan* (1960), drawn from sections of James T. Farrell's trilogy, is one such. Written and produced by Philip Yordan and directed by Irving Lerner (Haskell Wexler is billed as associate director), *Studs Lonigan* is actually more of an economical "independent" production than an out-and-out B from the quickie factory. Still, the lines between the two were blurring, though technically *Studs Lonigan* is far more accomplished than the merry messes that Corman was releasing at this time. Protagonist Christopher Knight is much too sensitive for Farrell's pool-hall wastrel, but the rest of the cast is apt and equipped, especially Jack Nicholson, a staple of the sixties B, as one of Studs's henchmen. Too, Jarrold (later Jerry) Goldsmith's sound-track score is highly ambitious, at times obtruding into our senses to heighten our reception of events.

Above all, it is Lerner's visual organization that makes *Studs Lonigan* special beyond its scale, as when the camera takes in the senior Lonigans' quarrel by jumping from one to the other like the referee of a tennis match, or when a Depression orator harangues a crowd in the rain and all we see, but for two hecklers, is a serene sea of umbrellas without people under them, or when Studs visits a sympathetic schoolteacher after a visit to a burlesque house. He's so horny that he "sees" her as a stripper, and when she puts something soothing on the Victrola, Goldsmith rings in bump-and-grind melody atop Mozart, the two musics aggravating the tension till Studs leaps up and tears the front of the teacher's dress. One notes the almost inevitable touch of generation war—even the dippy *Little Shop of Horrors* gets around to it, in wiggy satire—but in *Studs* it is a surprise, for as Studs is a wastrel ruining his life, his nagging father has a point. Best of all is the film's final scene, when Studs is reunited with his sweetheart. He had impregnated her but couldn't face marriage and so lost her. Now they are on a bench in the rain, and she rejects him still. "I gotta love you," he urges her. "I *gotta* love you." And the film immediately blacks out.

Another aspect of sixties cinema to consider in these first years of America's new wave is how easily realism and honesty adapted to all forms. It is not only that *Psycho* can be allowed to grapple with psychosis without the euphemistic shortchanging of earlier eras, that *Splendor in the Grass* is a more intently realized domestic chronicle than previous domestic chronicles, that *The Little Shop of Horrors* drops in on unfamiliar people. It is that *every* kind of film, from here on, has the option of making more of itself than was possible before, sifting its contents to fulfill its premise as no film could when whatever threatened the public's self-image could not be allowed.

Consider romantic comedy. This form, so endemic to the self-image of the embattled 1930s, barely survived World War II—isn't that ironic? But romantic comedy is frivolous in wartime—and was brain-dead by the 1950s: or do you think that 1940's *The Philadelphia Story*, with Katharine Hepburn, Cary Grant, and James Stewart, was improved in 1956's musical adaptation, *High Society*, with Grace Kelly, Bing Crosby, and Frank Sinatra? (Even Cole Porter was stumped on that one: or do you call "True Love" a great Cole Porter song?) Comedy, in the 1950s, was too loud and lumpy for romance; comedy was the unhousebroken Lucy, the emphatic Jerry Lewis. Where's wit? Where's elegance?

And where did *Breakfast at Tiffany's* (1961) spring from, the head of Zeus? Here, very suddenly, was a deft, adult, ambivalent romantic comedy with the bite of New York. It is funny, light and dark, tough and soft, as the city is. Its salient picture is the most chic woman alive in evening-gown black and jewelry-to-die bearing a cigarette in a holder about twenty inches long. It opens on Fifth Avenue, deserted at dawn: a cab pulls up and the woman, in dark glasses, slips out to window-shop at Tiffany's, then breakfasts on coffee and a danish to the strains of "Moon River." Already, the combination of the keen suave of the picture and the wistful mush of the music tells us that *la dolce vita* has its regrets. But then so does New York. This film catches that; and a taste of its day, its very moment; and a sense of the yearning for distinction, for love, for *fun* that the 1950s tried to drain out of us. Consider, too, that the most chic woman alive is a prostitute.

Where did this delightfully strange nonesuch—so hurt yet so game—come from, besides Blake Edwards's direction, George Axelrod's script, and Truman Capote's novella? Perhaps it came from New York

itself, the only part of the United States that resisted in the 1950s.*
Certainly much of *Breakfast at Tiffany's* runs on upscale Manhattan hip—
in Audrey Hepburn's "mean reds," "rats," and "super-rats," her pet, Cat,
and her manifestation into a cab in highest fashion to cry, "Grand Central
Station and step on it, darling!" But then Axelrod was careful to retain
as much of Capote's original as possible, taking in some of the film's
best-recalled lines—a drunken john's "You like me, baby, I'm a liked
guy"; or Hollywood agent Martin Balsam's "Is she or ain't she?"—meaning a phoney—and he adds, "She's a *real* phoney" because "she believes
all this crap she believes"; or Buddy Ebsen's epically deadpan "Son, I need
a friend."

Some of the film scants its source: in a more elfin, less earthy Holly
Golightly;† in a male vis-à-vis less like Capote's narrator and more like—
well, exactly like George Peppard, and particularly in an adjusted ending
in which the insistently evasive Holly finally gives in to romance instead
of fleeing it. Still, *Breakfast at Tiffany's* was filmed in a kind of alternative
Capote, taking in strains of both innocence and killer-instinct tension
that he brought into much of his New York tale-telling, if not *Breakfast
at Tiffany's* per se. A neighbor has called the cops on Hepburn's wild
party, and as she abandons it on a millionaire's arm, she meets the police
at the curb and happily points out her apartment at their request. Edwards
shoots this silent, from the distance, looking out a window of her apartment into the street. The picture, a virtual *New Yorker* cartoon, is absolute
Capote. So is the edgy elegance of Patricia Neal, her adultery with kept
boy Peppard very clearly noted, her checks and her suits and her purring
tone, sugared in venom, highly suggestive of the class of people Capote
enjoyed observing. Perhaps the most authentic moment in the entire film
is Edwards's fade on Hepburn's erotically platonic first night with Peppard, the two beautiful young prostitutes sheltering together like brother
and sister.

Breakfast at Tiffany's brings up another point of sixties revisionism,

*It should be noted that Broadway was the only sector of show biz that
withstood the blacklist, and the theatre mounted a number of anti-McCarthy pro-
tests, not only in Arthur Miller's *The Crucible* (1953) and a revival of Lillian Hellman's
The Children's Hour in 1952, but even in musicals such as *Flahooley* (1951) and
Candide (1956), which, in its original form, centered on a scene of Inquisition by
character assassination.

†Capote himself thought Marilyn Monroe should have played it. More earthy,
less elfin.

the newly polymorphic science of sound-track scoring. In the Studio Age, a universal tendency toward romantically symphonic accompaniment made the score to one film sound much like the score to another. A slight infusion of jazz widened possibilities in the 1950s. But it was the 1960s that explored the notion that a unique film needs a unique sound, a *colorito* that in effect translates its characters and setting into music. Henry Mancini's *Tiffany's* score is exemplary, then, for one couldn't imagine these tunes, in these orchestrations, making do in any other film. Just to cite the titles Mancini put on his cuts gives one a feeling for the jazzy, pensive, so hip and tender personality of the music: "Something for Cat," "Latin Golightly," "Hub Caps and Tail Lights" (as Hepburn and Peppard consider a pre–go-go dancer in a bar), "The Big Heist" (a kind of sneaky Debussy as the two pilfer Halloween masks from a five-and-ten), or the suavely soaring title tune, so soigné that it rises above the usual pasted-on lyrics for a wordless choral treatment. This is Capote's worldly innocence set to music, balancing the naïveté of "Moon River" with a very clear view of what Hepburn and Peppard do for a living.

One of the liberating factors in the sudden creation of this sophisticated sixties worldview is that the major censorship battles were fought in the 1950s. Later, from 1969 moving into the 1970s, the courts would harass radically sexy and outright pornographic films. But such very different movies as Roberto Rossellini's *The Miracle,* Otto Preminger's *The Moon Is Blue,* and Elia Kazan's *Baby Doll,* all in the 1950s, fought in court, in the press, and in the boardrooms of Hollywood to beat down repression. *The Miracle* is a religious fable, *The Moon Is Blue* an innocuous comedy with a no-no word ("virgin"), *Baby Doll* Tennessee Williams in full cry. Clearly, the *casus belli* was no one topic, no one treatment. The movies wanted the latitude of literature and the theatre, reasonable freedom for any and all topics.

Thus, again, the revolution of sixties cinema was an artistic and personal one, *not* a political one. However, one of the most introductory of sixties films is highly political, a product of both the anti-Communist cold war and of liberal anti-McCarthyism, thus conservative and innovative at once, a sort of shock of recognition somewhere between Yalta and détente: *The Manchurian Candidate* (1962). Working closely from Richard Condon's novel, director John Frankenheimer and writer George Axelrod tell us that the Soviets and their allies are indeed scheming to infiltrate and conquer the United States—and with a plot that would shock the most hardened devotee of loony-bin conspiracy theories. An American war hero, brainwashed while in captivity in Korea, has been programmed to follow any direction he is given upon viewing the queen of hearts playing card. A series of murders will lead to the assassination of the Republican Presidential nominee and the sympathy-election of his running mate, a Red-baiting idiot whose domineering wife is in fact a Communist mole. The Reds will run the country.

The infiltration thriller was established in the 1950s, but only in science fiction. Sheer fantasy. *The Manchurian Candidate* is suspenseful, eccentric, and intelligent, but this only makes it an unusually expert thriller. What makes it terrifying is the commitment of its sense of history. In the wrangling of calmly democratic Senator John McGiver and scattershot Fascist Senator James Gregory we have the 1950s in miniature, and Frankenheimer's use of such pleasantly familiar actors as Frank Sinatra and Janet Leigh connects us intimately with the action. (Isn't the use of Leigh as *Psycho*'s first murder victim extra horrifying precisely because she is not only a major star but a *likable* one—as opposed to, say, Joan Crawford or Ernest Borgnine, whose deaths might have left us with mixed feelings?) Gregory is perfect as the would-be next President, highly McCarthyesque in appearance and attack—not least in his habitual shouting of "Point of order! Point of order!"—and Angela Lansbury is at her most splendid as the mole. Oddly, Laurence Harvey's naturally wooden talent actually aids his portrayal as the controlled killer, not only because it accords with Condon's drawing—"Raymond stood as though someone might have just opened a beach umbrella in his bowels. . . . His resentment of people, places, and things was a stifling, sensual thing"— but because it vivifies the notion of a man not entirely connected to the rest of the world.

Most persuasive is Frankenheimer's depiction of the brainwashing exhibition in Korea, in which Harvey's squad is displayed, under absolute regulation, to a mixed audience of Communist dignitaries. The show is brutal. Harvey is told to kill two of his men as a dancer is told to do a time-step, and Harvey does what he is told. Yet the Americans have been conditioned to believe that they are waiting out a rainstorm in a hotel party room hosting a ladies' garden-club talk on "Fun with Hydrangeas." In the novel, Condon merely sets the scene. Frankenheimer *shows* us the effect of brainwashing in kaleidoscope technique, constantly "turning" the view so we take in now the soldiers' delusion, now the Communist au-

dience's view of things, here a real garden-club lady at the podium surrounded by soldiers, there a roomful of garden-club ladies (and the black
soldier sees a crew of black garden-club ladies). We get not the processes
of brainwashing, then, just the result; but Frankenheimer presents it so
convincingly that we understand how disoriented a mind can be unmade
to be.

The movies' real era of paranoia comes in the 1970s with *The Par-
allax View, Death Wish, Westworld, One Flew Over the Cuckoo's Nest, Dirty
Harry, The Stepford Wives, Sleeper, Play Misty for Me, The Conversation, Jaws,
Eyes of Laura Mars, Serpico,* and the slasher and alien-attack films that ran
on into the 1980s. These are what might be called "post-assassination"
movies. Strange that *The Manchurian Candidate* got there even before
John F. Kennedy's murder, with fiction that is widely believed to be
something like the facts of the Kennedy case. But then Frankenheimer
has said that he made *The Manchurian Candidate* to express fears that we
ourselves are brainwashed—"that our society is becoming manipulated
and controlled."

This is no doubt why the film inspired such a furor when it was
released. Frankenheimer tells us not only that we are trapped between
Fascisms of left and right, but that we can't even identify them. I was
in junior high school when *The Manchurian Candidate* came out, and I
remember how odd it was that some of my friends hadn't seen it. Ours
was a suburban, media-bound culture, and it counted certain events that
literally everyone except the usual schmudls sat in on—*The Twilight Zone*
and *Mr. Novak* on television, of course, and such movies as *Psycho, The
Time Machine, West Side Story, The Longest Day.* The ensuing discussions
were key social relations, our coffeehouse, yet about half my friends didn't
see *The Manchurian Candidate,* because their parents had forbidden them
to. Frankenheimer must really have struck a nerve.

He slips up, be it said, in the location shooting, another major
feature of anti–Studio Age procedure. The old moguls hated location
shooting, partly because of the expense and mainly because an entire unit
could thus drop out of supervisory reach. Fifties Hollywood, trying to
best television wherever possible, made location work a perquisite—better,
a convention—of most major releases, and by 1962 no important film set
in New York could make do with stock footage. *Breakfast at Tiffany's* is
Johnny-on-the-spot here, with a heavy taste of the East Sixties, Capote-
land. Its five-and-dime store and police precinct look studio-phoney, and

the *scène-à-faire* in Tiffany's itself, though authentic, feels like a commercial, even a Mass. Still, the film is dressed as persuasively as Hepburn is. *The Manchurian Candidate*'s New York has an air, but when Frankenheimer takes to the streets he carelessly catches theatre marquees—a rerun of Walt Disney's *Pinocchio* with *Pirates of Tortuga,* not released till 1961, when *The Manchurian Candidate* was shooting, or "Leonard Sillman's *New Faces*" (at the Alvin Theatre: the 1961 edition, obviously). Yet clues in the script tell us that it is about two years since Laurence Harvey was in Korea—in short, 1955.

Quibbles. Frankenheimer's forte is realism. He is one of the most anti-1950s of directors, because his gritty observations contradict the cultural pieties Hollywood most obdurately observed in the postwar era. One wonders how many directors in 1962—especially young ones like Frankenheimer, fresh from television—would have faithfully adapted a novel in which the mother is the villain. This may be why *The Manchurian Candidate* so dismayed Americans when it was new. Even today, after a quarter century's worth of bold cinema, Lansbury's portrayal terrifies, flighty and flinty on the surface but rigid with cold passions underneath. Her grandest passion is the Sino-Soviet advance, but her greatest, to our horror, is her son Laurence Harvey. "They" have destroyed him in the brainwashing, and she will avenge him. She is the Queen of Hearts. She is Mrs. Bates. And she is the Manchurian Candidate, the choice of the East, her regency to be guaranteed by assassination.

The film has taken on an added horror that Frankenheimer and Axelrod could not have foreseen, in its apparent prediction of the events of November 22, 1963, in Dallas. This was thought to explain the film's virtual disappearance till its rerelease in 1988: it vindicated our nightmares, filled in the outline of our paranoia. Actually, the film was put into limbo by a business disagreement among its owners. But there had been some fear, when the film was in pre-production, that its hardline view of the East-West conflict might hamper President Kennedy's attempts to reach a truce with Premier Krushchov. As it happened, Sinatra was a Kennedy insider, and could get the official view from the Chief himself at one of his Hyannisport weekends. It's the fate of the movie against the fate of the world; how will the great man take it?

So Sinatra tells the President that he's about to film *The Manchurian Candidate,* and Kennedy says, "Great! Who's playing the mother?"

Frankenheimer and Axelrod feel the cold war as ever hot; its soldiers have simply gone underground, as moles and dupes. Director Billy Wilder (with his constant co-writer I. A. L. Diamond) saw the cold war as silly, another example of how idiot man makes things difficult for himself, in *One, Two, Three* (1961). This comedy was set in the very center of East-West antagonism, Berlin in the late 1950s, and it troubled to mock the hypocrisy and scheming of all the local factions, the Americans, the Russians, and the suddenly universally non-Nazi Germans. No one holds the moral edge, because everyone—in Wilder's world—is a cheat. This is not democracy versus totalitarianism, not even given that star James Cagney is a Coca-Cola executive trying to negotiate a distribution deal with the Reds. Yes, the Soviets run a brutal slave empire: but Cagney is an adulterer and his boss, Howard St. John, is a redneck Fascist and his boss's daughter, Pamela Tiffin, is a selfish moron and Americans in general are racists—there are a number of allusions to the integration violence in Little Rock—and all the Germans, it appears, are former Nazis. Wilder loathes the whole cast, possibly excepting Cagney's wife, Arlene Francis; we can tell because she says things in a calm, dry manner and is a New York stage and television personality rather than a movie personality, as if, in the Wilder cosmos, a sensible person has to be imported from arcane places.

Soviet Russia, Eisenhower America: what's the difference? Everyone's hungry, everyone schemes, everyone takes. Coca-Cola's hometown, Atlanta, says Cagney, is "Siberia with mint juleps." No difference. Actually, the movie isn't about the capitalistic introduction of Coca-Cola to the East, but about Tiffin's secret marriage to a violently Communist East German, Horst Buchholz. How to reconcile him to our ways? It's farce, with the gangbusters tempo and giddy cynicism of a good revival of *The Front Page*. Cagney's secretary—what used to be known as a bombshell—is sick of Tiffin. Tiffin's didoes are interfering with the secretary's extra-office liaison with Cagney. Yankee, go home:

SECRETARY   It's August now. Won't school soon open?

CAGNEY   In Georgia? You never know.

Wilder's disgusted view of all sides in the war should be more shocking than Frankenheimer's if nothing else loyal view of the United States as the good guys. Yet *The Manchurian Candidate* was controversial and *One, Two, Three* a hit. Perhaps audiences were distracted by Wilder's furious pace, the keep-'em-coming aesthetic. They must have been bemused by the *Verfremdungseffektisch* insider's jokes, as when Cagney utters "Mother of Mercy, is this the end of little Rico?"* or, "The son of a bitch stole my cuckoo clock!"† or even, to a half-dressed and speechifying Buchholz, "Put your pants on, Spartacus!"‡ And they surely delighted in the jokes relating to Stalin's claims that Russians invented all sorts of ordinary Western items, and to the inferior quality of Soviet industrial production. In a chase through the Brandenburg Gate, the Russian car (modeled on a 1937 Nash) backfires every fifty feet; and the East German secret police force Buchholz to confess he is an American spy by playing a Soviet 45 of "The Yellow Polka Dot Bikini," the RPM cycle and sonics grotesquely distorted. Buchholz had stood up to the original American disc, but Soviet merchandise tears him apart.

This batch of early-sixties films is meant to define the era's positions, pretty much as the films did when they were new. *Psycho*'s naturalistically intrusive camera, *Splendor in the Grass*'s directness of sensuality, the anti-authoritarianism of the Kid films, the change-is-healthy restlessness of the B films, the confidential irreverence of *Breakfast at Tiffany's,* and the promise made in two very different ways in *The Manchurian Candidate* and *One, Two, Three* that solemnities will not be respected—all this forces upon Americans a new relationship with their movies, one of challenge rather than flattery, of doubt rather than certainty. The 1920s enchanted the public, the 1930s delighted and educated it, the 1940s heartened it. The 1950s lulled it. The 1960s disturbed it.

Or why else would a major studio make *The Hustler* (1961), the study of a ne'er-do-well pool player suffering a mean case of selfish in his heart and money in his soul? He has a gift: for the shooting of pool. Yet he flourishes it as a weapon, not as a boon. Paul Newman plays him ugly, casually uningratiating, with a grim territorial walk and a pride that hates all other men. "Even if you beat me, I'm still the best!" he cries

---

*A line from the Edward G. Robinson gangster film *Little Caesar,* alluding to the days when Cagney and Robinson were fellow toughs at Warner Brothers. *One, Two, Three* misquotes the text. It's *little* Caesar but plain Rico.

†A line from *The Front Page*—the curtain line, in fact: and the son of a bitch stole my *watch* (in the original).

‡An *hommage* to Stanley Kubrick's epic on the gladiator-slave uprising in ancient Rome, released the year before.

One, Two, Three. The East German police are miffed at Horst Buchholz's insurrectionary NATOist deviationism. Buchholz is startled himself—he had no idea. But that will happen in farce.

to Jackie Gleason's Minnesota Fats, the champ to be conquered like some aging gunslinger in a western. In this world, you don't just engage your rivals, *The Hustler*'s producer, director, and writer (with Sidney Carroll) Robert Rossen tells us. You destroy them.

No movie of the 1950s took such a brutal, clear look at the ego-affirmation of the one-on-one contest, at the inhumanity of the winner or the castrated vulnerability of the loser. A dark film emotionally and literally, *The Hustler* reminds many of forties film noir. But noir was fanciful, a mannerist form, an American expressionism, while *The Hustler* is realistic almost to a fault—you can smell the sweat and the fear. Nor does Rossen give us noir's Treacherous Woman or its relish in discovering crime among the bourgeoisie, hungry bank clerks and lusty wives. On the contrary, *The Hustler*'s arena is late-night downtown among the players and bettors. The woman, Piper Laurie, is the only decent element in Newman's life, and the crime belongs to criminals, chiefly George C. Scott as the "manager," who plays his own sort of pool with Newman's life—even unto bedding the unwilling Laurie with Newman's permission, a kind of trick shot that causes Laurie's death.

The very casting of these four leads is sixties casting—Gleason capping a decade of television sitcom on a vast turnaround as the methodically debonair Fats, Scott just launching his life's work of proving that you can be a star movie actor without being a movie star, Laurie preparing the glamorous anti-glamour that would revise the very look of stardom increasingly throughout the decade. Think of the famous kiss of Scarlett and Rhett at their parting on a back road near the end of the first half of *Gone With the Wind*: a reverberant emblem of the Hollywood that was. Compare that with the famous shot of Newman and Laurie embracing in their underwear.

Newman's Fast Eddie Felson, we should note, has a slight fifties ring, in a reminder of the Marlon Brando–James Dean–Montgomery Clift archetype that Newman also fit into. Or was fit into, for this type was the invention of reviewers who didn't know how to treat these new actors and lumped them together as "rebels." None of them was like any of the others. Could you see Dean as Stanley Kowalski or Marc Antony? Brando in Clift's roles in *A Place in the Sun* or *From Here to Eternity* (not to mention the pathetic cameo in *Judgment at Nuremberg*)? Brando in *East of Eden*? Sure: and what a sharp, vivid, enchanting film *that* would have been.

Fast Eddie is key Newman, not only unlike Brando, Dean, and Clift but unlike Newman—at least, the Newman he had till then presented. Coming on cocky, washing up punchy, all nose and teeth, Fast Eddie makes a decisive break with the extraordinarily *feeling* tough guys of the "rebel" era, with Brando's bellowing wail of *"Stella!"* and Dean's elated torments, the groanings of youth working its own rack, and Clift's brooding, cavernous wonders. Hollywood likes feelings in its heroes, whatever else they have or lack. "What beat me?" Fast Eddie asks, and is told, "Character." But he does end up seeking out his own emotions. "You're a loser," he tells Scott as he walks out on him, " 'cause you're *dead inside!*"

Hollywood likes its heroes to learn hard. Still, doesn't Fast Eddie start harder and learn harder than we are used to even in fierce naturalism? What's the worst ordeal a major star is put through in the Studio Age? Perhaps James Stewart's filibuster on the Senate floor in *Mr. Smith Goes to Washington*. And this is ritual humiliation, a communal shriving, Christian, ecumenical. The rituals of the 1960s are less comprehensive, less calculated on the public's identification with a hero in the first place. All might aspire to be a Mr. Smith in Washington, or a Jean Arthur powerfully in support. How much of *The Hustler*'s public connected to the spiritually unyielding Newman or the tragically abused Laurie?

Perhaps the films of the 1960s establish a new sort of transaction between art and audience. Once, the movies preached on the text of the safe place, the community, the patriarchy, the virtues. This is called uplifting. From 1960 on, the movies do not preach. They describe what their creators see in the world—partly, I think, to revenge themselves on the repressive authority that for so long enforced the lie of safety, community, virtue. The lie that there were such things. But mainly because what is true is always more appealing to artists than anything else, even though it is less appealing to their public. This is called humanism. The precision of the realism in sixties movies is above all what separates them from their predecessors, because realism is not what Hollywood liked. Realism is irritating, disorderly, unchurchly. It calls too much into question. But the industry has been in trouble since World War II ended, and it will welcome whatever proves profitable. Applehood and mother pie were dependable, and of course father knew best.

But from 1960 on, Mrs. Bates will be allowed.

Two

The New
Ten Commandments

Sometimes Hollywood's 1950s really do seem like a bland stream of westerns, weepies, religious epics, and Jane Powell musicals. Some vital new acting talent is introduced in Marlon Brando, Marilyn Monroe, and James Dean, but the directors and writers are largely hemmed in by the decade's fear of individualism and by what Arthur Schlesinger, Jr., citing as antecedents the Depression, World War II, the cold war, and the Korean War, called "the politics of fatigue." Thus Hollywood spent much of the 1950s running on empty, hoping to maintain worn-out genres, themes, and characters while trying to outdazzle television with technology rather than content.

So we truly sense a sudden change in approach when the change comes, and it comes very neatly, like it or not, in 1960. Still, from the early-middle 1950s on, Hollywood does release exceptional films that suggest a slight transitional sensibility, an eagerness to free American cinema of its inherited and newly applied restrictions. The brutal realism and fierce political subtext of *On the Waterfront* (1954) and the almost expressionistic violence of *Kiss Me Deadly* (1955), which treats America as a battleground between the Fascist muscle of Ralph Meeker's Mike Hammer and the egghead ineptness of almost everyone else, reveal an art of disturbing honesty, of the "no safe place" philosophy. *The Rose Tattoo* (1955) tries to give us a nearly actorless naturalism, a beyond-the-studio innocence of setting comparable to the neo-realism of Rossellini and De Sica, while *The Night of the Hunter* (1955) dares a kind of Griffithian visual stylization. *Baby Doll* (1956) takes on the censors. *The Killing* (1956) banks its chips on a hero who is an unmitigated crook, letting his smarts and energy lure us into admiration, disarmed as we are by, again, the persuasive location work. *Paths of Glory* (1957) and *The Sweet Smell of Success* (1957) emphasize the failure of virtue among those in charge: the men who run the French Army in World War I and the men who run New York after dark are monsters. *The Defiant Ones* (1958) treats racism so aptly it touches even racists, and *Gigi* (1958) reclaims the musical's moribund sense of style and panache. By 1959, we take in stride the frank looks at radical sexuality in *Suddenly, Last Summer* or *Compulsion,* even at the over-the-top sex comedy of *Some Like It Hot,* in some ways the most dangerous film in the group. The 1950s have been taking on the exceptional.

Foreign film greatly assisted. Put simply, it was a revelation. For decades Hollywood had colonized the world's theatres with its star system, its ethics of gallantry and self-esteem, and its often ambivalent notions about class, with Warner Brothers denouncing it, MGM quietly approving of it, and Paramount relishing it because everyone looks so neat in dinner clothes. Few foreign films caught America's attention during the Studio Age, but the court-ordered divestiture that took control of the nation's theatres away from the studio moguls in the 1950s encouraged not only independent production here but the independent distribution of cinema from there as well. Then, too, six years of headlines about a war that took place in many countries but not in ours might have made us curious about the various peoples who had become our enemies and our allies.*

And of course the films themselves astonished with their novelty. The more or less documentary observations of Italian neo-realism, the whimsey and bite of British comedy, the epic intensity of Ingmar Bergman, or, say, the parable-like purity of *La Strada* compared with the cynical wisdom of *Room at the Top*—here were styles of storytelling utterly unlike what Americans were used to and had always thought sufficient in

---

*It is illustrative that the Academy of Motion Picture Arts and Sciences began giving occasional awards to foreign films in 1946, but did not institute an annual one until 1956.

film. The world grew larger; many of the more discriminating moviegoers found it difficult to return to native fare after *The Red Shoes* or *Ballad of a Soldier.* Moreover, foreign films acquired a certain cachet, an opportunist's prestige, and for some there was the attraction of frankness in sexual matters.

Joseph Losey's *The Servant* (1963) typifies the appeal of foreign films: in the use of the newly prominent avant-garde dramatist Harold Pinter as writer; in the moody, oblique storytelling, which excites one's concentration as no Hollywood film ever wanted to; in the nuanced, anti-starish acting of Dirk Bogarde, James Fox, and Sarah Miles; and in the highly erotic nature of the relationship between a callow young playboy (Fox) and his manservant (Bogarde), who introduces a strange assortment of women friends into the household, first his "sister" (Miles) and later a bunch of gloomy floozies, plumed like birds of prey in high-fashion black.

By today's standards, *The Servant* seems tame, a little too implied from first to last. Odd clues here and there suggest a sadomasochistic homosexual liaison between master and servant—photographs of bodybuilders on the wall of the servant's bedroom, a kind of "marital spat" dialogue style when the protocols of class have broken down and the servant treats the master as a contemptible intimate, and especially a bizarre and apparently unmotivated scene in which the two play hide-and-seek, the master driven to terror when the servant finds him. Yet Pinter and Losey both draw back from anything more overt, and all the sex play involves the men with Miles, most fiercely when Losey catches Fox and Miles lolling in a chair. The camera shoots from behind the chair's back, so that all we see is their heads and limbs. The two are dressed. But they grow strangely silent, and as the scene fades, Fox's leg slides into view, naked.

In direction, writing, acting, and subject matter, foreign films seemed to a segment of the moviegoing public not only different from Hollywood's output but better, more searching and adult. And the growth of the metropolitan art-house theatre, which catered almost exclusively to the intellectual, emphasized the development of what might be called the "multiple audience," another innovation of sixties cinema. The old Studio Age belief held that there is one all-basic filmgoing audience. There were sectors within that audience, true—the women who attended Ruth Chatterton or Irene Dunne weepies, for instance, as opposed to the men who enjoyed George Raft's gangster pictures. Still, even such disparate publics

Foreign film had a sensuality and contemporaneity that Hollywood soon imitated. Above, the sex: Albert Finney and Joyce Redman in Tony Richardson's *Tom Jones*. Below, the contempo: *Weltstar* Anita Ekberg greets the international press in Federico Fellini's *La Dolce Vita*.

were assumed to be compatible elements of one great public that could in theory attend any movie made. From the 1920s through the Second World War, moviegoing was America's basic public event, the truest basis of its sense of community; not suprisingly, the number of paid admissions per capita was much higher then than it is today.

But then this alleged unity of moviegoers—of Americans, really— was another of Hollywood's attempts to create something by pretending to reflect it. The sense of community in the place that is safe was a delusion, a lie, like Clark Gable's casually swaggering outlaw sweetie or Joan Crawford's shopgirl princess, presented as exemplars of an American type. Nonsense. There were no such people except in the movies—or did you really think you lived down the street from someone coached by George Cukor, lit by William Daniels, dressed by Adrian, and written by Frances Marion, Joseph Mankiewicz, and Anita Loos?

The discovery that films could be so different from each other that they might profitably address totally different segments of the available audience supported the rise of the independent filmmaker—as witness that of the thirteen fifties movies cited seven paragraphs ago, fully half were released by United Artists, founded in 1919 as the house of talent too self-motivated to make kowtow to a mogul: Mary Pickford, Douglas Fairbanks, Charlie Chaplin, D. W. Griffith, and, later, Gloria Swanson and producers Samuel Goldwyn and David O. Selznick. Literally, the independent moviemaker was anyone who worked extramurally, beyond the walls of the major production factories. By the 1950s—with the old-time moguls dying out, their monolithic studios imploding, and United Artists' release schedule welcoming more and more contributors—independence meant sophisticated, eclectic, adventurous, unique. Osmotically, the independent's aesthetic influenced all Hollywood, even the honchos and employees of what was left of the studio system. Just as establishment Hollywood had no choice but to acknowledge the power of foreign cinema with an annual Oscar, the movie industry began to absorb the ideas and experiments of the rogue writers, stars, and directors. The revolution, then, is prepared in the postwar years. It builds in the 1950s. It pays off, it most apparently occurs, it *wins*: in the 1960s.

Consider how different all of Hollywood's output became even in their most basic aperçus, how strongly nonconformist and genre films alike revise the social and moral codes that had dominated Hollywood in the studio years. It is as if a new Tablet of Commandments had been handed down. For instance: *Thou shalt treat with irreverence that great American taboo, religion.* The classic entry here is Richard Brooks's *Elmer Gantry* (1960), right at the decade's start, a look at the huckster element in the backwoods divine. The picture wears its mission heavily, warning us, before the credits, "We believe that certain elements of revivalism can bear examination—that the conduct of some revivalists makes a mockery of the traditional beliefs and practices of organized Christianity! . . . However, due to the highly controversial nature of this film, we strongly urge you to prevent impressionable children from seeing it!"

It's a little late for that, as we're already assembled in the theatre by the time we read it. I still recall, as a respectably impressionable eleven-year-old, thinking something like, Hold on to your hats, upon reading Brooks's caveat. And *Elmer Gantry* did indeed have impact in 1960. But, unlike *Psycho* and *The Manchurian Candidate,* it has long ceased to shock. One problem is Brooks's coat-and-tie pacing; despite the antic nature of revivalism, this is a rather dignified production (perhaps in self-defense), from the grandly David Selznick–like opening on the first page of Sinclair Lewis's novel, pulled away as the prose comes to life, to the climactic conflagration of Jean Simmons's temple, drawn out in unnecessary detail. But then Majesty of Contents was a curse of the 1960s, as running times of two hours or more became a badge of importance and the 90-minute feature, once Hollywood's staple, fell into modified disrepute. Significant films bear not only significant messages but significant running times.*

Nor does Gantry himself enliven the epic. Burt Lancaster won his reputation for overdoing, like the stage actors who crowded their auditorium-filling gestures into the early talkies, mystifying the spectators. Is this an opera? Lancaster is an opera, luckily most often in operatic roles—natural overdoers like the soaring, flashing hero of *The Crimson*

Elmer Gantry runs 145 minutes; its action could easily have been accommodated in 100 minutes. One reason behind the inflation of the A feature was, once again, the war on television: the most notable video dramas filled 90-minute slots, thus degrading the very number. A better reason was that (some) movies were getting more complex and nuanced than had been usual under the Mayers and Zanucks. *The Hustler* lasts 135 minutes, not one of them excrescent. But some movies simply took their time. Elmer Gantry isn't crowded. It's slow, ponderous, *see how I run.*

Pirate (1952), the slob gunslinger of *Vera Cruz* (1954), or the con man
of *The Rainmaker* (1956).* Gantry, too, is an overdoer, a ham of God,
but Lancaster keeps trying to act him with his hair and teeth. Now he's
tousled: drunk. Now he's coiffed: fake reverent. Now he's wispy: unsure.
And that picket-fence smile! You wouldn't *sell* this man a used car. Worst
of all, neither writer-director Brooks nor Lancaster seems to have decided
whether Gantry is a scummy fake or a man of some belief. In the end,
Elmer Gantry is important not for what it says about people who live off
religion—it says nothing conclusive—but for daring to open the question
and, in the light of more contemporary developments in the world of
moneygrubbing evangelicism, presciently noting the like-unto-like attraction of the prostitute and the preacher.

But at least: *Thou shalt question the fairness of the American political
system,* and now our hats will fly, for one thing Americans pride themselves
on is the *limited* corruption of their government. The revelation of a bought
senator in *Mr. Smith Goes to Washington* or *Born Yesterday* is not intolerable;
every apple barrel has its rotter. However, *Advise and Consent* (1962) and
The Best Man (1964) suggest that it isn't a few scoundrels but the whole
system that rots. The best in man is anathema to the procedures of D.C.,
we learn. The worst—hypocrisy in particular—is not only appropriate to
but ideal in American politics. This is a basic rite of sixties rebellion:
unmasking the authority figures who advocate one kind of life yet live
another. The Bad Father not only doesn't know best; he is actively pursuing a code of deceit and aggression. Like Pat Hingle, Warren Beatty's
father in *Splendor in the Grass,* the villains of these pieces seem to regard
the world as their personal domain. They are Studio Age moguls let loose
in public life.

Interestingly, both *Advise and Consent* and *The Best Man* turn on
threats to expose a political opponent's homosexual past. This was startling enough on Broadway, where both projects began (*Advise and Consent*
in adaptation from Allen Drury's novel). On screen, it was sensation.
Advise and Consent even takes us into New York's gay underworld, as the
beleaguered Don Murray seeks out his former lover, John Granger. Director Otto Preminger added another check to his short list of Taboos to
Be Shattered in Murray's nervous visit to a repellent pimp (Larry Tucker)

---

*Lancaster also underplays—*Come Back, Little Sheba* (1952), *Gunfight at the
O.K. Corral* (1957). But then he isn't Lancaster; he's your accountant, or somebody's
uncle.

in an apartment of cats and beads and a needling cup of tea. Finally the pimp sends Murray to a certain Club 602, and, to Frank Sinatra's deceptively mellow reading of the kind of ballad that means one thing to homosexuals and another to straights, Don Murray and America get their first look at a gay bar.

It's a brief one, for instantly Murray sees everything his family life and political career were meant to erase—not least the blond, collegiate Granger—and flees. It's a telling scene, for the dark, crammed 602 contrasts with the sunny, wide-open terrain of Preminger's D.C., where most of the film takes place. Typically for this era, Preminger really exploits his location shots; the whole film seems to unwind in the shadow of the Washington Monument. And of course Preminger fills his show with the Hollywood great and near-great who have the dignity—at any rate, the pomposity—to carry themselves as statesmen. This includes such obvious choices as good guy Majority Leader Walter Pidgeon, swank President Franchot Tone, forthright Vice-President Lew Ayres, Folk Hero Henry Fonda,* who plays the would-be Secretary of State, and Charles Laughton, the Senior Senator from South Carolina. As actor, Laughton is unquestionably *Advise and Consent*'s best man, an obese slob in wrinkled coat and floppy ties, stoop-shouldered, prowling rather than walking, always ready to pause and admire a pretty woman, disturbingly articulate in defense of the old values and disgust with all else. This is a worrisome D.C., short of best men and rich in blackguards and fools, like the old duffer of a senator, used as a running gag, who sleeps through everything and shudders awake with "Opposed! I'm opposed!" And note that while Murray's sense of murdered honor drives him to suicide, the usual method of disposing of homosexuals in pre-Stonewall art, the film was really made to censure Senator George Grizzard, on the good guy's side but the man who organized the blackmailing of Murray. Similarly, *The Best Man,* set at a deadlocked Presidential convention, is less concerned with identifying that man—as a Studio Age movie would have been—than with showing how easily the worst men look good. Thus these two films do not treat right and wrong sides, really, but right and wrong methods of pursuing one's goals—a highly liberal notion after the hardline, cold-war 1950s.

Exposing the frailties of a system built on moral imperatives but

*Just as he was most apt in his youth as the juvenile hero of various historical sagas, Fonda in maturity proved indispensable as the land's ultimate senior citizens—he turns up also as *The Best Man*'s protagonist and as the President in *Fail-Safe.*

supervised by opportunists is daring enough. What if *Thou shalt question even the values of that most sacred place of all, Hollywood itself*? Cynical looks at the movie industry were inevitable in an age dominated by studio-system renegades, so thou shalt make *Two Weeks in Another Town* (1962), directed by Vincente Minnelli for MGM, most studio of studios, most Hollywood of places, where emperor L. B. Mayer humbled the greatest stars. Minnelli seems to be attempting a runoff of *La Dolce Vita,* seen in the U.S. only the year before. The town is Rome; we take a look at the expatriate cinema set. Kirk Douglas is a has-been actor, Edward G. Robinson a director, George Hamilton a difficult young actor, Cyd Charisse a temptress, Claire Trevor Edward G.'s angry wife, and exotic, beloved Daliah Lavi lends Continental charm. Where Fellini wonders and despairs at the baseness of the high life, its lack of a major theme, Minnelli cannot quite bring himself to swear off the Hollywood that was, cannot conceive of life without themes. For Minnelli, some people have a theme and some don't; he dare into *Angst* no more deeply go. Kirk Douglas's theme is regeneration, Edward G.'s is survival, and Minnelli's is even selfish manipulators (like Robinson) believe in the beauty of a great film.

This film is not great. It has its touches of *vita*. But when Fellini wants to show us a crazy mad reckless world, he shows us a crazy mad reckless world. Minnelli shows Douglas drunk, driving with Cyd Charisse, Charisse screaming in terror and Douglas grimacing (yes, but I mean even *more* than usual) while the camera revolves around the car as luridly as possible. It's an entirely ersatz film, two minutes in another town, to judge by the scanty location work.* Still, it affirms the era's patricidal metaphor in Douglas's climactic renunciation of Robinson, the actor becoming his own director, his own authority figure. And at least Minnelli does give us, in the character of an Italian producer, a coolly callous plutocrat.

Christopher Plummer, the producer in *Inside Daisy Clover* (1965), is yet more to the point: an insidious manipulator of human beings. He makes real life the way his employees make movies. Oddly, his smooth manner accords with Hollywood films' traditional view of the mogul as a nifty dandy (think of Adolphe Menjou in the 1937 *A Star Is Born*) rather than the booming, vulgar ogres they really were. We are in Hol-

---

*And must Douglas refer to Cinecittà as "Chīnnachētah Studios"?—a faux pas not challenged in American film till son Michael's stubborn "nucular" (for *nuclear*) in *The China Syndrome*, seventeen years later.

lywood in the 1930s, a ground zero of Studio Age tactics, and director Robert Mulligan and writer Gavin Lambert (adapting his novel) are most thorough in their distaste for the sheer business of Hollywood, the way it makes people into product.

Plummer's latest promotion, the title part, is Natalie Wood, a key sixties personality in her progression from the tragically love-struck teen in *Splendor in the Grass* in 1961 to her merrily "swinging" wife in *Bob & Carol & Ted & Alice* in 1969. Wood's ability to survive Plummer's tyranny (including a more or less staged marriage with a homosexual star) and say goodbye to Hollywood is made a moral lesson—one diluted, unfortunately, by the artificial quality of the background. This is a strangely sullen and empty film for a backstager about Hollywood in its dazzle days when all the world was a screen, and though Wood is touted as the latest song-and-dance sensation, she apparently only makes shorts built around André and Dory Previn's "You're Gonna Hear from Me," a pastiche of the typical Judy Garland up tune. Wood delivers it as her screen test, in an exaggerated tomboy outfit and painted freckles that make her look like Pippi Longstocking. Later, the tune provisions Wood's official debut, in a Herbert Ross staging that has Wood dancing through a sky of process shots (Saturn glides by at one point) in a lamé tomboy outfit. The 1930s simply did not look or sound like this—and shorts were used as program fillers, not as inaugurations of stardom.

Religion, two-party democracy, Hollywood—nothing is safe: rather, nothing, from now on, is exempt from revisionist examination. And *Thou shalt despise even warmaking,* an unthinkable act only a few years earlier in the depths of the East-West freeze-off. Fifties war films never liked but always accepted war. War was like the common cold: it may not be fun, but it's always going to be there. In the 1960s, *some* movies were notably ambivalent about war, not perhaps rejecting it but suspicious of its authoritarian hierarchy and its demand that ordinary men suddenly turn into heroes. "All he did was die," says Julie Andrews in *The Americanization of Emily* (1964), when her lover James Garner makes the cover of *Life* as the first man killed in the Normandy invasion. He's not a hero; he's a victim, as were her father, brother, and husband. It's World War II and everybody's dying. What, the film asks, is there to celebrate in that? Especially since Garner was the finagling moocher who got out of all the unpleasant duties that everyone else had to perform, such as dying for his country. But it seems that the Navy was being edged out of Europe by

The only good hero is a dead hero. James Coburn forces an unwilling
James Garner onto Omaha Beach in *The Americanization of Emily,* in a
macabre parody of the "I Want You!" recruiting poster of Uncle Sam. I
want you *dead!*

the Army and the Air Force, and needed some PR to break the ice at
the next appropriations summit. So Garner is forced—at gunpoint—onto
Omaha Beach, and duly shot, and duly honored. Garner's fellow Navy
officer James Coburn can't understand why Andrews doesn't respond to
his condolence call. He's waving *Life* at her, and all she wants is her
boyfriend back, along with "his cowardly, selfish, greedy appreciation
of life."

   The Americanization of Emily is a comedy, so of course Garner turns
up alive. But other films took a harder line—not, and this is significant,
fancy-pants items from the avant-garde catalogue but old-fashioned, big-
star entries that told their conservative audiences that war was *not* to be
accepted, that it shouldn't always have to be there. Consider what is
virtually a fifties war film reinvented by a sixties worldview, *None But the
Brave* (1965).

   The cast alone prepares us for a strait placement of genre: Frank

Sinatra (who also directed), Clint Walker, Tommy Sands, Tony Bill, Brad Dexter. Now, there are those who go by the rule that any film in which Brad Dexter appears is automatically out of the running. This is extreme. I go by the rule that any film in which Brad Dexter *has more than ten lines* is out of the running, and *None But the Brave* just makes the cut.

So let us consider. It's World War II, in the Far East. American soldiers have crash-landed on a remote island held by stranded Japanese. Early hostilities come to seem like folly to both sides: better to pool their resources for mutual survival. It's a delicate truce but, as time passes, a secure one, strengthened by respect and even affection. Most interesting is the film's complete lack of an absolute Us versus Them, a moralistic view of which side is right. In fact, the Japanese are naturalized for us almost to a fault, especially as they speak their own language to English subtitles, while *we* have Brad Dexter. Moreover, the movie is narrated (in English) by the Japanese commander (Tatsuya Mihashi), framing the action with a personable and philosophic tone. Fifties war films never forget that the Japanese fought on Hitler's side and attacked Pearl Harbor; this war film doesn't care. It sees war not as attack and defense but as a series of chance encounters among men who would be more profitably engaged in making friends than corpses. As in *Advise and Consent,* the issue is not the fairness of heroism but the heroism of fairness.

This is an extremely advanced attitude for a movie that otherwise follows the clichés—as when the Japanese commander, looking over the Americans on an intelligence sortie, identifies his opposite, Clint Walker, as "my colleague in the game of death." How can he tell, you ask? By "his lonely detachment from the others." (Easy for him to say. The wooden Walker would evince a lonely detachment from the others in a panty raid in Fort Lauderdale on the last night of spring break.) Naturally, Sinatra will be the wearily cynical corpsman and Tommy Sands the shrilly by-the-book lieutenant who twists his vowels into a kind of boot-camp Geschrei. And of course it is an American destroyer that turns up at the end to pick up our boys, forcing the Japanese to attack their erstwhile friends. We lose a few men and all the Japanese die. Finally, a title card: "Nobody ever wins."

The age is re-examining the received pieties. *Thou shalt question the beauty of marriage,* for instance, in Mike Nichols's filming of Edward Albee's play *Who's Afraid of Virginia Woolf?* (1966), as Elizabeth Taylor verbally racks Richard Burton in what their fans fondly hoped was a movie-within-a-movie. *Thou shalt question even the very nature of romance,* in William Wyler's *The Collector* (1965), in which working-class Terence Stamp courts condign Samantha Eggar by literally taking her prisoner and finally killing her, another butterfly like the thousands in his collection—and, at the fade-out, he is off with his net to snatch still another prize. In earlier times, *The Collector* would have been a thriller, distancing us from the horror. But William Wyler doesn't do thrillers.* *The Collector* is a love story in which the hero is a psychopath. Indeed, *Thou shalt be sympathetic to psychotic heroes,* which is the living end, in Frank Perry's *David and Lisa* (1963), perhaps the first American film in which the romantic leads are not only institutionalized loonies but spoiled idiot children. David (Keir Dullea) is a pompous coward who becomes hysterical if anyone touches him. Lisa (Janet Margolin) is a pert monster who speaks in (and professes to understand only) rhyme. *Virginia Woolf* is a star-powered Broadway adaptation, *The Collector* a Hollywood-sponsored English production derived from lit, and *David and Lisa* one of the new low-budget serious films. I take the broad sampling to demonstrate how influential the new code was becoming. Even forms that don't dare, as a rule, are daring now. Not that they *intend* to be daring, necessarily—it's that the possibilities for any film have become so wide that it almost cannot help but surprise us.

Some moviemakers had been waiting for the opportunity to surprise. Where fools feared to tread, devils rushed in: such as Billy Wilder. His personal commandment was *Thou shalt make merry comedies about disgusting people.* Sociopathic slime had long been Wilder's favorite class of people— the murderously cold-blooded adulterers Barbara Stanwyck and Fred MacMurray in *Double Indemnity* (1944), the undenazifiable Marlene Dietrich in *A Foreign Affair* (1948), virtually the entire cast in *Ace in the Hole* (1951). Even in the quirkily adorable *Some Like It Hot,* just one year before the 1960s begin, Wilder appears to be gearing up for a heavy decade of challenging a lulled and escapist public. Yes, *Some Like It Hot* was and remains widely popular, one of those rare American classics that pleases both the intellectuals and the mass public. Yet Wilder's characteristic misanthropy informs this farce no less than the Swiftian *Ace in the Hole,* only it is veiled. Veiled in Jack Lemmon's transvestite turn as Daphne, so flamboyant—so elated by its own grotesquerie—that we suspect that

---

*I know: *The Desperate Hours*. The exception proves the rule.

Wilder is dosing the audience with fierce medicine coated in sugar. Veiled in Tony Curtis's dead-on impersonation of Cary Grant as a mean-streets phoney dolled up in a yacht and an accent, an archetype of what so many of Hollywood's heroes really were: lit-up hoodlums. Veiled in Marilyn Monroe's most delightful and expert yet most stupid performance, a very icon of the bimbo bombshell she supposedly resented having to play. It is as if Wilder felt he can entertain us best by showing us how sinful and idiotic and fraudulent our entertainments are.

Still, *Some Like It Hot* is a fifties film in its outward show, its "adult" material held within the cultural expectations of a suburban family's Saturday-night movie habit and its agitations kept personal rather than Socialistic. Then, too, transvestism was one of America's fifties fascinations—think of *I Was a Male War Bride* (1949) and Jerry Lewis—as if the pressure toward macho typing of the male population were making men crazy for letting go and dressing up. ("Because I just went *gay*, all of a sudden," as Cary Grant explains, wearing a negligée in *Bringing Up Baby*, back in the 1930s.)

Some Like It Hot, above all, wants to forgive its principals. The sixties Wilder is *very* sixties, avid to exploit the new liberties; he won't find much to forgive. *The Apartment* (1960)—like *Elmer Gantry, Psycho,* and *The Little Shop of Horrors* an initiating piece, drawing us into the dawn of the age—is Wilder at his toughest. Who is there to admire here? The jerk who renders himself homeless for professional advancement, lending his apartment to executives for juju trysts? The cute elevator operator who is willing to throw her life away for an executive who is clearly only using her? The executive himself? Jack Lemmon, Shirley MacLaine, Fred MacMurray. These are apt Wilder people, all capable of encompassing the Wilderian paradox world of attractive goons, winsome losers, and sympathetic heels. Yet aren't they all at their least appealing here? *The Apartment* is merry: quick, funny, New York without the danger. We even get Christmas. But these characters *are* disgusting: such eerie goons, such total losers, such self-rationalizing heels. The difference between *Some Like It Hot* and *The Apartment* is the difference between a nonconformist in an age of conformity and a nonconformist in an age of breakout. In 1959, Wilder is a black jester, not largely understood, uncomfortable company. In 1960, Wilder is a *philosophe,* expounding the latest realities. He's supposed to be uncomfortable.

Well, it's an uncomfortable age, the one in which everyone finally admitted that America is made of unreconcilable antagonisms of rich and poor, intellectual and vacationer, lawyer-banker-manager Northeast and yeoman Midwest—and, mainly, sensualist and puritan.* Sex is the source of the essential American hypocrisy and it informed the most basic mandate in the new Tablets: *Thou shalt deal most honestly with sex in all its varieties.*

This is formidable. This, in America, is the last no-no, broader, touchier, and more loaded than even the sanctity of religion, the honor of war, and the purity of American government put together. And we are not speaking simply of poking a camera into a louche hotel room in Arizona or implying that Audrey Hepburn turns tricks. We speak of devoting the 125 minutes of George Cukor's *The Chapman Report* (1962) to female sexuality in such diverse forms that a number of the women stars play aggressive man chasers. Granted, Greta Garbo, Marlene Dietrich, Jean Harlow, and Mae West, among others, assumed this role in olden days. But these were exceptional personalities. Their fame was partly based on their reversal of what was thought proper—and were not all four restrained by the revitalizing of the Production Code in 1934, Garbo and Dietrich smoothed out and finally Americanized, Harlow tamed, and West virtually driven from the screen? Granted, also, we are not much shocked, even in 1962, when Shelley Winters spends her portion of *The Chapman Report* trying to tolerate her boring schmuck of a husband and throwing herself pathetically at Ray Danton. Shelley was born to throw herself at men, as pathetically as possible, and Ray Danton will do. But Cukor also gives us smashing Brit Glynis Johns—who suffers from an

---

*The populist and progressive eras of the nineteenth and early twentieth centuries of course politicized such antagonisms, but the troubles were not universally recognized, which is one reason why some historians argue that populism and progressivism were, ultimately, failures. Bryan, La Follette, Eugene McCarthy, McGovern. All pushed toward the Presidency; all failed. Even going back as far as the Jacksonian revolution, one can say that this great American liberalism was capped by the Presidencies of the two Roosevelts, who by reform policies built upon leadership-class probity were meant to unite the nation's warring factions. Still, the war was underground, seldom publicized. As the Pulitzer Prize–winning journalist Ray Stannard Baker noted in the early 1900s, "I used to be sure reform would sweep the country; that is, I always used to be sure until I talked to the man next to me on the streetcar." It was not till the 1960s that Baker and his fellow citizen really came to blows, most illustratively in 1968 in Chicago. Not till then, surely, does the appearance of fair compromise evaporate. Not till then have we proved that the nation comprehends no community, only sections and partisans.

Aggressive women of *The Chapman Report*. Above, admiring Efrem Zimbalist, Jr., Claire Bloom is saucy, Glynis Johns bewitched, Jane Fonda
bothered, and Shelley Winters Wintersesque. (Zimbalist is bemildred.)
Below, Johns, reciting Ernest Dowson, notes hunk Ty Hardin. Quoth
Jones, "What a magnificent animal!"

effete schmuck of a husband—spotting Ty Hardin on the beach and hiring
him to "model" even before that word had become a euphemism. And
lo, saintly Claire Bloom turns up as a nymphomaniac! Okay, marriage to
Rod Steiger would unhinge anybody, but what must the women in the
audience have been thinking? Aren't they all married to Rod Steigers?
Even Mae West, the most aggressive woman in Hollywood history, limited
her presentation of sexuality to verbal fun and the odd embrace. West
was a tease. *The Chapman Report* is illustration.

One of the things it illustrates is rape, and it is interesting that
Cukor, the "woman's director," allegedly unable to deal well with men
things, brings off perhaps the most persuasive rape scene of a decade that
would become fascinated with them. Claire Bloom is blearily kibitzing
at her sleazy boyfriend's all-male poker party, and Cukor exactly catches
the reckless heat of men just realizing, as they laugh and joke and look
at Bloom, that not only can they do it but they are just about to. "Here
we go," says one of them as they start.

If rape, why not abortion? *Love with the Proper Stranger* (1963) treats
one, with amazing realism for a Paramount picture starring Natalie Wood
and Steve McQueen. We see the empty apartment, the "doctor," the
insidious paraphernalia. We see Wood getting greatly spooked—she's
always at her best in the mad scenes—but it is McQueen who breaks
first, grabbing Wood and shouting out a cancellation of the deal. Again,
remember these are *stars* we see, stars as frigid or oversexed—*The Chapman
Report*'s Claire Bloom is shown the most disgusting lawless, unattractive,
sex-grubbing loser in all California and she still can't say no. She's the
kind of woman who inveigles delivery boys into her bedroom, even if
they're Chad Everett. Now we see Steve McQueen leading Natalie Wood
to an abortion and Wood almost going through with it. Anyone can put
an abortion into an independent *succès d'estime*. When the commercial stars
authenticate the breaking of taboos, then you *know* the times they are a
changin'.

Prostitutes, too, take stage. Audrey Hepburn's Holly Golightly may
have been the last of the touch-me-not hookers who somehow are never
quite seen actually plying their trade—prostitutes without sex. Barbara
Stanwyck runs a bordello full of the real thing in Edward Dmytryk's
Walk on the Wild Side (1962), and Shirley MacLaine plays a merry prostitute in *Irma la Douce* (1963), not surprisingly in one of Billy Wilder's
films, for here Wilder overturns an outstanding tradition. Hollywood

prostitutes, such as Bette Davis's "cabaret hostess" in *Marked Woman* (1937) or Mae Clarke and Vivien Leigh in the two versions of *Waterloo Bridge* (1931, 1940), were expected to pay the price, ideally die the death. They must never be content, willing, philosophical, as MacLaine is as Irma the Sweet. We get a last look at an out-and-out hard-core yet emotionally redeemable prostitute in Shirley Jones in *Elmer Gantry*—and how that dates the film, antiques it. Jones herself is excellent, closing in on the ambivalence of the tramp who wants out but doesn't believe in it, who sets up sideshow brother Lancaster without being certain, up to the last second, whether or not she can go through with it. She earned her Oscar. It's director Brooks who's at fault, trying to encircle the lurid events with an apology of melodrama: she's angry, she's hurt, she doesn't know what she's doing.

They know what they're doing over at *Walk on the Wild Side,* where prostitution isn't a refuge for the heartbroken but a living. It's a living, sister. "What are you doing here?" Laurence Harvey asks Jane Fonda when he encounters her at Stanwyck's pitch, the Doll House. Last thing Harvey knew, Fonda was a waif and petty thief. "I run the candy concession," says Fonda, half-sneering. Men can be so square. Dmytryk is square; he's trying to make a fifties-trim film in a sixties-heavy setting. Oh, the New Orleans bordello is presented directly from Nelson Algren's novel, complete with bar, black jazz band, black maid, and enforcer in a three-piece suit who likes to be tender with the girls when he beats them up. And Stanwyck has a legless husband. But the fetching swagger of Elmer Bernstein's swagger-rock title theme does not play out. There's too much of the movie-star show at work as Harvey busies himself with his Southern accent (more convincing, it happens, than his on-and-off North American in *The Manchurian Candidate*), as Fonda reveals but a shade of the actress she will become, as the tight budget keeps Dmytryk from giving us a single view of New Orleans or the vaguest idea of period—it's supposed to be the 1930s, but everything looks rather present-day. Capucine, Harvey's love and Stanwyck's prize doll, is dressed in absurdly high-modern clothes; at one point, deciding to leave the Doll House with Harvey, she starts to pack and it looks as if Pierre Cardin were showing off his spring line.

This is something the 1960s killed off: the movie-star "look" that invades period and locale with the perquisites of the Heavy Name, what we might recognize as the Alice Faye approach to costume drama (i.e.:

Always appear as if you were about to win at the Oscar banquet). No doubt Dmytryk was hampered by his producer, reportedly Capucine's lover—and it should be noted that the director does make it exceedingly clear that a bordello madam might easily be a lesbian. True, Agnes Moorehead had played a lesbian bordello madam in *The Revolt of Mamie Stover* in 1956—but the bordello was a "saloon" and the lesbian discreet. Stanwyck is damn quick open about her interest in Capucine, especially when Harvey turns up to take her away. Consider, in these very early 1960s, aristo Laurence Olivier's casual but unmissable come-on to slave Tony Curtis in *Spartacus* (1960), and a remake of *The Children's Hour* (1961), this time with the play's lesbian psychology restored, and we have another aspect of sex that this decade particularly brought forth, homosexuality. It can be subtle, insignificant, momentary, but it is—again, quite suddenly at the start of the 1960s—definitely present.

In one case, the gay infusion takes over an entire movie, and this is a mainstream, big-studio, major-names production, *The Roman Spring of Mrs. Stone* (1961). We have Warner Brothers, Technicolor, Vivien Leigh, and Warren Beatty, fresh from his major debut in *Splendor in the Grass*. Hardly an underground venture. Now, the film does treat the Widow Stone's decline into masochistic degradation in strictly heterosexual terms. But culturally, instinctively, and symbolically it appears to be a parable on the terrors of coming out in a pre-Stonewall era. Gavin Lambert's script, from Tennessee Williams's story, sets down the terms of the action so boldly only a fool or a straight could fail to comprehend, as when Leigh's best friend, Coral Browne, referring to the late Mr. Stone, says, "Everyone thought you'd married him to avoid . . ." "What?" asks Leigh. "*Love,*" says Browne, meaning sex, meaning the Stones' was a cover marriage. Or when procuress Lotte Lenya refers to Leigh as a "chicken hawk"—this is gay argot—or tells chicken Beatty, "This woman is only beginning to find out what loneliness is." Or, best of all, and very Tennessee, when Leigh observes, "People who are very beautiful make their own laws."

The entire film appears to urge "Mrs." Stone out of her bourgeois reticence into the fleshly underworld, to sever her ties with "legitimate" people—not just an inconvenient American couple, whom Leigh puts off with a lie, but even confidante Browne—and to sink, at last, to tossing her house keys out her window to be picked up by a piece of street scuzz who may kill her.

Gay prostitutes, one relatively open (Capucine in *Walk on the Wild Side*) and one "translated" (Warren Beatty, with procuress Lotte Lenya, in *The Roman Spring of Mrs. Stone*). Capucine's coy but Beatty's a cheat—for "Liar!" Lenya is crying. "Everyone knows that you never gave in to any of them. Not even Mrs. Jameson-Walker when she presented you with a pair of magnificent ruby cuff links—*which you tried to tell me were glass!*"

As a whole, *The Roman Spring of Mrs. Stone* lacks grip, partly because of the proportion of location work to studio mock-ups, which gives us more genuine Rome than the 1950s would have but too much imitation. Nor is José Quintero's direction as enlightening as, say, George Cukor's would have been. But then Cukor would surely not have wielded Quintero's amusingly coy camera, responding to the tense whimsey of Williams-Lambert by holding back on Warren Beatty's entrance as we wait to feast our eyes on this divo, or dwelling on a shot of a barber lovingly treating Beatty to a hot towel. Here is something unusual: a film that, but for the one character's switched pronouns, is entirely gay.

Most of sixties gay matter, however, is a libel, gays as insipid suicides and psychotic villains.* It will take another decade for Hollywood even to begin to accept gay as gay rather than as a metaphor for insanity and malice, in such exceptional films as *Little Big Man* (1970), *The Boys in the Band* (1970), and *Cabaret* (1972). So, for the time being, we have the hateful Stanwyck, the delectably lurid Olivier, the obligatory suicide without which *The Children's Hour* could not conclude—not to mention Lotte Lenya's vampire-like lesbian Rosa Klebb in *From Russia with Love* (1964) and Honor Blackman's Pussy Galore, the dyke-to-be-man-conquered, in *Goldfinger* (1964), the two helping to fill out the James Bond series' love of picturesque accessories. There are some nice surprises, though, such as Robert Redford's movie star in *Inside Daisy Clover,* played with a sharp observance of the type of actor who is never, never off camera. Working in the tiny space between mercurial and moody, between solid and tense, Redford's Wade Lewis runs exclusively on ego-fulfillment, on the need to charm everyone in the room, then move on to the next room, collecting worshippers. His sexuality is much less important to him than his ability to enchant the world; one has the feeling that Redford sees Lewis as pansexual rather than homosexual. He needs everyone. It was a daring role to take on, for with only two rather obscure films in his résumé, Redford was tending a highly vulnerable career. (He barely places an "also starring" credit for *Daisy Clover,* under the title, while Natalie Wood and Christopher Plummer ride above.) Perhaps it says something about the

---

*Gore Vidal, for one, attempted to pin the libel back on the bigots in *The Best Man,* wherein the politician whose homosexual past stands between him and a Presidential nomination is Cliff Robertson, playing a character otherwise apparently modeled on Richard Nixon.

era's expanding tolerance that a potential star could take on a gay part— a far from admirable one, at that.

Even *None But the Brave*—did Frank Sinatra really direct this movie?—yields a view of the Japanese commander's almost passionate love for one of his men, so badly wounded that Dr. Sinatra must cross over from the American side of the island to amputate a gangrenous leg. In fact, we see no more than the commander's paternal heartening of the stricken soldier, running his hand through the boy's hair and verbally caressing him. It's not precisely gay, but one notices it. One could hardly imagine Clint Walker doing that if Tommy Sands had got wounded. Of course, on an American movie screen the Japanese are foreigners even on a Pacific island, and foreigners have foreign ways. Still, comparing the manner in which *None But the Brave* executes genre agenda with the purer style of fifties war films leaves aficionados of the military format disconcerted. There has been no wholesale reconstruction of fifties technique or worldview, of the attitudes sounded in a major effort like *From Here to Eternity* or a mid-list special like *Battle Cry* or countless programmers like *The Girl He Left Behind, The D.I., Darby's Rangers, Take the High Ground,* or *When Hell Broke Loose.* Still, essential ideals are missing, and in between the cartoon panels, real people briefly emerge. Hollywood no longer sees war as inevitable because the rest of the world is made of Nazis and slant-eyed devils. War may not be inevitable at all.

This notion alone, which will be pursued a few pages hence in *Dr. Strangelove* and *Fail-Safe,* suggests that Hollywood's artistic revolution in the 1960s is to an extent linked to the revisionist politics of the age. However, like those politics, New Cinema will number opportunists, imitators, and running dogs along with the artists and expounders. Topics have been forced open for investigation, but not invariably by people of judgment and insight. Let us speak not of a better Hollywood, but a different Hollywood. How much better it proves remains to be seen as the decade draws on.

Three

Only Cream and Bastards Rise

More than any other decade, the 1960s is known for its archetypal characters and the stars who substantiated them. Other eras claim definitive figures—the gangsters and the gold diggers of the Depression, say, or the brat packers of the 1980s. But the 1960s seems to break most earnestly with Hollywood typing and casting traditions and to create its own personae and stars.

For one thing, most of the long-lived stars who had weathered shifts in public attention right through the Studio Age had finally passed on (Clark Gable, for instance, who made two last films in this decade, then died; or Gary Cooper, who made one and died; or James Cagney, who made two and retired for twenty years) or were bumped down to secondary or curiosity status (like the Lugosi sisters: Bette Davis, Joan Crawford, and Olivia de Havilland), or reduced to facsimile parts redolent of spent glamour (such as Vivien Leigh and Marlene Dietrich). Moreover, some of the most significant stars brought forth in the 1950s were dead (James Dean) or nearly so (Marilyn Monroe, washed up in the uncompleted *Something's Got to Give* in 1962, or Montgomery Clift, who made five films in the 1960s, playing his own shadow, until he died in 1966), or simply found themselves strapped for decent material (Marlon Brando, who scarcely took a worthy role till Don Corleone in *The Godfather,* in 1972).

Most important, a number of actors who had made at least some impression in the 1950s did not establish themselves before the 1960s—at that in parts that absorbed the nonconformist hero of the earlier decade but now put him forth not as a loser outsider but as an exponent of the American male: a jump, for instance, from *Rebel Without a Cause* to *Hud.*

Or, as Shirley MacLaine puts it in *The Apartment,* "Some people take and some people get took." The sixties avatar takes, which brings us to the tenth new commandment, *Thou shalt deconstruct heroism.*

Through sheer diversity of role, for example. In Old Hollywood, stars played type as strictly as possible, with occasional contradictory forays that in the end only affirmed type, as in vamp Theda Bara's Hansel and Gretel retractions, or straight-arrow Milton Sills's bad-boy adventures, or kidlet Mary Pickford's attempts to grow up. In the Studio Age, stars seldom contradicted but could *expand* type, as when Paramount's vamp Marlene Dietrich reformed over at Universal but retained a slice of her joy and a hint of her doom.

In the 1960s, however, stars may develop type as if experimenting, as if not finding but losing themselves. This is innovative especially after the 1950s, characterologically the most limited decade in Hollywood history. The 1950s is Rock Hudson for hero, Marilyn Monroe for blond idiot, and Burt Lancaster for serious and Jerry Lewis for comedy. That is the 1950s. The decade of the sixties is, for instance, aspiring star Robert Redford as soldiers in an offbeat drama (*War Hunt,* 1962) and an offbeat farce (*Situation Hopeless—But Not Serious,* 1965), as Daisy Clover's gay actor, as an escaped convict (*The Chase,* 1966), as a management hatchet man in a Depression-era Southern town (*This Property Is Condemned,* 1966), as a charmingly stiff young lawyer in contemporary New York (*Barefoot in the Park,* 1967), and as the Sundance Kid at the decade's end. The dossier is various, no more. What makes it unusually ambitious for an actor on the rise is Redford's keen edge on character—the bewilderment of the escapee, the deadly commitment of the hatchet man, the absolutely clipped, scornfully no-nonsense, contentiously logical delivery of the lawyer. All this in a man with traditional "movie star" looks—perhaps the only man in this chapter who could have been a big star in the 1920s and 1930s, the heyday of Looks Is Truth. But in the Studio Age a Redford would never have been able to realize a career on such a diversity of characters. A diversity of *parts,* yes—Gary Cooper came to light playing everything from blades to bandits. But Cooper smoothed them all into one character, into Gary Cooper. Redford played his 1960s as an actor, as a number of possible Redfords. Granted, his stardom was not official till he had played Sundance to Paul Newman's Butch Cassidy—as late as in *This Property Is Condemned,* Redford is billed under the title, after "with." Granted, too, supreme stardom dulls his edge, cuts back on the variety of portrayals. He becomes bigger and surer and less interesting. Still, it is the very nature of the 1960s and its sifting of unexplored possibilities that an actor could actually build a career by ignoring the building code, by making a reputation as an actor despite the looks.

An even more typical instance of the sixties leading man is Warren Beatty, for from his debut in *Splendor in the Grass* in 1961 he immediately counted as a major star, unlike the loitering Redford. Also, if Redford's broad range of role gave him plenty of traditional parts (*Barefoot in the Park* could have been made in the 1930s; I see it with Joel McCrea and Margaret Sullavan, directed by Gregory La Cava), Beatty's heroes really exploited the openness of the 1960s—his lavish, sullen Paolo in *The Roman Spring of Mrs. Stone,* with a brave stab at the Italian's macho style that treats men this way, women that way, and Lotte Lenya another way altogether; his selfishly destructive Berry-Berry in *All Fall Down* (1962), most sensitively filling in the outline of the terminally insensitive hero-lout; his nightclub comic in *Mickey One* (1965), a film so artistic yet so vigorously obscure that while many admire it only one person understands it—Beatty, to judge by the confidence of his performance. And this is not to mention *Bonnie and Clyde* (1967), which Beatty not only starred in but produced, and may be one of the four or five definitive films of the decade.

At first, critics likened Beatty to fifties stars. "He talks like Marlon Brando." "He has a startling resemblance to the late James Dean." "His style incorporates distracting elements of Dean and Brando." That one man could remind these jokers of two such dissimilar performers as James Dean and Marlon Brando shows what a nonsense this was, and tells us that as late as the 1960s some movie reviewers were still unable to comprehend the naturalistic revolution in movie acting.* Beatty did not talk like Brando, did not have a resemblance to the late James Dean, and his style incorporated distracting elements of the characters he portrayed. Beatty was a big, sexy, handsome leading man, and they're supposed to be derivative, empty paintings—at least they were in the 1950s. But Beatty wasn't. Beatty was, in fact, an actor of quite surprising gifts, and it is that element of surprise that marks him as a sixties personality, for surprise—reorganizing the game every job or so—is an energy of the 1960s. Gable did not surprise. Cooper did not surprise. Fairbanks, Gilbert, Grant, Tracy, Bogart, Taylor, Stewart did not surprise. Once they found their set of parts and an apt delivery, they stayed with them.† Brando and Dean surprised—especially in their realism of presentation. Next to them, just about everyone but Jo Van Fleet seemed ersatz, puppets pulling their own strings. Redford, too, surprised, in his measured way, faultlessly doling out the reality where Brando, Dean, and Beatty, no less admirably, turned spendthrift. Other actors would fall into step, ridiculing by their very numbers the critics' monotonous invoking of Dean and Brando at each appearance of a naturalistic actor. Oddly, Beatty, for all his new manners, was one of the last of the old Movie Stars, last to see his life turned into a performance by a very predestination of celebrity. The dozen or so actors offered in this chapter as fundamental sixties people can challenge Beatty's fame, but not one of them sees his professional projects, romances, and even politics chronicled as Beatty's are.

Like Beatty, Paul Newman was compared to Brando and the other available names of fifties acting naturalism, but Newman is more like Redford and Beatty in the almost studied diversity of his roles, from working-class tough to Philadelphia socialite to jazz musician, from American Southerner to Israeli to Mexican outlaw. Moreover, if Beatty

---

*There have always been naturalistic movie actors, especially women, especially voluptueuses—Nazimova and Garbo, most notably. But the changeover from artificial depictions, made of indications and attitudes, into fully developed Stanislafskyan replicas of real beings, occurred in New York in the 1930s, thanks to such various influences as the Group Theatre and the Lunts, and it moved into Hollywood along with such Broadway veterans as Elia Kazan and, again, Brando and Dean. (You didn't know Dean started on Broadway, did you? His *curriculum vitae* takes in the very American *See the Jaguar* and the very French *The Immoralist*; and Brando played Shaw and *I Remember Mama*.)

†I think James Cagney surprised; but that needs another book.

was proclaimed the Next Star right at the start of the 1960s and Redford took the decade's length to emerge, Newman had started deep in the 1950s. Yet he is anything but a fifties figure. Though he enjoyed leads in three Broadway hits, touching base with both Williams and Inge, Newman made little impression in Hollywood, slogging from the ancient Rome of *The Silver Chalice* (1954), a vast inane, to *The Helen Morgan Story* (1957), outrageously disingenuous even for a Hollywood bio.* Newman's Rocky Graziano in *Somebody Up There Likes Me* (1956) is seemingly a very contemporary act, the Brooklyn hood turned boxer brought off with the typical naturalistic actor's "surprise." But the public hardly knew Newman then; one surprises not by showing up but by leaping through a succession of tours de force. So the public took Newman for granted— till *The Hustler.*

We have considered this film and Newman's performance already; what matters here is not how fine a film it is and how well Newman plays it, but how neatly character and actor came together for the public in 1961. Fast Eddie's "Even if you beat me, I'm still the best!" revises a long tradition of Hollywood underdog winners with a combination of arrogance and recklessness that blows the trope apart. Newman's hustler is an underdog loser, with the blind, destructive self-love of the jerk who sees himself as a hero. Shirley MacLaine's "Some people take and some people get took" in *The Apartment* could be the caption for Newman's portrayals from *The Hustler* on, as he moves into a dark world of opportunists struggling for power while the innocent sink in despair. The few neutral characters, like Jackie Gleason's Minnesota Fats in *The Hustler,* seem to be there for decoration, removed from this moralistic cosmos of the bruisers and the battered. "Fast Eddie, let's play some pool," says Fats, dapper and cool, twenty-five hours into a marathon bout with Newman and $18,000 down—but, if not a winner, nothing like a loser. Losers have no cool.

Newman's next film success, *Sweet Bird of Youth* (1962), written and directed by Richard Brooks from Tennessee Williams's play, redoubles the stakes. There are no neutrals here. Everyone in Williams is a dreamer or a realist, and the realists murder the dreamers. It's a curious film, half fifties and half sixties. Broadway saw the play in 1959, first of all, and

---

*An old movie-buff trivia question runs "Who plays Helen Morgan in *The Helen Morgan Story*"? Answer: "No one."

Brooks took along four of the stage players—Newman, Geraldine Page, Madeline Sherwood, and Rip Torn. (Be it said that while Ed Begley assumes Sidney Blackmer's role as Boss Finley, president-for-life of a small Southern town, Sherwood's keeper, Torn's father, and Newman's nemesis, Begley was active on Broadway at the time and could easily have originated the part.) A play from 1959 cannot be said to antedate the 1960s by enough to measure with tweezers, but *Sweet Bird* as filmed is technically backward, its sets so soundstage that even modest interiors—any studio's first cinch in art direction—seem false. And Page's envisioned recollection of the first night of her last premiere is violently fake. Even an early talkie, wrestling with the microphone and the crippled camera in its immobile booth, wouldn't have dared a scene this phoney-looking, this . . . well, fifties.

But *Sweet Bird of Youth* does usher in what will be a prevailing view in the 1960s, and one that Newman, more than Beatty or Redford, helps articulate: that the image of a community, of a people respecting some emotional and cultural bond, is a delusion. Hollywood fostered this image, from Warner Brothers' backstage musicals ("Two hundred people! Two hundred jobs!") through Frank Capra's Americana fables ("The people—try and lick that!") to the "we're all in this together" war sagas. Now Hollywood is exposing it as cant. If there is no one true people, how can there be heroes? There would be no heroic stock for them to derive from, no responsive populace to be led and redeemed by them. There would be nothing but oppressors and victims.

So Williams and Brooks show us, in a portrait of a miniature America, power and privilege overwhelming every decent instinct. Brooks even enlarges *Sweet Bird of Youth*'s stage script to show key features of Boss Finley's regime, such as a scene in which he and his coterie screen a piece of video made by Finley's political opponent, exposing Finley corruption. The solution, of course, is to firebomb the opponent's house. Even better is a scene in which Finley presents a gift of jewelry to girlfriend Sherwood after he has learned that she drunkenly scribbled a critique of the Finley bedtime manner in lipstick on a ladies'-room mirror. In the play, we only hear what happened. Brooks shows us Begley snapping the case shut on Sherwood's fingers before he throws her out of town; and Begley's gleaming grin, as the score is about to be settled, is something to see.

Well, okay. Where does Newman fit into all this? At the very center.

And there's the rub. For Newman, this time out, is no hero but a lover boy, Geraldine Page's pickup* and Shirley Knight's old flame. Knight is Boss Finley's daughter; a Studio Age film would have demanded that Newman not only win Knight but beat Finley as a Capra hero beats Edward Arnold. By 1961 this was unusual, even—tragically—unnecessary. It is enough that Newman challenge Begley for the right to love his daughter; since a belief in love is about the only ideal that Hollywood can still count on.

Hud (1963) doesn't even believe in love. Here's Newman as the embodiment of The Self Is the Center of the World, disillusioning his nephew, disgusting his honorable father, and trying to rape the woman indicated as his spiritual and physical match. Here is Newman, really, beating out Beatty and Redford as the era's dark lord through force of meanness. *Hud* was a hit not because people came to gape but because they came to admire. *This* is the 1960s—admitting, at last, that Hud's reckless amorality is what Americans like in a man. In the world of the takers and the taken, Hud is a winner. He's a cheat, sure—but, he explains, "I always say the law was meant to be interpreted in a lenient manner." Even Hud's nephew Brandon de Wilde adores Hud's cheating ways, though de Wilde is obviously the film's moral figure—which explains why de Wilde died young. Hollywood is losing its moral figures. Melvyn Douglas, as Hud's father, balances de Wilde's youthful wonder with a senior's wisdom, but he is powerless, in the process of passing on, like the morality of the Studio Age itself. The trouble with Douglas is that he stands for what is right. Hud stands for what feels good—as does, at first, de Wilde, exhilarated after a night in town when he helps Newman beat up two men in a bar. De Wilde has had a taste of being a winner, too, of being on top. But, as Newman observes in the Raymond Chandleresque *Harper* (1966), "Only cream and bastards rise." Ten years before *Hud,* de Wilde had called out to hero Alan Ladd, "Shane! Come back, Shane!" Now it is de Wilde who departs, at the end of *Hud,* too offended by Newman's self-seeking to bear him anymore. Bastards rise, so there is no hero, no community.

Steve McQueen is possibly even more exponential in this era than

*She was blitzed when they connected and doesn't get a good look at him till the following morning, when she finally puts on her glasses: "I may have done better, but God knows I have done worse"—straight from the original stage text and one of Tennessee Williams's most autobiographical lines.

"Paul Newman is Hud," the posters gloated. Note how authentic Newman's audience looks: real people are replacing the professional extras as
Hollywood intensifies its naturalism.

Newman, for while McQueen began in the 1950s* and continued to work
right up to the last year of his life, 1980, the movies with which he is

---

*In *Somebody Up There Likes Me,* by happenstance, in a small part as one of
Newman's Brooklyn gang. McQueen's introduction to movie audiences is notable for
its prediction of the persona McQueen would eventually assume, the coiled-spring
jester punk. Touched from behind while making a pool shot, McQueen whirls, his
hand slicing through the air—but hey, it's Newman, back from prison, and as
McQueen shoots him a grin we suddenly notice the open switchblade in McQueen's
right hand.

most identified all fall into the 1960s: *The Magnificent Seven* (1960), *The Great Escape* (1963), *The Sand Pebbles* (1966), and *Bullitt* (1968). Moreover, while Newman's sixties attitudes derive from the roles he played, Mc-Queen, a far less able actor, seems to have worked up his roles by applying his own attitudes to his parts. Newman adapted to the 1960s, portrayed them. McQueen *was* the 1960s.

The 1960s at their worst, perhaps. Here was an attempt to present a heroless world with its choice hero manqué: a sullen, lazy, lawless hooligan, angry yet dispirited, a drifter and a loner, sometimes humorless and capable of noble acts although fundamentally heedless of the world and its various moral codes. "Life is a scam," McQueen often said offstage, and on screen he generally treats life as if beating the system comprises cheating everyone he meets up with—even, in *Bullitt,* a newspaper-vending machine. We are supposed to find this charming, just as McQueen's real-life associates tried to, accepting the star as a kind of errant kid brother who was always getting into trouble, only to wave the trouble aside with a grin that hides a desperate need for love. One of those myths. McQueen the orphan, the runt, the casualty who fights his way to the top. Indeed, he was that: a virtually fatherless boy raised by elderly relatives, then reunited with his mother and a stepfather he loathed, a hard-knocks "problem kid" in and out of police detention and, as a Marine, a frequent visitor to the brig. Life is a scam. Life is disobedience and mockery, taking lumps with a grin and grinning back for more. Life is, in effect, scamming the authorities, hustling them in a kid-brother manner.

Much as one may admire McQueen's individualistic system-baiting, one may resent his sneering distaste for any feeling but McQueen's. Does this guy have to rob even a vending machine to express his need for liberty? There is something uncompromisingly crass about McQueen. If Beatty is most often bewildered, Redford pensive, and Newman intelligent, McQueen is brutish. His action roles give him a heroistic scope, escapades in dangerous places, but he is very like the loudmouthed jerk who gets into fights in movie theatres two or three rows behind you. McQueen buffs insist that, in his films, it is not the tale or the dialogue or the co-stars but the star's personality that makes the movie. There is, they say, a wonderful sense of familiarity in his style, a sense that one is seeing one's beliefs affirmed. But McQueen has the sort of personality that makes you feel, after five minutes in his company, that you have hated him all your life.

Stardom this major cannot be fluke. Perhaps McQueen articulates the average American male's dream of himself. If Gable and Cooper were role models, McQueen is a replica. He spends nearly all *The Great Escape*'s 168 minutes in chinos and a cut-off blue sweatshirt, the American male's ideal go-everywhere attire. Gable and Cooper had to wear costumes—or, at least, clothes. (When McQueen gets into suit and tie and plays golf and polo, in *The Thomas Crown Affair* [1968], he looks absurd, not least because of the self-conscious brooding cool he adopts to suggest an Ivy League personality.) Then there is the typically McQueen expression of macho in a love of machines, especially motorcycles. McQueen makes his share of the Great Escape on one, and, in *The Sand Pebbles*, walks into the *San Pablo*'s engine room to caress the casing and say, "Hello, engine. I'm Jake Holman."

Then there is McQueen's extraordinary success with women, which other men would resent in real life but accept by proxy-identification on screen. Has any other actor enjoyed such immediate and lasting attraction for women characters? Even Gable—Gable the King!—frequently had to work overtime to get his opposites to concede an attraction. Claudette Colbert, in *It Happened One Night,* is ever so chilly almost to the fade-out; Vivien Leigh, in *Gone With the Wind,* can't see Gable for squash till the film is almost over. And Jeanette MacDonald, in *San Francisco,* is positively virginal, but then that's not saying much. Still, one is struck by director Norman Jewison's description of the McQueen–Faye Dunaway romance in *The Thomas Crown Affair* as "a love story between two shits." How many movies made in the days of Astaire and Shearer and Colman and Davis—barring film noir—could one say that of?

The Magnificent Seven is not a love story, but it has seven shits. Worse, it has Brad Dexter, *and* he has more than ten lines, so we'll move along except to note that McQueen is as yet only making stabs at his image. Yul Brynner is the muscle on this picture, and Brynner sees to it that the other six come off considerably less magnificent than he. One aperçu, however: of them all, only McQueen survives to ride off with Brynner at the finale.

The Great Escape put McQueen over as a star as the comic rebel, rude to his superiors as a rule and unbreakable even after spells in the

"cooler"—solitary confinement—which he whiles away with the some-
what masturbatory use of a catcher's mitt and baseball. The film, directed
by John Sturges from a novel based on fact, follows the attempts of British
and American soldiers to sneak out of a high-security Nazi prison camp.
McQueen, top-billed for all three pictures he had made between *The
Magnificent Seven* and *The Great Escape,* retained first credit over James
Garner, Charles Bronson, Donald Pleasance, Richard Attenborough,
James Coburn, and David McCallum. He is clearly meant to embody the
film's salute to courage, resourcefulness, gallantry, never-say-die individualism. In short, to be a hero of heroes. Thus, when a British officer
offers a toast of homebrew "To the colonies," McQueen responds, "To
independence," with an air of "especially *mine.*" And thus Sturges centers
the climactic series of escapes into Germany on McQueen's motorcycle
steeplechase, in which, pursued by what looks like three divisions of the
German Army, he attempts to hurdle not one but two barriers of barbed-
wire fencing into Switzerland. He doesn't make the second barrier, but
when the Germans reach him, he's still at war, struggling in the barbed
wire. A hero of heroes.

However, McQueen is not actor enough to keep up with the coolly
natural Attenborough and Bronson, the expertly colorful Pleasance and
Coburn, even the competent Garner. Or do we believe in McQueen's
personality all the more *because* he can't act? Since he is unable to fake
anything, all of him must be real. But then all the rest of the film must
be fake. In fact, though *The Great Escape* was filmed on location, right
there in Germany, it suffers from leftover fifties finagling, as in Attenborough's scarred eye, supposedly from Gestapo torture but all too artfully
made up to emphasize Attenborough's nobility; or in the absurd notion
that escaped Brits carrying forged documents can speak convincing German to suspicious German policemen. Their German might be excellent,
but surely not native.

Still, *The Great Escape* was a tremendous hit, and it bore McQueen
along with it. Five contemporary and somewhat romantic roles led him
to *The Sand Pebbles,* and here the comic rebel turned serious, underlining
the hero's alienation, even his tragedy: he dies. The Oscar people were so
impressed they nominated McQueen as Best Actor; surely the citation was
rather for Best Attempt to Reconstruct Heroism. There were too many
hustlers, too much Hud around.

McQueen, then, must reform, and does. Suddenly his instincts are generous, his valor permanently on call. An old-fashioned hero? Yet one cannot imagine an old-fashioned star—or anyone but McQueen—as Jake Holman, for his heroism awes us precisely because it must be built upon the established McQueen archetype of the selfish loser slob. Here, crisp and alert and methodical in his Navy whites, McQueen retools his loner from a wastrel into a deity, trades defiance as a personal eccentricity for defiance out of moral necessity, and thus the all-time great taker becomes one of the ones who get took.

Interesting that this should occur in perhaps the first of the major "Vietnam films"—not about that country per se but reflecting our changing attitude toward intercessory martial junkets. This is China in 1926, and the "sand pebbles" of the title, the crew of the *San Pablo,* are cruising the Yangtze River to keep red-white-and-blue order in a disorderly time and an anti-American place. Director Robert Wise gives the film the atmosphere, the historicity, that *The Great Escape* lacks—not just because Wise shot every minute in Taiwan and Hong Kong, but also because his cast clarifies the series of confrontations-within-Confrontation that the tale turns on: the West versus the East, visitors versus natives, sex versus romance, missionaries versus the secular state, capability versus incompetence, and, of course, independence versus authority.

McQueen stands at the very center of all this. An expert engineer, he must serve under the demanding but at times unknowing captain Richard Crenna. A realist, McQueen endures a romance with a Christian proselytizer, Candice Bergen. A tolerant man, he outrages his fellow sailors by treating too kindly the coolie (Mako) who assists him, and intervenes in a red-light joint when a young Chinese woman is unwillingly auctioned off for a one-nighter. "Strip her! Strip her!" the men joyfully shout, whites and Chinese alike. When someone rips off her bodice, McQueen tears the place apart.

This brings on the tragedy. The anti-imperialist Chinese torture the xenophile Mako to death within yards of Crenna's ship, forcing an international incident; then they murder the Chinese girl, finger McQueen as the culprit, and demand that Crenna hand him over. To our horror, most of the crew second the motion. "*Hol*man, come *down!*" they chant. "*Hol*man, come *down!*" There could be no more instructive view of the mob's lack of empathy for the loner—better, of their hatred for him. But Crenna is an officer of honor, and *The Sand Pebbles* moves on to its *scène-à-faire,* an epic face-off between the *San Pablo* and the Chinese, who rope off the river with a bridge of boats in hopes of trapping the ship and slaughtering the crew.

This is McQueen's meat. Truth to tell, *all* of Jake Holman is his most successful part yet, the one that best folds what he can do into what we want to admire. Hacking away at the cords of rope with which the Chinese have secured the water, chopping and screaming at the enemy while protecting his own, McQueen *must* inspire us—not least when, job done, he disobeys Crenna's orders and slips off to save Bergen and her fellow missionaries from the Chinese. "This is desertion in the face of the enemy!" Crenna objects. "I ain't got no more enemies," McQueen tells him. "Shove off, Captain." Rebellion above all, but re-bellion for good.

At 179 minutes, first-run on a hard-ticket release,* *The Sand Pebbles* disappointed. As a Steve McQueen picture, it *wasn't* a Steve McQueen picture; as an epic, it was—well, rather like a Steve McQueen picture. Television viewings unfortunately rob Wise's original print of its pan-oramic camera setups, particularly in the climactic set piece of the battle over the boat bridge, the majesty of the Yangtze broadening the tension as the Americans approach the Chinese for some wide-screen hand-to-hand violence. Nevertheless, *The Sand Pebbles* was a necessary film, a chance for Hollywood's most hip, most loose, most inarticulate, and most in-tractable—most sixties—persona to reclaim some of Hollywood's lost dignity. From the mere rebel, thence to the rebel loner, McQueen now became the valiant rebel loner. He brought his hero home from Germany and China to San Francisco in *Bullitt,* Peter Yates's *policier* on one of the good and also incorruptible but mainly unbeatable law officers who stand between us and Robert Vaughan, the Edward Arnold of the 1960s.

At least Arnold, Frank Capra's Fascist of choice, looked and acted like a monster. He was coming to get you, and you knew it. The poli-ticians Vaughan portrays fool voters and run the world and never get caught—except by McQueen, a cop trying to protect a witness in a criminal trial. The witness is killed—possibly by law-and-order Vaughan—and the fun begins, as Yates fills *Bullitt* with doubles, glimpses

---

*The 1960s was the last great era of the "road show": movies presented on a higher-priced, reserved-seat basis, two or (at most) three shows a day. The intent was to give film the prestige of theatre, make movies less available and thus more respectable. The embarrassing collapse of a number of road-show musicals later in the decade put the approach in such bad odor it has never recovered.

of someone, strangers who suddenly look (strangely) familiar, cabdrivers who behave like assassins, a celebrated car chase through San Francisco, and, even better, the less celebrated but climactically suspenseful chase between planes along night-lit airport runways. For *Bullitt,* in the end, tells us of the dark side of the system, the thug honchos and arrangements we know nothing of: the night of our society—better, its "sewer," as one character calls it. San Francisco is no more safe a place than the Bates Motel was. But McQueen can handle it, as he continues to reintegrate his character elements, running a steamy love affair with Jacqueline Bisset (*The Great Escape* was all boys, and in *The Sand Pebbles* Candice Bergen was a missionary; missionaries don't do steam), reminding us that Real Men Don't Have Life-style when he goes grocery shopping and hefts a load of TV dinners without even looking to see what kind they are, and allowing Bisset to cry, "Do you let anything reach you? I mean, really *reach* you," because even in a sewer a hero scarcely blinks, let alone feels. And of course comes the great moment when McQueen cuts through all the con jobbing with a well-placed *"Bullshit!"*—the source of his character's name, surely. It is as if the 1960s were saying, life is *not* a scam. If we are short of safe places, then there must be heroes though we may have lost our belief in them.

There can't be heroes, however, if one argues that Lee Marvin is even more fundamental a star of the times than McQueen. And I so argue. In Marvin we have the exponent of the era's very relative morality, moving from villain to hero from film to film, and in one of them literally playing both—not simultaneously but one after the other. In Marvin we have as well a figure to centralize the decade's growing belief in violence as an expression not of villainy but of humanity. And in Marvin we find a star who could not get graduated from the 1960s. A heavy in the 1950s, a sparring partner for such as Marlon Brando, Glenn Ford, Spencer Tracy, and Randolph Scott, Marvin hit his fame on Oscar night in 1965, yet never quite weathered the 1970s as Warren Beatty, Robert Redford, Paul Newman, and Steve McQueen did. Marvin belongs to an age.

It is a paradoxical age, beating down post-fifties bourgeois Fascism with a Fascism of the left, trashy, intolerant, picnicking with demons. Was the 1960s a time of Camelot or Nixon, of civil disobedience or riots, of the rise of a New Left or the destruction of traditional American liberalism? It seems apt, even ingenious, that Marvin won his Oscar for the western *Cat Ballou* (1965), in a highly dual role, as both the film's

villain and its hero: the beastly, noseless gunslinger Tim Strawn and the
drunken klutz Kid Shelleen, who takes Strawn on and vaguely cleans up
the town. Marvin's sixties career follows this path, veering from good
guy to bad and often blending the two. An interesting dossier for the
man who, when he began, looked like the all-time great absolute villain,
an identity Marvin maintained into the early 1960s, in *The Man Who
Shot Liberty Valance* (1962). Marvin is Valance, morally a black hole, a
creature who, given the rules of traditional American cinema, was born
to be shot by John Wayne (though James Stewart gets the credit, as if
Marvin's villainy were so loaded it takes two heroes to take him down).
If Steve McQueen catches the era's need for a hero, expanding his junkyard
show-off to an almost hieratic grandeur of gesture, Marvin affirms the
era's ambivalence about the heroic.

So in *Ship of Fools* (1965) Marvin plays a coarse, loudmouthed American, humiliating our national self-esteem by comparison with such swank
fellow players as Simone Signoret, Oskar Werner, and Vivien Leigh. After
them, it would take an entire Jerry Lewis retrospective to make Marvin
seem even human. But no; in *The Dirty Dozen* (1967) he is smooth, tough,
and commanding—a commander, in fact, more or less overwhelming
twelve atrocious soldiers into pulling off a mission impossible during
World War II. *The Dirty Dozen* is far more of a cartoon than *The Great
Escape,* but rather like it—in the martial setting, the conservative action-
picture linear structure (working up to the escape through the tunnel;
working up to the blowing up of various Germans), and the hokey Dis-
tinguishing of the Principals by Their Colorful Personalities. As in *The
Great Escape* one of the team is The Scrounger, one The Forger, one The
Mole, and so on, so in *The Dirty Dozen* one of the team is retarded, one
is a streetwise manipulator, one is Telly Savalas, and so on. Still, note
that Marvin is playing the kind of hero that Americans used to love, the
Errol Flynn–John Wayne *Ur*-hero who always wins because he never sac-
rifices his (actually, our) principles no matter what the odds. A very un-
sixties kind of guy, right? Unreal. A movie man, not a man of the world.

But then this is that paradoxical side of the 1960s, that "of course
I hated the 1950s but I fear what may happen in the 1970s" air of
distrusting one's own distrust. McQueen is easier to categorize because
McQueen hones in on one aspect of the time, its belief in loser heroes.
All McQueen's parts stand as variations on that image. But Marvin, a
very sharp actor, reinvents himself from role to role. He is richer than

McQueen, reflecting eight or nine ambivalences to McQueen's one or two. If McQueen centers the age, Marvin extrapolates it. He contains multitudes.

He is even fine in comedy—even in musical comedy. (Well, no one else got a hit single out of *Paint Your Wagon*.) But the most pertinent of Marvin's roles is Walker, the protagonist of John Boorman's thriller *Point Blank* (1967). A cult of admirers regards this as one of the most typical of sixties films, a weather vane for the age, indicating tendencies toward rage and suspicion and the new high-tech violence that seemed increasingly to be shaping American life as the decade's end approached. This is the movie in which Lee Marvin shoots a bed to death, beats up an automobile, punches a guy in the crotch, and throws another guy off the balcony of a high-rise. This is violence as a rhetorical device, as endemic to Marvin's character as dance is to Fred Astaire's and gloom is to Garbo's. We'd have to go back as far as James Cagney—the very early, circa 1931–33 Cagney—to find another star so connected to aggression as a style of communication and self-definition. It throws the other sixties men stars into some relief. The essentially non-violent Warren Beatty and Robert Redford come off as dandies by comparison, and even Steve McQueen is more the gadfly, the come-on-I-dare-you clown, than the aggressor that Marvin portrays.

Marvin is the absolute aggressor. *Point Blank* follows his hunt for the man (John Vernon) who betrayed Marvin in a heist, cheating him of $93,000 and, incidentally, his wife; throughout the film Marvin lashes out, now hot, now cool. This is our sixties archetype. He has passions, but he knows what he's doing. Good thing someone does in this age of upheaval, assassination, withdrawal. Who's in charge here? Not Beatty, not Redford, not McQueen.

Marvin is. There's steel in his mad, even charm in his tense. No regrets. No opinions. When you deal with cheaters and liars and "the organization," violence is like breathing: necessary. Marvin can even take it as well as he dishes it out—when romantic interest Angie Dickinson, outraged at his ruthless calm, spends a good fifty-five seconds whacking at him, and with such energy that she beats herself to the floor. Marvin just stands there for the whole thing, then turns on the television, switching from channel to channel by remote control. All television is one television. All feeling is no feeling. All women are broads. This is Marvin. At least Cagney's violence was a release of the little guy's frustrations, an almost political statement of hitting back at the hitters. Marvin, caught between the smooth of the fifties beat and the suspicion of the seventies paranoid, is anti-social, beyond politics, a heavy-metal hero, not moralistic but post-modernist, a glide of images looking for the exit. He bursts into John Vernon's honeymoon house (which comes complete with Marvin's bride) and murders—literally *murders*—the bed. He test-drives a car, pumping the salesman for directions to the fleeing Vernon's whereabouts, and when the salesman demurs, Marvin jumps, bumps, and crashes the car to ruin. His punch to the crotch is so lethal that we not only see it very clearly but hear his victim gasp and watch him clutch himself. We *have* to see, hear, and watch; this is how *Point Blank* tells us it's the 1960s. And when Marvin catches up with Vernon, he doesn't just toss the guy off the balcony; he degrades and denudes and defenestrates him in a kind of abradant chivalry. Baiting a bed with the willing Dickinson, Marvin surprises Vernon in his sheets, so to speak. Interrogation follows, and Marvin doesn't like the answers. He pulls on Vernon, wrapped in his bedclothes. *Pulls* on him, thrusts and spins him across the room toward the balcony, unwrapping the sheets to skyrocket Vernon into the air to fall to earth, nude, in one of the most spectacular murders in movie history.

This unleashing of violence is partly a response to the violence in the news, but also an artistic gambit, a facet of the new realism. You film a thriller, you film the thrills; everything can—must—be allowed. Or perhaps Marvin's contradictory balance of eerie villains and both inviolably competent and irredeemably incompetent heroes, centered on *Point Blank*'s admirably self-possessed criminal protagonist, demonstrates the sixties fear of heroes. Heroes are dangerous; they attract violence. Newman, Redford, and McQueen, too, draw fire simply because they are better than the men around them. Are the toughs who break Newman's thumbs in *The Hustler* punishing him for cheating with his expertise or for being the expert, good-looking, special amid small-town mediocrities? Are the laid-off railroad workers who beat up Redford in *This Property Is Condemned* expressing Depression fury or sexual jealousy? Why do McQueen's fellow sand pebbles so instantly dislike him?

Marvin never played such roles, was never martyred. He is the sixties hero who corrals *other* men, with a blend of con and menace. Marvin doesn't get took. This is his link with the Gables and Coopers of a more heroic age. But note that while they were natural lover boys, born for romance, Marvin spent his first decade in Hollywood typed as heavy—this is the man who scarred Gloria Grahame with boiling coffee in *The Big Heat* (1953) and threatened Spencer Tracy more thoroughly than all the rest of the bad guys put together in *Bad Day at Black Rock* (1954). Here is a villain with a demon's ontology, a wolf in wolf's clothing, Vlad the Impaler pointing at you and saying, "That one." This is the sixties—cruelty is sexy. It's the way out.

On the other hand: Dean Martin. Casual and content whether in western or spy thriller, the sort who would laugh at himself if he had the energy, Martin spent the 1950s foiling for Jerry Lewis, then came into his own just when Lewis's following of eight-year-olds grew up and went on to other things. Martin was a presence in the 1960s, then. Yet can anyone name another actor who built a major career on such dreadful movies? Here is an old-fashioned Hollywood star, the kind who invariably plays himself. Lee Marvin changes characters; Dean Martin changes costumes. But the 1960s is not a time for stars. It's a time for certain characters that the stars portray. Martin is less useful than, say, Jack Lemmon, another fifties person who became more substantial in the 1960s, perhaps because his good-guy loser—a "schnook," in the vernacular of the day—seemed a relief amid the life's-a-scam takers. In the 1950s, Lemmon couldn't get arrested, even in such surefire parts as the screwball Ensign Pulver in *Mister Roberts* (1955) and Clark Gable's role (re-tailored) in a musical remake of *It Happened One Night, You Can't Run Away from It* (1956). But then schnooks were despised in the limited 1950s, when anything less—or more—than a he-man (red-blooded, of course, whatever that means) was one of the usual suspects, probably a homosexual or a Communist.

Lemmon dared the disapprovers as the she-man Daphne in *Some Like It Hot,* on the verge of the 1960s, revealing color and élan he had kept hidden till then, and launching a partnership with Billy Wilder that totaled seven films, including the very epochal *The Fortune Cookie* (1966), in which Lemmon's schnook runs up against Walter Matthau's life's-a-scam lawyer when a black football player, a kind of he-man schnook (Ron Rich), accidentally crashes into television cameraman Lemmon during a game and Matthau pops up to organize Lemmon's lawsuit and make Rich miserable. A good role for Lemmon: well intentioned but ineffective. Many people felt so in the 1960s—one wants to, but one can't.

It was *The Apartment,* back in 1960, that most persuasively offered

Lemmon as the answer to the scammers. His neighbors, Dr. and Mrs. Dreyfus, aren't sure how to take him. Doctor thinks he's a "nebbish." Mrs. takes him for "a real Ivy Leaguer," and that's Mrs. Dreyfus's idea of a compliment. However, after noting the procession of women gliding in and out of Lemmon's place, Doctor gets a little awed and Mrs. calls Lemmon a "beatnik," especially when he uses paper towels as napkins. Actually, the girls are not Lemmon's, but the dates of executives of Lemmon's firm, who use his flat as a rendezvous on the promise of Lemmon's promotion. This is Wilder's comment on ambition within the Corporation; this is how to get ahead. But Lemmon is not a hustler, not a taker: "I'm the kind of guy," he explains, "who can't say no." True, he does delight in getting his own office, swanking around in a bowler, and, best of all, making the executive washroom. True as well, letting out his apartment was how he finally connected with Shirley MacLaine, who tried to kill herself there after having been seduced and abandoned by Fred MacMurray. And, truest of all, when MacMurray demands Lemmon's apartment key and Lemmon refuses and MacMurray threatens to fire him, and Lemmon sadly hands over his key, it is the key to the executive washroom, an elatingly tender moment for the crusty Wilder and a relief from the invasion of the taker heroes. One wants to, so one can. For all his nebbishy manners, Lemmon personified for the era a protagonist whose instincts are reconciliatory rather than divisive.

The foreign influence on Hollywood, elitist in the 1950s, became general in the 1960s, and placed new stars on the scene both in films imported from abroad and in films made or sponsored in America. Truth to tell, the development of the studio from Hollywood's exclusive source of output into merely a source of capitalization and distribution ushered in international "co-productions" that often made it hard to decide just what nation had produced a particular picture. From the mid-1960s on, America would see "Italian" films made in Spain with all-American principals, "British" films directed by an American for an American look, and "American" films made in England with multinational casts.

Still, the most noticeable wave from abroad washed over from Britain, in movies made in and about Britain, or in a heavy presence of British actors in films of quite various origin. Such stage veterans as John Gielgud and Ralph Richardson acquired a sudden new fame in sixties cinema, though they had been in movies since the 1930s—Gielgud had even made a few silents. Doubtless it was their Shakespearean majesty, set into the typical Hollywood mélange of so-so actors and can-do personalities, that provisioned their cachet. They were Superb Stage Brits, brought in to dress the scene whenever a producer was feeling disreputable.

They stood out in the most expert company. Orson Welles's *Chimes at Midnight* (1967), on the relationship of Falstaff and Henry V as he grows from princeling into king, offers Margaret Rutherford's Mistress Quickly, Jeanne Moreau's Doll Tearsheet, the very young Keith Baxter's Prince Hal, and of course Welles's own Sir John, cavernous and gamy, so confident of the royal favor the better to be excruciated with despair when his friend turns against him. As if the rich casting were not enough, Welles turns the Battle of Shrewsbury into a fifteen-minute set piece of spectacular horror: the Shakespearean chronicle of history as a confrontation of great men's egos illustrated as a carnival of blood, history as sheer waste of life, the opposing sides reformed by tight and yet tighter editing into an atrocious, churning, exhausted mass of golems melting back into mud. On paper, Richardson and Gielgud should be lost in so packed and grand a show, the one merely a narrator's voice-over and the other given but five minutes as Henry IV. Yet both men make their impression. Perhaps there was something reassuring in their zest of entitlement. They ooze with expertise—not only in Welles's fine company, but most especially amid the Hollywood crowds, as in Richardson's temporizing General Sutherland, trapped between the people he admires and the nation he loves, in *Exodus* (1960), or Gielgud's tyrannical father in *The Barretts of Wimpole Street* (1957), which tenders us the unique delight of sampling Jennifer Jones as a Victorian poet.

Hollywood had been making love to British actors ever since talkies made the voice primary, but a new movement seemed under way now, perhaps in reaction to the debased hiring policies of Hollywood starmakers in the 1950s, when anyone, even John Derek, could take the lead. Richardson and Gielgud actually became necessary, and a number of their younger countrymen crowded in along with them—Laurence Harvey, Richard Burton, Albert Finney, Peter Sellers, Michael Caine, Terence Stamp, Richard Harris. Yet where Richardson and Gielgud remained somewhat accessory to the obsessions of the era, these younger men fell right in with the sixties worldview and characters in roles that questioned the most basic tenets of traditional heroism. Callous womanizers, rotters of opportunism, disgusted class-conscious louts, or doers darkened by self-doubt, they easily joined up with the Fast Eddie Felsons and Jake Holmans.

Peter O'Toole, however, seemed to combine the features of the Superb Stage Brit and the contemporary non-hero. Richard Burton might have beaten him to it, with his imposing theatre credentials combined with Jimmy Porter in the film version of John Osborne's *Look Back in Anger* (1959), the very first of the Angry Young Man parts. This gave Burton the outline of the thespian who lends a touch of class to his film work. But in the end he proved something of a Welsh John Barrymore, declining in things like *Cleopatra* (1963), *The V.I.P.s* (1963), *The Sandpiper* (1965), and *Boom* (1968), all with Elizabeth Taylor, his partner in this peculiar backstage fame based more on one's appetites than one's roles.

O'Toole was something of a scandal, too, if the whimsical authenticity of *My Favorite Year* (1982) is to be taken seriously. But O'Toole was also unique, more the lord high thespian than his coevals—more pungently, ingeniously, delivering his portrayals—yet just as able in comedy, potboilers, a thriller. Looking over his credits, we are not surprised to find *Becket* (1964), *Lord Jim* (1965), and *The Lion in Winter* (1968), all vehicles for the Stage Brit in a charismatic mood, titanic yet an enigma, romantic yet bizarre. Even Albert Finney, who won first notice in the theatre for truly biting into the title roles in *Billy Liar* and *Luther* (for promising to be, in fact, the angry young actor that the angry young playwrights were going to write for), glided into film with the uninflamed naturalism of the born screen actor, taking the gestures and profile and grand-slam emphases down to one-twelfth.

O'Toole did not. He is one of the few modern movie stars to wallow in bravura. His romping, bellowing, larger-than-death Henry II in *The Lion in Winter* is one of those rare movie performances that would seem just as big live on stage. On the other hand, when you've got to confront Katharine Hepburn's Eleanor of Aquitaine, it doesn't do to stint yourself. If Spencer Tracy simplified Hepburn's mannered style in their MGM 1940s and 1950s, O'Toole reliberated it; Hepburn's Eleanor is a last look back at her wild youth at RKO, when to be mannered was sport; and who cared *what* Hollywood thought?

O'Toole is not unlike that young Hepburn, especially in the variety of his roles—the neurotic lady-killer of *What's New, Pussycat?* (1965), the title, so 'tis said, derived from Warren Beatty's favorite opening line on the telephone; or an angel in *The Bible* (1966); or the fastidiously morbid Nazi of *The Night of the Generals* (1967), an aficionado of decadent art and an active devotee of decadent murder. Yet, in a way, O'Toole loaded all this versatility into the part that made him a major star, the hero of *Lawrence of Arabia* (1962).

And here *is* a hero, at least—a superhero, even, not to mention a romantic enigma, the British soldier who more or less turns into an Arab chieftain without quite knowing why. "Who are you?" he is asked at one point. For starters, he is someone writ large, as the scope of the original release made clear in its dazzle of sandy vistas and in Omar Sharif, a conventional hero and conventional Arab, on hand to proportion O'Toole's magnificence for us. Sharif is reasonable, O'Toole passionate. Sharif is prudent, O'Toole a daredevil. Sharif is a natural son of desert ways, O'Toole learning them. And learning what else?

Who he is. Did any other actor of the 1960s quest so existentially? In the Studio Age, the quest was not Who are you? but Whom do you love? Who likes you? Heroes were known by their romances and their comrades—not only by the company they kept but the values that supported them. A sixties hero is not rooted in his beliefs; he discovers them, as O'Toole's Lawrence does, or he loses them, as O'Toole's Lord Jim does, or he is forced to abandon them, as O'Toole's Henry II (in *Becket*) does.

Not that all this turns O'Toole into a Hamlet, so mired in quest he never arrives anywhere. *Lawrence of Arabia* is, among other things, an action picture, filled with set pieces designed to reveal the true Lawrence even as they ever more heavily mask him—Lawrence getting into his first desert robes of spanking white; Lawrence riding back into the wasteland to save one of "his" people; Lawrence settling a dispute by summary execution . . . of the man he saved; Lawrence leading the victorious attack on Aqaba; Lawrence, wild and shaggy in his sheik raiment, forcing his way into a British officers' club to order lemonade for himself and an Arab boy as the club "natives" fume. ("Throw the wog out!" one cries, as likely referring to Lawrence as the Arab boy.) "What are you thinking of, coming here dressed like that?" Jack Hawkins asks O'Toole. "Amateur theatricals?"

Of course O'Toole answers, "Yes."

What most distinguished British stars from Americans was their birthright gift as thespians. They were mostly actors who had gone into film, while the Americans were more frequently people who had gone

The essential sixties victim. Tom Courtenay, his face scarred and his ideals shattered, in *Doctor Zhivago*. This was a decade of spectacular losers.

into movie acting. In a phrase: Peter O'Toole as compared with Steve McQueen. What drew all these stars together was a complicity in the new divisive protagonist of sixties narratives, the man who explodes the notion of community that Hollywood doted upon. O'Toole *as well as* McQueen, then: all these men helped raise up the new bastard hero, from hustler to enigma, from Life is a scam to Who are you? And, in this, perhaps the most exponential actor was Tom Courtenay.

At first an art-house favorite for *The Loneliness of the Long Distance Runner* (1962) and, taking over Finney's stage role, in *Billy Liar* (1963), Courtenay was graduated to the all-together-now international monster star show in *Doctor Zhivago* (1965). Yet it was in the very nature of his persona that he could never properly break into international stardom, for

Courtenay was the eternal victim of society, of history—the martyr, really, to O'Toole's titanic grotesque and McQueen's back-alley chiseler. Movie-goers are not buffs of the victim mentality. Worse yet, Courtenay is almost always a moralist, as certain of his principles as Cassandra was of her prophecies—and as poorly heeded. No one listens; no one sympathizes. No one *cares*, really—yet what burdens Courtenay takes on! He is the closest thing to a genuine hero in this time, but he's a loser—and our values are so skewed in any case that Courtenay comes off as a loony simply for believing that right is right. Let a soldier throw down his arms on the battlefield because he saw a vision of God, and it has to be Courtenay, in *Private Potter* (1963). Let another soldier desert World War I because war is socially objectionable and this, too, will be Courtenay, in *King and Country* (1964). Let a Japanese prisoner-of-war camp ooze with corruption as officers and rascals jip their fellows of rations and privileges, and let but one man try to enforce regulations and keep everyone equal, and that man shall be Courtenay, in *King Rat* (1965), driven to a nearly psychotic despair as ace rascal George Segal lives it up while finer men starve and die. Courtenay is class war, hopeless righteousness, and a kind of Dos-toyefskyan raw youth of doom rolled into one. Give any other actor a shower scene and all he'll do is get wet. Give Courtenay a shower scene, in *The Loneliness of the Long Distance Runner*, and he'll present anomie.

What, now, of women stars? The 1960s was not their great era; the decade seemed to welcome a decline in the importance of women head-liners that has held ever since. One reason was the collapse of the woman's picture—the weepie, more or less—that such stars as Irene Dunne, Ruth Chatterton, Norma Shearer, Joan Crawford, and Kay Francis made a staple in the Studio Age. Another reason was a lack of the kind of men whom such women could play opposite in *any* genre, the relatively elegant and witty personality such as Cary Grant, William Powell, Leslie Howard, and Melvyn Douglas. Heart-of-darkness cinema tells of hustlers, not dan-dies; it is, moreover, largely about men in the first place. Women, in such tales, are accessories, like Patricia Neal in *Hud* or Jacqueline Bisset in *Bullitt* or Angie Dickinson in *Point Blank*, handy to set off a man's impenetrability ("Do you let anything reach you?") or to allow him to relate at least on a sexual level, as when Angie Dickinson lightly but very thoroughly smiles after a pillowing with Lee Marvin in *Point Blank*. Okay, he's good in bed. Got it. Maleness.

Thus the most successful women leads were those who best complemented the men, in a kind of permanent co-star status, even when the women were important enough to get first billing. Natalie Wood was prominent here, thanks to a go-everywhere freshness amazing in someone who had been in movies without a break since making her debut at the age of five in 1943. Wood communicates with everyone, not only Beatty in *Splendor in the Grass* but the glumly dominating McQueen in *Love with the Proper Stranger* and the deviously reticent Redford in *Inside Daisy Clover* and *This Property Is Condemned*. She even handles Charles Bronson at his heaviest, in a skinny-dipping scene in *This Property*, when Bronson—a bully here, but a steamy one, let's admit—wafts over to Wood to grip her head and pull her close for a kiss. She manages to stop him and the moment passes, but the point is made: she is vulnerable because every man wants her. This is about as strong a position as a woman star could hold in the 1960s, when most stories were men's stories, including this one, for while Wood is technically the protagonist, Sydney Pollack's direction and even James Wong Howe's photography concentrate on framing Redford's tale, not Wood's.

Wood was versatile, far more able in the musical *Gypsy* (1962) than her miscast *West Side Story* Maria would suggest. Caught between the titanic Rosalind Russell as her mother and the underplaying Karl Malden as the manager of the mother's atrocious vaudeville act (all this in a movie so theatrical it comes complete with the original Broadway overture, played under the credits *in front of a theatre curtain*), Wood nonetheless makes much more of the young Gypsy Rose Lee than her stage counterpart did. After all, Gypsy is a no-talent kid who is first ignored in favor of her adorable sister, then thrust unprepared into the spotlight; Wood's very lack of musical-comedy know-how places her portrayal, gives us the nice girl who has to make it the hard way. Comedy, too, found her in season, in *The Great Race* (1965), a parody of old-time slapstick concerning an automobile race, with good guy Tony Curtis in white and bad guy Jack Lemmon in black. (Note that the idea of old-fashioned heroism versus villainy is by now so outdated that it's fit for spoof.) Yet how can a star maintain status by basing her profile on her abilities as an all-purpose trouper, or on survival, or on how well she folds herself around the available male icon?

True, *Love with the Proper Stranger* is technically Wood's picture, not McQueen's. She was the bigger star then, and took first billing as well as the role that is the film's proper protagonist. This is her story, her theme of love (she doesn't really believe in it; she calls it sex masquerading as "bells and banjos") that is explored. This is, even, her second nomination for an Academy Award. Yet it is not the old-style star vehicle the title and stars suggest. The scenarist, Arnold Schulman, was an adherent of the ethnic-working-class New York text introduced in the 1950s by Paddy Chayefsky, and the director, Robert Mulligan, assembled *behind* Wood and McQueen a cast of expert ethnic working-class New York specialists. Herschel Bernardi. Harvey Lembeck. You know, Italians. There is a lot of location work—but real location work, not just on the sites but with the people who dwell on the sites—and the scenes in Wood's home of absolute mother and three smothering brothers are so realistic that the last time I saw the film on television I found myself screaming advice to Wood, mostly "Move out!" But also "Kill them!"

Unfortunately, neither Wood nor McQueen fits into the ethnic atmosphere. They're as Italian as Rasputin. Nor are they the kind of actors who can compete with Herschel Bernardi in a naturalistic mood. Here was a problem for the Woods of the day: how to keep up with the infiltration of New Cinema? *Love with the Proper Stranger* is in effect two movies at once—one a romantic comedy with Natalie Wood and Steve McQueen, the other a study in urban naturalism with Herschel Bernardi. The two films come together in the aforementioned abortion scene, when Wood and McQueen rise to the naturalism. Still, we worry that New Cinema is going to leave some of our favorites in the lurch. Stars like Wood had it hard. The times—again—are a-changin'.

Joanne Woodward had it harder, as an actress rather than a personality, the kind of star only critics care for. Worse yet, she was married to one of the icons, Paul Newman, and thus did a lot of relating to him, too often in films that weren't good enough in the first place. David Thomson likens Woodward to "a dutiful wife who goes along on the husband's fishing trips"—specifically for *WUSA* (1970), but applicable to all the Newman-Woodward teamings. *Sola,* she would take on acting challenges, but her "scandal of the county" in *The Fugitive Kind* (1960) still finds her playing foil, to Marlon Brandon's flashy vagabond in a snakeskin jacket. And Woodward's best scene, a eulogy to the slain Brando at the fade-out, is, you notice, all about Brando and not about Woodward.

The worst of it was that Woodward's films without Newman could be as dull as the ones with him. *The Stripper* (1963) is dicey but potential: Franklin Schaffner directing (his first film) an adaptation of William Inge's play *A Loss of Roses* (which flopped), about the tragic liaison of a horny youth and a sensual older woman, he of the bourgeoisie and she of the demimonde. It would make a good opera—it did: *La Traviata*. Unfortunately, Woodward's Alfredo is Richard Beymer, constantly trying to smolder in the Warren Beatty manner. (This is at least authentic, as Beatty originated the part on Broadway in 1959—his audition, more or less, for *Splendor in the Grass*). Beymer gives Woodward as little to play to as he gave Natalie Wood in *West Side Story*; he is a candy bar. This role wants cocaine, glory, something slashing—how else can his rejection of her destroy her life? "You'll be cruising street corners looking for any trick you can find," Robert Webber crows as Woodward despairs. She has become The Stripper, in a costume of balloons that burst to the delight of leering galoots. Yet the film is soap opera. It lacks dimension. Bored, one begins to notice the decor, a fatal sign in a movie set in the dreary parlors of a Midwestern town. The folk I screened *The Stripper* with became fascinated with Woodward's oversize wicker purse in the shape of a blowfish. This is not the reaction that great careers are built upon. There is, then, something terribly telling about *The Stripper*'s first scene, wherein tourists in Los Angeles spot someone from a bus. Is it Jayne Mansfield? No, Kim Novak! No, the busdriver tells them: "It's *nobody*."

Actually, it's Joanne Woodward.

The British invasion produced a notable woman star in Julie Christie, less for the variable quality of her work in *Doctor Zhivago*, in François Truffaut's *Fahrenheit 451* (1966), and as the bizarre heroine of *Petulia* (1968) than because *Darling*, the film that put Christie over (complete with a Best Actress Oscar), was regarded as the ultimate contemporary piece, avidly *now*. *Darling* is an English *dolce vita*, from John Dankworth's reedy, light-jazz instrumentals to the holiday on Capri where serious sunbathers turn over in exact synchronization as an alarm clock rings the half hour. Christie plays a fashion model whose idea of sexual fidelity, as boyfriend Dirk Bogarde puts it, "is not having more than one man in bed at the same time." The director, John Schlesinger, was to take heavy fire at the decade's end for his ruthless satire of Americans in *Midnight Cowboy*, but here he is ruthless with his own people, catching a charity benefit at which a speaker enlarges on malnutrition among the less fortunate as a doughy matron scarfs up a last finger sandwich; zooming in on the middle-class politesse that fronts for a hostile rejection of anything beyond the mediocre; reveling in a television commercial for a line of chocolates filmed in fake medieval with Christie as a damsel on a horse, so reticent yet so vulgar, so English; and sticking his camera and a mike in the faces of (apparently) real people to ask what they are most ashamed of in Britain today and unmasking nothing but bigots and jerks—one man cites "traffic congestion." But Schlesinger (and his writer, Frederic Raphael) is hardest on Christie, who earned her Oscar for being contradictory, loose, and tormented. This was contemporary woman in the 1960s: being *now* comprised undergoing rituals of humiliation. *The Hustler*'s Piper Laurie and *All Fall Down*'s Eva Marie Saint kill themselves when romance and self-respect sour; Christie survives. But the triumphant—or, at least, self-confident—heroine of the Studio Age, the kind of woman personified in Myrna Loy, Claudette Colbert, or Rosalind Russell, is becoming an endangered species. In the 1960s, women are men's paraphernalia or their own victims.

What we have, in all, is an era that has ceased to believe in the character archetypes that the movies had been (at best) admiring and (at worst) peddling for sixty years. On one level, this is generational war. The moguls who had run Hollywood since the 1920s were overthrown; and youth has its rights. On another level, this is simply more honest moviemaking. You know it's honest by all the controversies it engendered: only honesty is that subversive. There have been controversies throughout Hollywood history—over *The Birth of a Nation*'s racism, for instance, or the wild private lives of some stars in the early 1920s, or the loaded sexual content of Mae West's and Garbo's and even one of Miriam Hopkins's films that led to the revitalization of the Production Code in 1934, or the glum directness of *The Best Years of Our Lives,* which ran contrary to the official postwar optimism, or the purge of liberals immediately after. And of course there was the censorship war of the 1950s, almost entirely relating to sexual material.

Nonetheless, no earlier era saw so many controversies over the sheer content of the films themselves as did the 1960s. It was *The Best Years of Our Lives* over and over, picture after picture, furors over what should be allowed—*The Manchurian Candidate, Lolita, Dr. Strangelove, The Pawnbroker, Blood Feast, Bonnie and Clyde, In Cold Blood, 2001, Midnight Cowboy, The Wild Bunch,* not to mention such foreign entries as *Blowup* and *The Damned.* Interestingly, many of these controversies weren't based on objections to a film's content but on objections to its success: on the rage of people who frantically attempt to dissuade other people from seeing films that the parties of the first part found threatening in some way. The problem wasn't that the films they hated were trash; the problem was that they weren't. A chance alignment of devotees, prudes, and worms could tolerate this New Cinema only as long as it remained marginal, an intellectual's caviar rather than popular fare. Even some of those intrigued by Hollywood's long-overdue sophistication thought it a mixed blessing. There was a gain in insight into the human condition, but a loss of delight in being human. The sheer gladness, the sense of fulfillment, evoked by such classics as *Sunrise, It Happened One Night, Top Hat, Ninotchka, The Wizard of Oz, The Philadelphia Story, Meet Me in St. Louis,* or *It's a Wonderful Life* was missing. Was it possible that there would be no classics as such from now on? Would one come back to *Psycho* or *The Hustler* with joy in one's heart? Wasn't an ecstatic affirmation of life and love precisely what Hollywood was born to provide? If its new movies can't provide them, why attend?

In desperation, certain reviewers began raving about second-rate but inoffensive films, like a corrupt teacher promoting favorites. However, so ingrained were the tenets of New Cinema that the most empty nonsense might be tense with observation, the most unassuming forms deal in contraband. There was no escapism left, it seemed. All cinema was New Cinema.

Or no. Smack in the middle of this self-hating and system-questioning era, let us set forth a true hero, one of those gallant, invincible characters who right wrong not for gain or celebrity but for the utter fairness of it. Here, at length, we will find the moralist of the era—best of all, an unshakable one. He cannot lose. He cannot die. He cannot suffer a loss of belief. He is violent only when necessary. He has impeccable manners, in fact an infallible sense of style, which puts him one up on Paul Newman, Steve McQueen, Lee Marvin, and even—let's face it— Buster Crabbe. This hero is the Superman of the free world. And here's how we'll do it: upon the framework of the forties adventure serial we'll lay a high-tech, slightly futuristic spy-versus-spy climate, add sex and wit, the whole to be played with a touch of theatrical *Verfremdung,* because the package is frankly too loony to be real. The public will accept this hero, even worship him, only if they can laugh, at least slightly, at his comic-book world.

It worked. Indeed, it engendered the most successful series in film history, the James Bond films, which were consistently lucrative even when the Superman himself begged off and had to be replaced several times. This is interesting, for surely what made the Bond films so compelling when they were new was Sean Connery's thug-dandy charisma. Here was no scion of provincial rep or West End masque, but a working-class Scot who drifted from the Navy into bodybuilding and soccer, odd-jobbing his way into the theatre to hunk around in a touring company of *South Pacific*. Then the movies, bits and featured parts, usually as a heavy. "I wanted something stable," he later said, "but not too emotionally demanding."

And is *that* not James Bond, the ultimate anti-romantic? Never has a movie hero been so secure treating sex as sex rather than as love, or so ruthless in his derring-do. Not that he'd get the job done more efficiently if he longed for a mate and a cottage, or waxed indecisive about his license to kill. On the contrary—isn't it Bond's very heartlessness that makes him marvelous? He is flawless. Inhuman. Literally a superman. Still, it is noteworthy that even escapist Us-versus-Them genre cinema did not come up with the traditional ice-and-fire hero but one, instead, all of ice. Is this a cartoon view of the action hero, or a comment on the apocryphal nature of postwar hostilities? Is everything less than an absolute superman useless when battling the enemy in a nuclear age? There is something of the con man in Connery's Bond, even a tinge of life's-a-scam cynicism amid the do-or-die efforts for Queen and Country. Yet in no way does Bond— Ian Fleming's creation, but known to us primarily through the film's slightly revisionist interpretation, Fleming-Connery—bear on any of the stars and characters discussed in this chapter. They are the new-style protagonists, scaled to human size, reinvestigated and expanded from the tactfully admirable heroes of old. Bond is beyond the sixties conception of hero and anti-hero, a god-redeemer in an age that doesn't think it deserves one.

Perhaps Bond was the antidote to the era's entropy of ideals. Yet the first of Connery's Bond movies, *Dr. No* (1962), did only moderate business. Fleming's books were not widely known then (though they had been coming out at the rate of one a year since *Casino Royale* in 1953), and the film itself lacks the whirlwind pace and gadgety plotting that would characterize the Bond cycle right through its recent installments with Timothy Dalton. But the second and very profitable Bond entry, *From Russia with Love* (1964), like *Dr. No* directed by Terence Young, established the format that provisioned the series' almost epidemic popularity. We get the paranoid frisson of a paramilitary organization (Spectre) juggling cold-war establishments, the macguffin being a code machine that the

The all-basic sixties knight errant. Sean Connery in a PR portrait early
in his run as James Bond. Once an era, there is *perfect* casting: Greta
Garbo as Ninotchka, Margaret O'Brien as Tootie Smith, Johnny Sheffield
as Bomba the Jungle Boy—and Connery as 007.

Russians have and that both the Americans and the Brits are after. We
get the picturesquely diabolical villains—not only the Mack-the-Knife
Lenya but a faceless archfiend we only see fondling a cat, a chess whiz
("Number Five") who schemes for the archfiend and is liquidated when
a scheme fizzles, and, mainly, Robert Shaw as Spectre's hired gun. We
get the uniquely Bondian black comedy, as when Lenya, sizing up Shaw,
smashes him in the solar plexus with a set of brass knuckles and, when
he doesn't react, observes, "He seems fit enough"; or when Lenya goes
after Bond with a poisoned blade in her shoe, her foot furiously jabbing
till he fells her and says, "She had her kicks." We get the gimmick

props—an attaché case, which, if opened by the uninitiated, lets off a neutralizing gas, for the set piece of Connery's big battle with Shaw on a train. We get the profusion of cuties for Connery to bed and the dangerous jazz of Monty Norman's theme music,* so endemic to the feel of the whole that it was retained as an overture in many of the Bond films.

James Bond is larger than the 1960s, for the adaptation of Fleming's books created a genre that is still very much with us, the pop action thriller. There had been adventure films before, of course, even adventure films based on the exploits of invincible heroes in a strictly construed moral universe. But the churning pace, cliff-hanger overturns, high-tech material, and, above all, the colorfully diabolical villains, though siphoned out of the tank of the Saturday-afternoon serial, were all elementally recombined into this new form, at first for spies like James Bond and his imitators Matt Helm (Dean Martin) and our man Flint (James Coburn), later for Indiana Jones and Rambo—but above all for Superman and Batman, who stress the pop action thriller's derivation out of comic books into cinema.

As we'll shortly see, cold-war and even wishfully post–cold war worldviews of the 1960s countered Bond with work in a highly corrective style, scorning the Bonds' intemperate *joie de tuer* for intellectual thrillers in which all spying is equal, all governments are devious, and agents are not icy warriors but enervated uncles who want only to come in from the cold. And by the 1980s, movies regard even the free world as so corrupt a place that pop action heroes such as Sylvester Stallone and Arnold Schwarzenegger often have to fight two enemies, Them . . . and Us. At least Bond had the confidence of his chiefs; Stallone and Schwarzenegger must outwit our own immoral authorities in order to reinstate a good-guys-against-bad-guys mentality.

So James Bond may have been the last hero, the last to function in what his public perceives as a moral climate. And note that he could only pull it off with a systemic lack of feeling, ice his natural condition and fire merely a hypertension for use in emergency conditions in the field. He is suave but he is a barbarian.

Only cream and bastards rise.

---

*John Barry composed the bulk of the sound-track score, but not the James Bond theme itself. Lionel Bart wrote *From Russia with Love*'s title song, heard and forgotten. *Goldfinger,* the following year, had a more memorable title song, memorably delivered by Shirley Bassey.

Four

What Ever Happened to Bette Davis?

Fifty-seven years old, heavy, and as gnarled as an old stump, James Cagney struts and prances through *One, Two, Three* (1961), helping to relate the new era to the old. He had come to Hollywood as far back as 1930, direct from Broadway, for *Sinners' Holiday*; *One, Two, Three* was his sixty-second film, planned to be his last. Yet there is nothing tired about him. He still has the energy, the self-spoofing arrogance, the fast eyes of the street fighter, and the loose hands of the hoofer, now rifling the air, now shooting out to a point. Fifty-seven and fresh. And notice that Cagney chose a distinctly new-style film to go out in, satiric and irreverent in the breezy new freedom, and one of Hollywood's consistently contemporary directors, for Billy Wilder had the knack of producing epochally definitive cinema, framing his age even as he dodged each age's conventions—think of *Double Indemnity, The Seven Year Itch,* or *Kiss Me, Stupid.* "Acting is not the beginning and end of everything," Cagney told *Newsweek* some years into his retirement. He did make a last hurrah in *Ragtime* (1981), but by all that matters *One, Two, Three* was the end of it; he went out not only in a hit but a hot one, something of the here and now.

Not everyone did. Bing Crosby, who had reached Hollywood the same year as Cagney, went much more gently into the good night of retirement, appearing in the kind of movies he could have shot in the 1930s. Yea, Crosby's last film *had* been shot in the 1930s—*Stagecoach,* remade in 1966 with Crosby embarrassingly unconvincing in Thomas Mitchell's old role of the alcoholic doctor. Crosby also remade a forties-style film in a final *Road* picture with Bob Hope and Dorothy Lamour, their seventh in the series, *The Road to Hong Kong* (1962), one of the year's most successful releases.

There was life in Crosby, and market value, and an amiable refusal to participate in New Cinema. His lowish-budget vehicle *High Time* (1960) even corrects the postwar views on the generation war. Here the kids have nothing to complain about. Fathers are tolerant, generous, and perhaps daring, as father Crosby elects to cap a career as a Howard Johnson–like restaurateur by getting a college degree. The fun, apparently, will lie in Crosby's interaction with his young fellow students, all of whom turn out to be drearily nice and supportive: Fabian, Richard Beymer, and Pat Adiarte, so clean they squeak when they smile. At least Tuesday Weld is on hand as a hip co-ed. We know she's hip because she disdains jocks. What ever happened to the explosive generation, the rebels with plenty of cause? Crosby's thirties films for Paramount sometimes dealt in mean realities: unemployment, class war, greed, irresponsibility. But *High Time* is so unreal that Crosby and his three roommates are all tapped by the same fraternity—Adiarte, cast as an East Indian, included. What, no racism? In a *fraternity*? And the frat initiation hazing comprises polishing shoes, washing floors, and wearing Southern-belle drag to an antebellum-theme party—this at a time of fraternity-hazing scandals and inquiries into students' suspicious deaths.

Crosby was fifty-nine when he made *High Time*; so how does it feel to be old? Just fine. Bing sings "The Second Time Around" to reassure us and observes, "Love, like youth, is wasted on the young." Then what is *Splendor in the Grass* about? True, Crosby fits in a romance with Professor Nicole Maurey between attending swimming meets and pep rallies, and encores *Holiday Inn*'s "White Christmas" with "It Came Upon a Midnight Clear" to wrap up *High Time*'s tone of glad serenity. No, there's more: Crosby, B.A., delivers the commencement address for the Class of 1960.

So the Old Cinema had not vanished. It proposed to coexist with *Psycho, The Manchurian Candidate, The Little Shop of Horrors.* However, New Cinema was becoming Hollywood's major cinema, where the prestige and profits lay. Tradition began to seem dowdy. A business-as-usual item was still good for a run—the dully fifties war film *P.T. 109* (1963), with Cliff Robertson as the young John Kennedy (who preferred Warren Beatty among candidates for the role); or *The Carpetbaggers* (1964), from a Harold Robbins best-seller about trashy rich people; or *The Sons of Katie Elder* (1965), a formula western on how the Elder boys (John Wayne, Dean Martin, Earl Holliman, and Michael Anderson, Jr.) fight for their late mother's estate. But no one in or out of the film world cared about these titles. Hollywood likes *hot* above all—the kind of excitement that Cagney and Crosby, for instance, generated in their youth, when Cagney's back-alley boulevardier and Crosby's distinctively soothing way through a tune promised the movie business what it loves most, something that is completely different and absolutely popular. First, because a smash hit can spawn an industry-wide cycle that may last for years;* second, because a number of smash hits in fast succession gets the on-and-off moviegoer into a steady moviegoing habit.

Thus, Cagney, making his valedictory in the very of-the-moment *One, Two, Three,* went off a winner while the unreconstructed Crosby appeared to peter out. Bette Davis and Joan Crawford had less choice than Cagney and Crosby. With offers for prominent, or at least reputable, or even minimally acceptable projects down to zero, they accepted the leads in Robert Aldrich's *What Ever Happened to Baby Jane?* (1962), as two has-been actress sisters driving each other nuts in a gloomy old mansion. At least, that's what the script is about, as composition. The movie, as a screening experience, is a lampoon of the kind of movie stars Davis and Crawford were, of the freakish exaggeration that informed their aura— Davis's bellicose consonants or Crawford's Adrian-to-die fashions. At 132 minutes, *Baby Jane* is spendthrift with put-down and degradation and riffraff glamour. It's very sixties: a ritual humiliation of the religious aspect of Studio Age Hollywood using two of its most formidable icons.

And yes, the film hit it big enough to inspire a cycle of old-time movie-star Grand Guignol that ran right through the decade. Better yet, because Aldrich had had so much trouble financing *Baby Jane,* he had filmed it cheap and fast, so here was a series in the making that could

---

*The best among countless examples is the flash success of *42nd Street* (1933), which not only re-created the backstager as an infinitely workable format but rein-stituted the movie musical, almost totally dead by 1931 because of a glut of idiotic musicals in the first two years of the talkie.

She's written a letter to Daddy. Bette Davis reviews her past—as do we—in *What Ever Happened to Baby Jane?* Note unsavory Baby Jane doll in chair, right.

be connived out of shoestring and paste and cast with unemployed veterans who would work for pin money. Sure enough, quickie artist William Castle signed Crawford up for *Strait-Jacket* (1964), which edged the cycle beyond horror spoof into outright gore porn.

The subject is ax murders, especially Crawford's. No doubt she was relieved to get a more vital role than the wan Blanche of *Baby Jane,* for Davis, as the demented Jane, got all the attention. Publicly, Crawford thought *Baby Jane* redeemed the two of them equally, completely missing the point. *Baby Jane* didn't redeem; it *reviled.* "Toward the end of production I finally realized it was a good film," Crawford told Roy Newquist years later. "The great actress [Davis] hadn't totally defeated the mere movie star. Sure, she stole most of my big scenes, but . . . she stole them because she looked like a parody of herself and I still looked something like a star."

Crawford looks something like an animated model of herself in *Strait-Jacket.* Maybe even cheesy horror shouldn't run this cheap. It's a shameless piece of work, right from the six-pack of Pepsi-Cola prominently displayed in Crawford's kitchen to the final shot of the Columbia logo statue, headless, in honor of Joan's way with an ax. The fans thrill with a joyful noise when Crawford strikes a match on the grooves of a playing LP to light her cigarette, though her entire performance is pitched to this note of callous overemphasis. All right, how else does one play an ax-murder shocker? And didn't Crawford specialize in comparably absurd parts in all her MGM runaway heiresses and sleep-to-the-top shopgirls and, later, her Warner Brothers queen bees? But this Crawford is suddenly graceless, wooden, and loud. She has even forgotten how to overact. Worse yet, Castle has folded about her the limpest of companies, the most subterranean surroundings. If we must sit through anti-star horror camp, give us Victor Buono, not Diane Baker, Leif Erickson, Howard St. John, and George Kennedy. One moment in this nonsense catches fire, when Crawford's daughter Baker is revealed as the real ax murderess. We had hoped it was Crawford, and in a way it still is, for Baker makes her rounds in a Crawford costume, mask, and wig. The real Crawford catches her in the act, and they fight for the ax: *dueling Joans!* Too bad Aldrich wasn't in charge; what a picture he might have made of this confrontation of new-old and old-new.

Aldrich did return for Davis and Crawford's second joint horror show, *Hush . . . Hush, Sweet Charlotte* (1965), but Crawford didn't. Ailing, she was replaced by yet another bygone grande dame, Olivia de Havilland. Perhaps because de Havilland was too classy to fall entirely into the series' trash-thyself sensibility, Aldrich filled the scene with grotesques—Agnes Moorehead, lurking and moaning as Davis's housekeeper (who gets thrown down the stairs); the dangerously impish Cecil Kellaway; Bruce Dern, whose hand is chopped off (very graphically, and he holds up the stump in case somebody missed it); and Victor Buono, now so authenticating a figure in camp Guignol that he's touted as a "guest star" in the credits. Joseph Cotten joins de Havilland over the title, dull but guilty. De Havilland is guilty, too. Even Mary Astor—invalid and little more than an eminence at this point in her career—is guilty. Bette Davis isn't, but everyone thinks she is, and in this series that's guilty enough. It is as if it didn't matter who is innocent or evil. The thriller's mandate—restructuring amoral chaos into moralistic order through the unmasking of disorderly malefactors—does not apply in camp Guignol. Yes, Davis drops a piece of sculpture on de Havilland at the end, but this is less retribution than an act of symmetry, balancing out the violence. We get the feeling that simply to be a movie star, especially an old one, is to be guilty: of having more than one deserves and wanting ten times more; or being famous for being there as much as for doing something; of being so vastly seen and so little known. Maybe Billy Wilder's *Sunset Boulevard* (1950) was the first of the sixties films for its view of stardom as psychosis—but *Sunset Boulevard* exposes Norma Desmond, not Gloria Swanson. *Hush . . . Hush, Sweet Charlotte* exposes everyone it can get its hands on. Its many characters are either vicious or mad, but even this is phoney. "She's not really crazy," Sheriff Wesley Addy says of old Miss Charlotte, Bette Davis. "She just acts that way because people expect it of her."

We no longer love our stars as we used to in the golden youth of Crawford, Davis, de Havilland, and Cotten—not to mention Astor, from so far back that when she made her movie debut, D. W. Griffith was still working with the Gish sisters. Audiences knew how to love then. Certainly there was an odd mixture of fascination and alienation in the public's reaction to John Huston's *The Misfits* (1961), New Cinema with old stars. A literate and persuasive saga of the victims of social change, cast with some of Hollywood's most notable victims and produced just when Hollywood was both experiencing and portraying social change— shouldn't it be a classic? To some it is: as Clark Gable's and Marilyn Monroe's last movie; as a fierce example of Huston's work as a reader of humanity or of the importance of a first-rate screenplay (by Arthur Miller); or for the stunning climactic sequence of the capture of the wild mustangs in the dry-lake desert of Nevada—like *Psycho*'s shower murder or *Bullitt*'s car chase, one of the sights of the age.

But to many *The Misfits* must have seemed less a timeless masterpiece than an all too timely document, another of those depressing sixties realism things—and with Gable and Monroe! The film did somewhat disappointing business and found few partisans. The fans thought it Serious; the intellectuals couldn't dig the stars. Yet it is a unique film for this very combination of merit and glamour, this coming together of what Hollywood had always represented and what Hollywood could (now) do.

Clearly, *The Misfits'* makers regarded it as unique from the first, and they set out to make it uniquely, shooting the script scene by scene in story order rather than in the usual method of "bunching" particular scenes by logistical convenience—shooting, moreover, entirely on location, even for simple interiors that might have been duplicated in the studio— and treating playwright Miller's script with such devotion that the author was encouraged not only to witness filming and insist on letter-true deliveries but to advise director Huston. Granted, Miller was something of a Broadway Goethe by this time, not to mention Monroe's husband. He could hardly have been barred from the set. Still, this is reverence for the word unprecedented in Hollywood, where writers had long been re-garded as dime-a-gross hirelings, permanently replaceable no matter how respected they might be in other climes.

This is not to suggest that moviemakers of the 1960s learned to respect writers. The *Misfits* production was nonconformist even in a non-conformist age; Hollywood proper took it for a folly, and the *Misfits* honchos treated Miller with deference entirely because Huston himself had started in Hollywood as a writer and because the film's producer, Frank Taylor, was a Hollywood outsider and, in fact, Miller's publisher. But this does help point up the unusual nature of *The Misfits*, both in production and as the film we screen; and this is very sixties, for it was becoming an era known for unusual movies. In the Studio Age, genre and stars were what kept the industry minting. Unique cinema was eventful, prodigious, exceptional above all: *The Thief of Bagdad, The Crowd, Cavalcade, The Informer, The Wizard of Oz, Gone With the Wind, Citizen Kane, The Best Years of Our Lives.* Most—not all—are expensive, longer and grander than the usual. They know they're ultra and they capitalize on it. In the 1960s, when star power and the safety of genre had lost their purchase, unique cinema became coin of the realm, not the odd extraordinary outing but film of the day: *Psycho, The Apartment, Elmer Gantry, The Hustler, Splendor in the Grass, Summer and Smoke, Judgment at Nuremberg, Breakfast at Tiffany's, Walk on the Wild Side, What Ever Happened to Baby Jane?, The Manchurian Candidate, Dr. Strangelove, Fail-Safe, Mickey One*—an interminable list running right up to *Easy Rider* and *Midnight Cowboy* at decade's end. Anything goes, on a regular basis.

So we should not be surprised to find Clark Gable and Marilyn Monroe in another of those depressing sixties movies. This is precisely where the biggest stars would now be found. As for *The Misfits* itself, it is excellent but it's not delightful: another of those depressing sixties movies, exactly. Huston comes through best; he has the measure of these people and their place, the far edge of a society that cannot tolerate, can only contain. Thus the title. Perhaps Huston saw himself as something of a misfit, too. Though he cooperated with the all-containing studio system, he was something of a rogue. Certainly his treatment of Miller's characters is sensitive, comprehending, and his ability to build up atmosphere is intrepid whether out of the amiable tension of two men and one woman in a room or at a crowded bar where Monroe holds forth as a paddleball champ, one of the sexiest scenes she ever put on film.

Miller, too, is in form, though his writing is not the showy kind. No wit, no poetry. He has an O'Neillian concentration of theme that edges the lines toward a central premise, as in Monroe's "We're all dying, all the husbands and all the wives," or Gable's "A man who's too afraid to die's too afraid to live," or Eli Wallach's "Dropping a bomb is like telling a lie." As Huston told reporter James Goode on the set, "I don't know how good a writer [Miller] is, even at this moment. You go along boxing as I did when I first read Miller's script, keeping your left out, and suddenly there is a kick in the groin. I don't think Miller cares about writing *per se,* but rather what's behind it."

Miller can think *movie,* can aim his lines at a confrontation that is entirely visual—the war of misfits out in the dead-on wasteland of mustang territory, where one gang of society's holdouts (the cowboys) attempts to subdue another (the wild horses). The sequence is not only exciting as sheer sensation, but dramatically absorbing, because Miller has forced his three last heroes, Gable, Wallach, and Clift, to prove their valor by corrupting it: the beautiful horses will be sold to be ground up for dog food. "I *pity* you!" Monroe screams at Gable as he ropes down the mustangs with cold fury. "You're three dead men!" Huston catches her in a telling isolation, a small figure in a long shot of the desert—as sharp a perception as any of Miller's laden lines.

It is the cast that sometimes lets us down. Eli Wallach and Thelma Ritter are fine, and Monroe is superb. But Montgomery Clift is uncomfortably realistic as a burned-out wrangler. I keep worrying that he isn't acting; he's really burned out. Nor is Gable comfortable off his turf of MGM tailor-mades. Having played Gable vehicles for twenty-five years, he isn't entirely ready for New Cinema. But then, nor was the public, not if Gable was in it. Spectators conditioned by the Studio Age star system found it difficult to see past Studio Age stars and take each film as it came. The Cinema was New, but the audience wasn't.

What were they to make of John Frankenheimer's *Seconds* (1966), a devastatingly naturalistic horror picture starring—Rock Hudson? Here was even Newer Cinema than *The Misfits,* with a far more traditional star, the ultimate non-actor who makes it on looks and promotion. What else are we to say of a performer who builds a career on films like *Magnificent Obsession* (1954), *A Farewell to Arms* (1957), and *Pillow Talk* (1959), not to mention *Bengal Brigade* (1954) and *Taza, Son of Cochise* (1954)? But surely this was why Frankenheimer wanted Hudson for *Seconds*—to bring the horror home to us through the agency of a general favorite. Here is no glamour-besmirching farrago like *Baby Jane,* but an absorbing fantasy on a theme of wide appeal: the possibility of eternal youth. The Davis-Crawford freak shows distance us. Frankenheimer wants to draw us in.

He starts with John Randolph, polite, respectable, well-to-do, and greatly aging. Again, this is sound casting, for Randolph is familiar but not famous, virtually a neighbor. James Wong Howe's camera work veers throughout from near-documentary to expressionism; his hand-held tracking shots and fish-eye perspectives turn Grand Central Station into a Piranesi. Already, then, Frankenheimer has the real and the fantastic at his command, and lures us, along with Randolph, into an under-the-counter operation in which people like Randolph are sucked out of their over-the-hill lives and rejuvenated on the surgery table. Lewis John Carlino's script (from David Ely's novel) sends Randolph first to a laundry, then to a meat-processing plant—in effect, they clean you, then they cut you up.

And when they're finished, you're Rock Hudson. It's a fascinating premise, so meticulously developed that it comes off not as fantasy but as menacingly probable: in the strangely nondescript staff of the rebirth corporation, all workaday lumps except for their chief, an avuncular bow-tied hayseed, grimly friendly, a piece of freeze-dried slime; or in the cheerlessly bracing jump in locale from Randolph's Manhattan and suburbs to Hudson's Malibu beachfront; or in the grape-stomping festival in a monstrous vat that turns into an orgy as Hudson is stripped and pulled into the thick of it, crying "Please! Please!" because he looks like Rock Hudson but he feels like John Randolph; or in our realization—as Hudson fails to adjust and enjoy his new identity, to the disgust of his fellow "reborns"—that the white Halloween mask we saw under the credits was in fact Hudson just after the operation, his face covered in gauze and his mouth agape in a silent scream.

If the public shrugged off *The Misfits, Seconds* was actively despised. But then Frankenheimer is working on perhaps the most unpopular theme available to an artist: that whatever external changes you make in your life, you remain what you were. This was an especially "hostile" viewpoint in an age that cultivated a belief in limitless self-regeneration, but it is spit in the face at any time. *Seconds* was a disaster as the American entry at Cannes, and failed dismally at home. Did another of those depressing sixties movies have to be *this* depressing? Even *The Misfits* faded out on the likelihood of a Gable-Monroe mating. *Seconds* ends in terror.

Because it happens to Rock. He's a movie star, not an actor, not protean. But then if *Seconds* had happened to Henry Silva or Richard Beymer, it wouldn't have been *Seconds*. It is persuasive—*punishing*—precisely because it happens to someone likable and handsome, someone with what we had assumed was the *invulnerability* of the icon. Oddly, faced with one of the few thespian challenges of his life, Hudson comes off quite well. Not as a movie star. As an actor.

He came off better in sex comedies with Doris Day, needless to add, but here was the form Hudson and Day were born to work in, romantic comedy in an era torn between the appearance of chastity and the stirrings of the erotic. In the 1930s, sex registered as wit—Cary Grant and Katharine Hepburn. In the 1940s, sex registered as crime—Fred MacMurray and Barbara Stanwyck. There was no sex in the 1950s. Now, in the 1960s, sex is very diversely expressed—here directly, there allusively, now only verbally, then all in a visual. But in producer Ross Hunter's Hudson-Day series for Universal, sex registers as a kind of mass-market locker-room whimsey. There is something violently elfin, something silly and stupid and crassly glamorous and very, very horny about this series, roughly: *Pillow Talk* (1959), the central pair sparring over their telephone party line as Hudson's business partner (Tony Randall) and Day's maid (Thelma Ritter) comment, respectively, with innocuous bemusement and tart wisdom; *Lover Come Back* (1961), on advertising, Hudson and Day as rival account executives and Hudson smugly disguised in a risible beard and horse-blanket suits as a mild-mannered scientist inventing an irresistible product, again with Randall; *That Touch of Mink* (1962), with a gray Cary Grant in for Hudson and a case of acute sex terror for Day; *The Thrill of It All* (1963), Day now paired with (and married to) James Garner, the plot hitch not seduction but career competition, and ZaSu Pitts is the maid; *Send Me No Flowers* (1964), Randall returning, as hypochondriac Hudson, believing himself terminally ill, morosely plans to fix up the Widow Day with a suitable second husband.

These films are like a tactfully psychotic nun in a Fellini movie— no, a tactfully psychotic Fellini in a nun movie. Yes, these are nun movies,

Avatars of the 1960s. Rock Hudson, breezily in command of Doris Day (and Nick Adams, drunk, on shoulder) in the first of their Universal sex comedies, *Pillow Talk*; then a casualty of his own despair in *Seconds*. Next (opposite), two tuff guys. Above, Lee Marvin. The shot is technically from *Point Blank* but it could be Marvin in general, loner in the dark. Below, Steve McQueen (on fife) assisting in the "Spirit of '76" mock-up for a Fourth of July celebration in *The Great Escape*. Note, on drums, James Garner, one of the era's few he-men who, like Hudson, played expert comedy as well—from *Move Over, Darling* (with Doris Day) to Raymond Chandler's *Marlowe*.

because they act like nuns and they think like nuns and they smell like nuns. They want to be risqué, but they are about getting married, not getting laid. They want to be hip, but they take middle-class consumerism to such ends that they are like commercials for the breeding of yuppies. They want to be debonair—and they are, and in this lies the main reason for their great and lasting success. Amid all the trashing of stars and the grimy naturalism and the depressing truths, here was a series devoted to the advantages of being healthy, good-looking, and well-to-do in a land of plenty. Everybody dates and nobody dies. Anyone can be debonair on those terms.

Granted, the Hudson-Day and comparable teamings never challenged the velvet of the leading romantic couples of thirties comedy, and, for all its leers, the form as a whole seems to regard sex the way Judy Garland regards "home" in *The Wizard of Oz*: as something you only get to after the fun is over. One has only to compare Garson Kanin's *My Favorite Wife* (1940) with its remake, Michael Gordon's *Move Over, Darling* (1963), to see how vitiated it becomes in its transformation into a Universal Hudson-Day farce. Actually, Day went over to Twentieth Century–Fox for this one, James Garner again standing in for Hudson. But the generic elements had become so, uh, universal that the studio and the male co-star didn't matter.

What matters is the loss of subtlety and honesty. *Wife* is stranded for years on an island, husband remarries, wife shows up complete with hunk from island sojourn: in *My Favorite Wife,* Irene Dunne, Cary Grant, new wife Gail Patrick, and hunk Randolph Scott. This is classic prewar casting, Dunne's brave worry and Grant's gentlemanly regret facing off the chicly rotten Gail Patrick and the unbearably confident Scott. *Move Over, Darling* would be typical sixties with, say, Vera Miles and George Hamilton assisting Day and Garner, but instead we get Polly Bergen and Chuck Connors, pleasantly offbeat. Still, *My Favorite Wife* is about how the two leads regard each other, how they sift their feelings after the physical separation and during the legal one. *Move Over, Darling* is about Day trying to keep Bergen out of Garner's bed. It's bad enough that she's afraid of sex—she doesn't want *anyone* having it.

Universal's genre has its moments. One laughs, enjoys the personality tug-of-war between Hudson and Day, dotes on the sardonic maids if not on Randall. As an attempt to counter the hustlers and psychos with a dear view of the upper-middle-class quest for love and prosperity, the series is definitely preferable to coeval sex comedies. Billy Wilder's *Kiss Me, Stupid* (1964) is vulgar. Richard Quine's *Sex and the Single Girl* (1964) is stupidly sexist even for the day, as hack writer Tony Curtis sets out to debunk Helen Gurley Brown runoff Natalie Wood. A screwball comedy? No, a glut of smoking-car stories, filthy, old hat. Every hang-up of the 1950s comes up for an airing, as when a tuba bleeps for Wood's cursing out of Curtis, or when, after an accidental dip, Curtis dries off in an implausibly flouncy bathrobe.* And what fun when Henry Fonda, after a quarrel with wife Lauren Bacall, asks Curtis, "What do you call it when you hate the woman you love?" and Curtis answers, "A wife." In Richard Quine's *How to Murder Your Wife* (1965), Jack Lemmon doesn't hate Virna Lisi—he just wants to kill her.

This film has a problem with women. It sees marriage as the death of (a man's) soul, a bachelor party as the funeral. "I've been married for forty years and I don't regret a day of it," says Sidney Blackmer at Max Showalter's night-before-the-wedding party. "The one day I don't regret is August 2, 1936. My wife was visiting her ailing mother." But the bride sends back Showalter's ring, and the mourning breaks into a Rabelaisian brawl, complete with Lisi coming out of a cake. The next morning, Lemmon wakes up married to Lisi. What heterosexual male doesn't dream of finding Helen of Troy in his bed? All Lemmon can focus on is that he'll lose his butler Terry-Thomas, who, like *The Servant*'s Dirk Bogarde, only works for bachelors. As Lemmon is a cartoonist, he writes Lisi into his strip—and there snuffs her out.

This is a long haul from thirties gender-war comedy, which saw sexuality as most hot when two extremely disparate people are thrown together. This was the essence of screwball: opposites don't attract, they make each other crazy. Sixties gender-war comedy sees sexuality as most ruined by marriage, but we don't see anything hot to begin with. Jack Lemmon is unhappy to find Virna Lisi in his bed? Whom is he kidding? Perhaps even more telling is the opening, under the credits, of Bud Yorkin's *Divorce, American Style* (1967): the angry voices of couples over a long shot of suburbia as a symphony conductor directs the Great American Symphony of spatting marrieds. It's all so familiar and charmless that

---

*Yes, Cary Grant did it in *Bringing Up Baby*, and even used the word "gay." But Grant was up against Katharine Hepburn (and Howard Hawks) in the ultimate screwball comedy, and you can't make an omelette without breaking eggs. Curtis and Quine just give us dithering gender neurosis.

while the Hudson-Day series at least has the honor of being notorious, the other sex comedies of the time are never mentioned today. Yet they were popular once. They were even thought relevant—more relevant than *The Misfits,* whose backward glance at a near-vanished breed of men now seems an act of sixties historicism; or than *Seconds,* whose brinkmanship exploration of mortality underlines the boldness of the sixties; or than *What Ever Happened to Baby Jane?,* whose loony-bin capering marks the beginning of our modern parody and *hommage,* of self-conscious film-within-film.

It was as if there were two contradictory cinemas, one based on what was more or less working in the 1950s and one defying and shaping Hollywood tradition. Yet even the contradiction yielded paradox: when Rock Hudson made *Send Me No Flowers* and *Seconds* only two years apart, or when Bing Crosby made *High Time* but Bette Davis made *Baby Jane.* The difference between Old Cinema and New is one of technique and attitude but not necessarily one of participants, whether one speaks of the pros or the public. Some actors simply go where the jobs are and some moviegoers will see anything that sounds hot.

Nor can we identify Old and New by form, for New can be devious. Some of Hollywood's least enterprising genres were seized by New people—the B movie became virtually a safe house for revolutionaries in the 1960s, and the big-budget western, a very conservative form by nature of its moral code and strict narrative construction, would in the hands of Sergio Leone and Sam Peckinpah greatly influence all Hollywood.

Even kid film, a founding form of post–Studio Age revisionism, suffered delineations that ran to the square. George Sidney's *Bye Bye Birdie* (1963) is downright counterrevolutionary in its view of teenagers as immature and their music as loony tunes croaked by debauched rednecks. Granted, parents are spoofed as well. But the only people the film respects are Dick Van Dyke and Janet Leigh: grown-ups. Of course, *Birdie* came from a Broadway still steeped in the echoes of Jerome Kern and Cole Porter and the aesthetic of Rodgers and Hammerstein. It was a time when if you heard a song you liked, you'd ask, "What is that from?" because all good pop music was written for a show or a movie. To Charles Strouse and Lee Adams, the authors of *Birdie*'s score, American pop was that of the great Broadway masters; the stage *Birdie*'s immediate coevals include *The Sound of Music* and *Camelot.* Next to these, rock and roll was dumb, and the film *Birdie* honors the show's up-to-the-minute *passéisme,* its tendency to seem hip and unliberated at once.

Bye Bye Birdie is an important film—not a great one, but a big hit that, for many, expressed the entropy of *tempora* and *mores* in an America of the U-2 incident, James Meredith's matriculation at Ole Miss, the Bay of Pigs, *Who's Afraid of Virginia Woolf?,* the Cuban missile crisis, and the Beatles, who first toured the United States the year *Birdie* was filmed. Its *casus artis,* however, is rooted in the 1950s: the drafting of Elvis, or, here, Conrad Birdie (Jesse Pearson), who in a final PR flourish will kiss a typical American teenager (Ann-Margret) on Ed Sullivan's Sunday-night television show, to the awe of her father (Paul Lynde) and the fury of her boyfriend (Bobby Rydell). Wisely, Sidney and his crew didn't attempt a replica of the stage production (though preservations of Broadway originals had become habitual in Hollywood, from *Oklahoma!, The King and I,* and *South Pacific* in the 1950s to *The Music Man, Gypsy,* and *My Fair Lady* in the 1960s). Anyway, Gower Champion's staging was too theatrical to transfer. But the movie *Birdie* expands the stage show somewhat faithfully. So "The Telephone Hour," in New York a construction of boxes containing chatty teens, is filmed through quick cuts and split screens to range through Sweet Apple, Ohio, to catch the kids at home and school and ballet class, in the car and shower and soda shoppe, all of them, everywhere, on the phone—there's an extension for each seat at the soda counter. Then, too, Sidney's choreographer, Onna White, can fill the town square with "Honestly Sincere," to show, more brazenly than Champion was able to, the Dionysian impact of rock, especially in the closing crane shot (to "John Brown's Body") of a thousand kids passed out all over the plaza. "Put on a Happy Face" yields mixed media, as Van Dyke draws cartoon faces on the screen with his finger and dances with a merry, double-exposed Leigh to energize the real, grumpy Leigh. "Kids," Paul Lynde's Charleston lament, bears new lyrics for Van Dyke and Maureen Stapleton (as his mother) to emphasize the generation war, with a witty twenties orchestration to point up the characters' reactionary psychology.

Generation war fuels the movie *Birdie* far more than it did the show. Lynde presents the same professional groucher he played on Broadway, but Stapleton is even more manipulative than Kay Medford had been on stage, constantly referring dilemmas to her late husband, a canasta enthusiast. "Lou! I'll be right up!" she cries, shoving her head in the oven. "Start dealing!" The kids have become yet more self-important about trivial things, and the camera troubles to show us that rock not only lacks the intelligence of, say, "Put on a Happy Face" but is actively disruptive. It even exacerbates the East-West conflict, when Sullivan's airing of the "Moscow Ballet" is chemically speeded up to insure time for the Birdie slot. Dance, a highly old-fashioned art as shown here, is made ridiculous, as the dancers hit hyper-space and fall all over and a Russian diplomat exclaims—in correct Russian, by the way—"капиталистический комплот" ("A capitalist plot!"). Perhaps we take the film's measure most securely in the Van Dyke–Leigh romance, so innocent they go out of the way to make it clear that they won't cohabit till they're married. And it has been a *very* long engagement.

Welcome to the 1960s? At least *Bye Bye Birdie* encompasses a certain naïve charm, not a worldview as much as a rec-room view. And, if only because it was a musical, it did dramatize the new and very fundamental valence of music in America's youth culture, even its link with sex. *Birdie*'s farewell song may be entitled "One Last Kiss" but, like much of rock and roll, it sounds like balling.

However, a cycle of college-weekend films thrust the subject of the music aside to treat mainly the sex. Here is another piece of what is now viewed as a sixties mythology, tales of the sexual freedom of youth. But *Where the Boys Are* (1960) is really something of a Fox threesome musical without Alice Faye (or music): new girls in town seek love. The town is Fort Lauderdale during spring break and the love is pure—except in the cautionary adventure of Yvette Mimieux, who Goes All the Way for one boy and finds herself passed from friend to friend like a box of popcorn. *Palm Springs Weekend* (1963) is cleaner; it even has a disapproving father who is also the town's chief of police, to exert a restraining force on adolescent rebellion by arresting everyone at a climactic party.

A Warner Brothers production, *Palm Springs Weekend* was filled with the stars of Warner's television series—Connie Stevens, Robert Conrad, and Troy Donahue of *Hawaiian Eye,* Ty Hardin of *Bronco,* Andrew Duggan of *Bourbon Street Beat*—all more or less playing their usual characters (except Conrad, here cast as a really nasty rich boy) and all well into voting age. These are not really kid movies. They don't contain kids—Ann-Margret was twenty-two when she played *Birdie*'s ninth-grader—and they aren't concerned with the reality of kids. Weekends in Palm Springs

The Big Broadway Musical. *Can-Can* (1960), with Shirley MacLaine in Hermes Pan's S & M apache spoof, is unfaithful to the original, but *My Fair Lady* (1964) and *The Music Man* (1962) are more or less runoffs of the New York stagings. Above right, Jeremy Brett, Audrey Hepburn, Rex Harrison, and Wilfrid Hyde-White at the races—"Come on, Dover! Move yer bloomin' arse!" Below, assistant choreographer Tom Panko (left, in street clothes) musters Shirley Jones (center right) and the corps in "Marian the Librarian."

and a guest shot on Ed Sullivan are swank events. Most kids just bop around the neighborhood.

As it happens, one kid cycle did feature relatively youthful performers and centered on a popular kid recreation, summertime sporting and dating on the beach. At the same time, this series saw kids as sweet do-nothings, mindless and carefree, chortling at the occasional interfering grown-up and shrugging off the odd bully. None of these kids seems to have a home or parents, much less a summer job. Where do they live, if all the world's a beach? Worse yet, the kid actors are without exception flavorless and dreary, despite their energy mere facsimiles of teenagers. *Birdie*'s Ann-Margret has a sexy vitality; *Where the Boys Are*, for all its sins, produces the always welcome back-street blonde Barbara Nichols; and *Palm Springs*'s weekenders at any rate have money or attitude problems we can believe in. But the real-kid beach movies belong to a Cinema so Old they make the 1950s look new wave.

This is American International's B-budget "beach party" musical cycle, built around Frankie Avalon and Annette Funicello and directed by William Asher: *Beach Party* (1963), *Bikini Beach* (1964), *Muscle Beach Party* (1964), *Beach Blanket Bingo* (1965), and *How to Stuff a Wild Bikini* (1965). Unlike most of the fifties kid films that exploited rock, these are story musicals—like *Bye Bye Birdie*—in which characters burst into song to tell us how they feel, rather than waiting for a chance to jive at a party or dance. The music is *very* light rock—in fact, bubble gum—but it piles up the numbers as if American International were doing prestige adaptations from Broadway. *How to Stuff a Wild Bikini*, for instance, opens with a title tune, by the boys, and moves on to: "How About Us?," when the girls want advertising executive Mickey Rooney to use them in his next campaign; "He's the Greatest on Madison Avenue," the executives' salute to Rooney; "A Healthy Girl," the boys' salute to Beverly Adams, Rooney's bikini girl; "I'm the Boy Next Door," by the comically villainous Eric Von Zipper (Harvey Lembeck) and his motorcycle gang, the Rats; a concert interpolation by the King's Men; Annette's "When Love Comes Swingin' Along" and "The Perfect Boy"; the Rats' "Follow Your Leader"; and so on. There's more sheer score in these films than in any Astaire-Rogers RKO, yet one never thinks of them as musicals. No doubt that's because the RKOs really use music while everyone in the beach-party series is merely hanging out. There is no texture to this life, no up and down, no Fred meets Ginger and great bells go bong. It's all a party and it's all on the beach.

This everything-is-nothing philosophy centers on the personalities of Avalon and Funicello, the David Manners and Zita Johann of the 1960s. Funicello especially may be seen as a key figure in the clash between fifties white-bread style and the richness of the 1960s. She is not transitional. She is reactionary, mandated by old values. She is prim. Yet she is not a moralistic figure, because she is utterly uninvolved in what she is doing. Where's the *intensity* of youth? I don't ask for political commitment, just for a sign of life. Annette, called Deedee throughout the series (Avalon is Frankie), is presented as an average American girl, but so average, so ordinary, so lacking in inflection, that she comes off not as average but bizarre. Reaction shots designed to connect her to the action distance her, so limp is her sense of focus. At least we get a chance to relish her costume. Everyone else is in briefs, but Annette models hostess pants and a fussy top, as if afraid of sun poisoning, an arresting eccentricity for the heroine of a beach cycle. Nor do the scripts flesh her out. The most awful moments are those calling for a snappy comeback. In *Muscle Beach Party,* a territorial dispute between the kids and Don Rickles's corps of body-builders inspires two of the latter to drag a kid by the feet through the sand to—so to say—draw the line. The kid screams for help, but fun-loving Frankie cries, "Hey, Johnny, that's a cuckoo way to travel!" Blithe, helpful Annette adds, "Next time try the train." No sweat.

The presumable heart of the series—the surfing action—is in fact so extracurricular that American International simply rings in stock foot-age every now and again as someone calls out, "Surf's up!" The real heart is exploring the adolescent love of goofing off. Oddly, these films do articulate certain teenage fears—of the menace of brutes, the outside world's rage for money, the engulfment of sensuality. *Muscle Beach Party* states this most completely, for the kids' beach is invaded not only by Rickles's bravos, but by plutocrat Buddy Hackett (who picks up a phone and says, "Buy Sicily!") and his *favorita* Luciana Paluzzi, an aggressive sex goddess. But the drastic mediocrity of the kids enervates one's senses, blinds the vision. All we are left with is bubble-gum musicals that seem to have been created to slow the revolution.

One might say the same of Elvis Presley's films. Here was an avatar of hard-core rock and roll who, on screen, became an exponent of MOR, the easy-listening contemporary sound pitched between rock and Muzak. Presley's films are usually musicals, but they are seldom about music the way Fred Astaire's or Eleanor Powell's are about dance or Mickey Rooney and Judy Garland's are about performing. Presley's movies are somewhat comparable to Bing Crosby's Paramount vehicles, in which the star plays a wide variety of characters, all in the same style and generally with assistants rather than co-stars—actors who never quite made it, like Lizabeth Scott, Wendell Corey, Barbara Eden, Gary Lockwood, Julie Adams, Mary Ann Mobley, and Will Hutchins, or actors on the rise, like Walter Matthau, Juliet Prowse, Ann-Margret, Angela Lansbury, and Mary Tyler Moore, with the odd imposing appearance by such as Barbara Stanwyck, Burgess Meredith, and Rudy Vallee. Crosby played a college professor, a sailor, a rancher, a priest, a Victrola salesman in old Vienna. Presley plays a boxer, a pilot, a pineapple heir, a lifeguard, a racing-car driver, a cowboy, an Indian, a fashion photographer—all about as believably as Crosby ran *his* gamut.

Actually, Presley's first four films, in the late 1950s, made some attempt to come to terms with the paradoxical hot innocence of the singer of "Lawdy Miss Clawdy," "Hound Dog," and "All Shook Up." The character is not yet defined. *Love Me Tender* (1956) "introduces" (below Richard Egan and Debra Paget) rather than stars Presley, and he is bewildered in *Loving You* (1957) and surly in *Jailhouse Rock* (1957) and *King Creole* (1958). Two years later, demobilized from the Army, Presley embarked on an itinerary of twenty-seven films, but the journey is fixed, for the character is in place and the music has been tamed, locked up. Presley is amiable, generous, tolerant, and rich in natural wisdom. In *Girl Happy* (1965), he admires a woman in a bathing suit and some dopey dude says the physical is of no matter because all the elements in the human body are worth $1.98.

ELVIS (*cool and dry*) I'll take fifty dollars' worth.

Yet the music gentles out this redneck prince. In the 1950s, Elvis's rock was dangerous. It was *rock and roll,* sex shaking down the pillars of the social structure. By the 1960s, the sole dangerous element in Elvis's films is Elvis's obligatory fight scene, usually with two or three criminals or at least a tactless bully.

It must be said that the Elvis series provided the early 1960s with the only consistent source of enjoyable original film musicals. Almost all other musicals were from Broadway, whether a relatively faithful reproduction like *Bells Are Ringing* (1960), *West Side Story, Flower Drum Song* (1961), or *The Music Man* (1962), or an idiotic debauch like *Can-Can*. No doubt Presley's films seem bald, flat, uninflected. *Bells Are Ringing* is daffy. *Can-Can* is bawdy. The Presley musicals consist of Elvis's girls and Elvis's buddies and some major problem that Elvis can solve.

He has enemies. He takes on white racists (as an Indian) in *Flaming Star* (1960), conservative parents in *Blue Hawaii* (1961), federal welfare agents in *Follow That Dream* (1962), gangsters in *Kid Galahad* (1962), and himself (in a dual role) in *Kissin' Cousins* (1964). Yet the films have a leisurely air and the music smooths everything over. Thus, even *Kid Galahad*'s picture of Elvis, just out of the Army, having to fight his way into the boxing game and then protect his associates from mobsters, has a score made of mild rave-ups and ballads, as if this were *Rebecca of Sunnybrook Farm*. "This Is Living," Elvis sings, to a choral backup of other Army boxers, and there's "Riding a Rainbow," sung to a car-radio accompaniment, and "Home Is Where the Heart Is" for a quiet beach date, and "I Got Lucky (When I fell for you)" at a picnic, as the jes' folks clap and Elvis tries the twist. And so on. The music doesn't reflect the story; the music takes turns with it.

These must be the most amiable musicals in history. Yet Presley was a rich figure—too rich for his placid Old Cinema to encompass. As Greil Marcus observes in *Mystery Train*, "Elvis has emerged as a great *artist*, a great *rocker*, a great *purveyor of shlock*, a great *heart throb*, a great *bore*, a great *symbol of potency*, a great *ham*, a great *nice person*, and, yes, a great American." Not, however, a great movie star. A popular one, yes: not a unique one. This is Old Cinema in a New Age; it cuts the unique down to acceptable size. Even the most rebellious of kids can be enlisted on the side of the traditions and the pieties and the cautions.

These were best expressed in the all-star epic, a form so young it was pioneered as late as the 1950s and did not proliferate until the 1960s. The casual moviegoer may find this startling. Were there not spectacles way back in the silent days—*The Birth of a Nation* and *Ben-Hur*, for instance? And surely all-star casts are no postwar novelty—what of *Grand Hotel* and *Gone With the Wind*?

But with the genuine all-star epic, we are dealing with Big Film, not only vast in size but in star value, especially if all sorts of fancy people can fill in the supporting parts—a passel of Brits, or some lavish veteran whom everyone over forty will recognize with pleasure. *The Birth of a Nation* and *Ben-Hur* were spectacles, certainly, but without heavy star pull. Griffith didn't even list his players in the titles (many of them did become stars, years later) and *Ben-Hur*'s Ramon Novarro, Francis X. Bushman, May McAvoy, Claire McDowell, Carmel Myers, and Nigel de Brulier are somewhat less than an all-star contingent.

In fact, in the silent era, a major star seldom appeared with another major star, let alone in packs. It was simple economics: one major star alone can sell not only a given picture but an entire line of pictures (in the procedure known as "block booking"). Why waste a second or, worse, third star on the same title when they should be selling their own pictures (and lines therefrom)? Not till MGM's Irving Thalberg put Greta Garbo, John Barrymore, Joan Crawford, Wallace Beery, Lionel Barrymore, and Lewis Stone into *Grand Hotel* in 1932 had Hollywood turned out an indisputably all-star film, at that an intimate drama, no spectacle. The studio pursued the concept with *Dinner at Eight* and *Night Flight,* and Paramount chimed in with *Alice in Wonderland* and *If I Had a Million,* all four within a year of *Grand Hotel.* Again, these are not epics; and Paramount, though it mustered more contractees than MGM, lacked the ultimate in star power. *Grand Hotel*'s leads were more or less the most intensely prominent actors available in 1932. Just the proximity of Garbo and Crawford on a single marquee gives us summoning words of a very wild magic.

There could not be many such events in the Studio Age, with all the stars tied to contracts at highly competitive studios, and with a limited number of stars in any year who could fairly be called major. Anyway, talkies had ushered in a new approach in which two or three stars per picture became almost routine. All-star epics seemed less necessary than ever. David Selznick's *Gone With the Wind,* at the end of the 1930s, would seem exceptional, but only by hindsight. Here is a spectacle, no question, but not quite all-star: one hot star (Clark Gable), one debutante promising to get hot real quick (Vivien Leigh), and two warm stars, one still on the rise (Olivia de Havilland) and the other over the hill (Leslie Howard). Note that Selznick had to borrow Gable, de Havilland, and Howard, and discover Leigh to complete even this quartet— and the film's many other roles went to players of sure ability but unquestionably minor note. Attempting to outdo himself, Selznick assem-

bled a more imposing cast for *Duel in the Sun* seven years later, for now
the names of the great, near-great, and once-great run way down into
the minor parts.

Still, the concept of Big Film took hold slowly, even in the 1950s,
when Hollywood was trying to make Big its ordnance in the war on the
little home screen. Cecil B. DeMille's *The Greatest Show on Earth* (1952)
and *The Ten Commandments* (1956) were Big, albeit with mixtures of first-,
second-, and third-rank stars. *This Is Cinerama* (1952) has sights, not
stars, and *The Robe* (1953), with Richard Burton, Jean Simmons, Victor
Mature, Michael Rennie, Jay Robinson, and Richard Boone, has class and
types rather than major names. However, the ongoing breakup of the
studio complexes and the resulting growth of the free-lance pool made
all-star groupings more feasible. We sense a turning point in *Around the
World in Eighty Days* (1956)—significantly, Michael Todd's independent
production, released by United Artists. Todd's four leads, David Niven,
Cantinflas, Shirley MacLaine, and Robert Newton, stand virtually at par
with Selznick's *Gone With the Wind* quartet on the fame chart. But Todd
filled his adventure with some forty great stars of all kinds, turning up
in roles so small some of them could have danced on the head of a pin:
Noël Coward, Buster Keaton, Hermione Gingold, Peter Lorre, Victor
McLaglen, Edward R. Murrow, George Raft, Fernandel, Glynis Johns,
Ronald Colman, Andy Devine, Jack Oakie, Red Skelton, Joe E. Brown,
John Gielgud, as well as Beatrice Lillie as a Salvation Army revivalist,
Marlene Dietrich as a saloon hostess, and, seen face-on for seconds, Frank
Sinatra as Dietrich's pianist.

Note the international frame of the casting. Big Film's grandiose
budgets made worldwide success essential. They also made Big Film
conservative. Simple economics again: to attract the most people, these
movies must offend the least. So when maverick Stanley Kubrick takes
on *Spartacus* (1960), there is almost nothing to alienate, confuse, or outrage, even in a film on the tragically failed revolt of the oppressed. Yes,
there is Laurence Olivier's come-on to Tony Curtis, but it's over so quickly
that anyone who didn't want to see it missed it. Otto Preminger's *Exodus*
(1960) and John Wayne's* *The Alamo* (1960) are even less bold. Note the
sudden occurrence of three Big Films in one year, all at the start of the
1960s. This is a sixties form, partly out of post-Studio exuberance, partly

*Don't ask.

out of ambition, and partly because Hollywood was in a kind of controlled chaos. The war on television has been lost. The energizing moguls who kept their hosts of cameras turning are almost entirely defunct. The audience-baiting stars are dispersed. And New Cinema continually beats out Old. So why not pour fortunes into gigantic versions of Old Cinema, Big Film? Why not raise up such a noise with the *size* of the thing that the crowds will come simply out of curiosity?

Why not make, for instance, *Cleopatra* (1963)? MGM had cleared a truly tremendous fortune on *Ben-Hur* in 1959; now Twentieth Century–Fox will take its turn. In fact, Fox's *Cleopatra* project was announced before *Ben-Hur* went into production, as a relatively tidy costume romance suitable for filming on the back lot and upon a divan or two. But Big Film was in the air; a cycle was in the making. Isn't *Cleopatra* an ideal subject for spectacle and stars? A series of mishaps and screwups dogged the project as it grew in size, lost its original Caesar, Antony, director, and script (after six million dollars had been spent and but ten and a half minutes canned), moved from Rome to London and back to Rome, and ended as the most expensive film made till that point, surely a folly. But all this is the industry's viewpoint. The public, drawn by the thunder of inadvertent backstage publicity, finds the premise appealing. The public likes Big Film, even this one.

If ever a movie star had dibs on Cleopatra, it was Elizabeth Taylor. Rex Harrison was virtually indispensable as Caesar—this is Gable-as-Rhett casting—and by the time the movie was released, Richard Burton had gossip-sheet headline entitlement as Taylor's Antony. True, the whole thing rather barges down the Nile, to borrow an old Broadway joke. But surely no one was expecting anything admirable, just very expensive fun. Is it a good bad movie? No—wait one chapter for *The Oscar,* a classic good bad movie. *Cleopatra* is an amusingly boring movie.

The Fall of the Roman Empire (1964), on the other hand, is a boring boring movie, though it is also the first of the vigorously international all-star films. In the opening minutes, we get not only Alec Guinness and James Mason but Stephen Boyd, his hair dyed blond and marcelled; in his jerkin and greaves he looks like a demented Robin Hood. Then, to Dimitri Tiomkin's pensive cello, Sophia Loren prays to Vesta in a fabulous fur-trimmed cape. But for Boyd's armor, it might be a dress rehearsal for *Doctor Zhivago*; and in quick course we greet Christopher Plummer, Omar Sharif, Mel Ferrer, Anthony Quayle, and John Ireland, the closest thing to a star the Americans can field in this one. Just as well; it's not a career-enhancing movie. Director Anthony Mann makes it a heavy two and a half hours—even the action scenes seem talky—and the cast doesn't work very hard, though the great Mason has to suffer torture by fire to prove to a pride of Visigoths that God is stronger than Odin. The moment looks absurd because we see Mason's grimaces but not the fire, prudently kept out of camera range. It is one of Old Cinema's most basic tenets that extremes are forbidden.

But New Cinema has spoiled us, and the traditional half-measures and tasteful facsimiles don't work anymore. We have seen Paul Newman assault Patricia Neal, Mrs. Bates stab Janet Leigh to death, James Mason gloat over the passing of the one obstacle to his obsession with his step-daughter: his wife. Of course, we also saw Mason faking his way through a torture test, but foreign-film watchers of the time had seen Jean-Luc Godard's *Le Petit Soldat* (1960; released here in 1963), which takes in a torture scene that looks and—within the cold Godardian *regard*—feels like torture. Old Cinema is in a lot of trouble.

Exhibit A: George Stevens's *The Greatest Story Ever Told* (1965), on the life of Our Lord. Here is mass-cult at the acme, provided no special-interest groups or the odd fanatic can find anything to object to. The adaptation shall be devotional. The characterizations shall be insipid. The visuals shall, wherever possible, imitate reverent and familiar Old Masters. And the eyes shall fill with stars—not just Max von Sydow's Christ, Dorothy McGuire's Mary, Charlton Heston's John the Baptist, and José Ferrer's Herod, but Carroll Baker, Angela Lansbury, Sidney Poitier, Telly Savalas, Ed Wynn, Claude Rains, Van Heflin—dare I go on? I mean, think of it: Ed Wynn in the Holy Land. It worked for *Around the World in Eighty Days,* but it lends a Brechtian alienation to what should be a highly involving pageant. How can we sink into the Mystery when we're so busy counting our blessings? Chuckling over the manifestation of Sal Mineo as the cripple whom Jesus heals, we might miss Shelley Winters's eighteen seconds as another of Dr. Christ's patients ("I am cured! I am cured!" crieth Shelley). After a while, it becomes a game: try to predict the next cameo. Natalie Wood as the Magdalene? Barbara Nichols as Mary, Queen of Scots? Yo, how about John Wayne as the Centurion managing the Crucifixion? But good heaven it *is* John Wayne as the Centurion managing the Crucifixion, uttering the deathless line "I believe this truly was the Son of God."

The hard part of it was that the narrow vision and one-size-fits-all aesthetic seemed to afflict the epic in general, as if all of them were *The Alamo*, as if even a first-rate director could make no more than a kitsch of history and a soap opera of human affairs in the epic form. The Italian critic Giovanni Grazzini, writing about another adaptation of sacred writing, John Huston's *The Bible . . . In the Beginning* (1966), said, "This *Bible* is exactly what one expects of an industry that, according to its own logic, understands God as a consumer product for the great international market and can not or will not run the risk of innovation, to work against the feelings and images of traditional popular illustration, to challenge the commonplace that gives an infantile sense of security to the mob." Considering the outrage that greeted both Pier Paolo Pasolini's grim version of *The Gospel According to Matthew* and Martin Scorsese's passionate *The Last Temptation of Christ,* one sees why the epic will not risk innovation.

Then why have epics at all? Big Films seemed virtually determined to be the worst films—the least artistic, the least stimulating, even the most boring. Huston's *Bible* was not the worst of them. Some of its special effects come off nicely, especially the Tower of Babel sequence, closing in a spectacular view looking down from on high as a terrified multitude dispersed over the earth in all directions. It was a process shot; had it been filmed live, only God Himself could have held the camera, so Lordly was the perspective. And Huston, the occasional actor, makes a delightful Noah. But Grazzini pointed out the absurdity of giving "blond hair and shaved cheeks to Adam, soft locks to Eve, a tough-guy look to Nimrod, and Ava Gardner's face to Sarah." But what else, with such a motley crew—Americans here, Italians there, a Norwegian Eve, a German Shem, Peter O'Toole (playing it straight) as an angel, and, matching Gardner's Sarah, George C. Scott's Abraham?

Not only was the epic's crush of stars becoming platitudinous, the view of windy running times as prestigious was dragging Big Film out to anything but heavenly lengths. *The Bible* ran 174 minutes, *The Greatest Story Ever Told* 225 minutes (cut to 141 for general release), and *Cleopatra* lasted a bit over four hours. *Gone With the Wind* at least endeavored to comprehend a sizable novel in virtually all its principals and events. Epic was written into the project from its conception. But *The Bible* was a vulgarity, *The Greatest Story* a series of paintings littered by celebrities, and *Cleopatra* little more than three people and a scandal.

Comedy worked better than history and Scripture in the epic, if only because it could work around the epic's salient flaw, self-reverence. Stanley Kramer's *It's a Mad Mad Mad Mad World* (1963) piled just about every prominent American comic actor (except Bob Hope) into 162 minutes' worth of chase after boodle, while Ken Annakin's *Those Magnificent Men in Their Flying Machines; or, How I Flew from London to Paris in 25 Hours, 11 Minutes* (1965) favored an international cast in a "great race" romance. Still, the point of view is Anglo-American. Kramer sees the world as a menagerie of crooks; Annakin sees it as a menagerie of crooks to be tamed by the strenuous self-esteem of the American and the gallantry of the Brit. Stuart Whitman is the American, a lazy showboater, walking into the sea in suit and tie just to give Sarah Miles a glass of champagne and losing the race when he pauses to save an opponent from a burning plane. James Fox is the Brit, ramrod straight, affable and fair, first to reach Paris but insisting on calling the race a tie because of Whitman's sporting concession. So who is Annakin's hero? Whitman: he gets Sarah Miles, giving Fox a chance to display gentlemanly grace when he bows out of the triangle. In fact, *Those Magnificent Men* gets a lot of mileage out of ethnic lampoons. If the American is a cowboy and the Brit a square, the German (Gert Frobe) is arrogant, the Italian (Alberto Sordi) dishonest, and the Frenchman (Jean-Pierre Cassel) a womanizer. There is even a cad Brit, Terry-Thomas. But then *Those Magnificent Men*'s grandiose logistics need these stereotypes. This is fantasy film, not just exaggerated but bizarre. Just the differing quaintness of the competing airships is a study, and the shots of the fliers sailing over Paris are wonderful, a kind of visual *joie de vivre* we saw little of in the 1950s.

All the epics mentioned here are color films, which brings us to one of the most lasting alterations of the film industry in the 1960s. Setting aside the worldview of sixties cinema, the stories and characters it uniquely favored, we find a number of purely technological innovations: the standardization of jazz (in all its forms) as narrative sound-track material after strictly novelty use in the 1950s; the perfection of the matching shot, so that an editing cut does not surprise an actor in a position that fails to correspond to his previous one, a bane of the 1930s at all Hollywood studios, a chance irritation for about twenty years thereafter, and totally conquered, even in the quickie, by about 1962 or 1963. There was as well the pre-credits "prologue," touched on in earlier decades but almost a cliché in the 1960s in nearly every kind of film, whether to set atmosphere, jag a plot into motion, or reveal a key character. *How to Murder*

Your Wife's prologue sets atmosphere: Jack Lemmon's valet, Terry-Thomas, runs through his morning duties while introducing the location (New York), his boss (unseen), and boss's high style of life (as a make-out-king bachelor in a town house), all this directly addressed to the audience in the light, soigné manner that the film hopes (vainly) to maintain throughout. *Hush . . . Hush, Sweet Charlotte*'s prologue handles plot duties, showing us, at a ball thirty-seven years before the movie's main action, how Bruce Dern jilted Bette Davis and was promptly chopped to death, and how Bette then wandered into the ball with blood on her dress, and how difficult it is to film Bette Davis so she looks thirty-seven years younger. (Director Robert Aldrich takes the easy way out, wreathing her in shadows.) *No Way to Treat a Lady* (1968) does not as much reveal its key character as disguise him, for Rod Steiger opens the film as a whistling Irish priest, ruddy and fully brogued, strolling the streets of New York. He's off to Mrs. Molloy's for a glass of wine. But Steiger's no priest. He strangles Mrs. Molloy, then kisses her and caresses her cheek. As the credits start to roll, he executes not a holy office but a demented serial killer's *modus operandi,* setting her corpse on the toilet, drawing a mouth on her forehead with lipstick, and blowing her a kiss as he leaves. And we're off with Detective George Segal on a grotesque murder case.

From Russia with Love's prologue must be the champion, since it sets atmosphere, launches the plot, and introduces a key character all at once, as Robert Shaw stalks Sean Connery in the night. Shaw kills Connery. Lights blast on—a mansion, loudspeakers, rushing men. It was only an exercise: the dead 007 was an anonymous prey wearing a James Bond mask. It's a bit farfetched (why the mask, except to shock us?), but the flamboyance, even exhibitionism, suits the Bond series—the 1960s, in truth, as a whole.

As we'll see, a spirit of "movies for movies' sake" seizes sectors of the business. In Old Hollywood, when the silent was relatively young, the first generation of stars still expanding the dimensions of fame, and the full-length feature yet contending with the two-reeler, moviemaking was the exuberant self-realization of a bunch of kids striking it rich. In the Studio Age, moviemaking was one of America's most profitable industries, with a hierarchy and protocol. By the 1960s, the kids are taking over again, with—for perhaps the first time in Hollywood's history—a genuine love of film not for what film can give them but for what film is. In the Studio Age, directors revered success and wanted to win Oscars; in the 1960s, directors revered D. W. Griffith and wanted to write their own scripts. This new breed of filmmaker is one reason for the movies' sudden change from the public's flatterer to the public's critic, and why its technical accomplishments appear as acts of self-esteem rather than as simple expertise. Maybe the flourishing of a prologue before the credits is a director's imposition of his stylistic signature in front of the studio logo: an act of arrogance. But maybe it is sheer delight in the discovery of yet another exercise in the practice of making movies.

However, the institution of color as virtually mandatory in the marketing of films was one development that was not regarded as an advance. On the contrary, it was forced on the industry. Color features had been on the scene since the 1920s, very sparingly applied. In the first years of the talkie, it was thought appropriate only for musicals and cartoons: color was frivolous. Technicolor's improved three-strip process reimposed the possibility of the color feature, and after 1935's *Becky Sharp,* a rare romance or drama would use Technicolor as a credential: color was prestige. *Gone With the Wind,* as David Selznick's movie of movies, would have been unthinkable in black and white. Yet the 1940s generally avoided it, except for Arthur Freed's musicals at MGM and Fox's Betty Grables.

Color made progress in the 1950s. It was, again, the war on television: color was good box office. Still, if it was no longer special, it had not become common—and this held true in the first half of the 1960s. Consider how many full-budget Hollywood features came out in black and white: *Psycho, The Apartment, Inherit the Wind, The Hustler, The Children's Hour, The Misfits, Judgment at Nuremberg, One, Two, Three, Days of Wine and Roses, Walk on the Wild Side, The Manchurian Candidate, Advise and Consent, To Kill a Mockingbird, The Miracle Worker, Lonely Are the Brave, Hud, America, America, The Victors, Dr. Strangelove, Kiss Me, Stupid, Fail-Safe, Seven Days in May, The Best Man, The Americanization of Emily, Mickey One, A Thousand Clowns, Ship of Fools.* Many of these films have an artistic claim on black and white as opposed to color—*Psycho*'s shadowy ambiguities, *The Hustler*'s nighttime underworld, *To Kill a Mockingbird*'s antique setting, and *Fail-Safe*'s documentary precision all report more ingenuously in black and white. And that's just the point: most moviemakers didn't want color. It was expensive. It was associated with musicals, comedy, and romance; wouldn't it trivialize a thriller or social commentary? Imagine *The Grapes of Wrath* in color. Cinematographers especially loathed it, after logging a half-century of craft in black and white. Color was unsophisticated.

But color was good for television sales. After a decade of resisting and hating TV, the studios now threw open their vaults to it—and since color was becoming absolute on television, black-and-white movies generated smaller sales. Color movies facilitated amortization of any project: and that's why virtually all films today, whatever their ambiguities and documentary precisions, are made in color.

But Darryl Zanuck's *The Longest Day* (1962) was not, and this, for an epitomization of the all-star epic, is startling. No doubt the black and white is meant to suggest a newsreel-like witness to this look at Americans, Englishmen, Frenchmen, and Germans during the Normandy invasion, for the realism runs so heavy that everyone speaks his own language to English subtitles. Nevertheless, the inevitable parade of stars upsets the realism as surely as it does Roman antiquity and Biblical mythology. We get seniors John Wayne, Robert Mitchum, Peter Lawford, Robert Ryan, Eddie Albert, Red Buttons, Rod Steiger, Richard Todd. We get teen heartthrobs—Robert Wagner, Fabian, Richard Beymer, Paul Anka, Sal Mineo. We get Richard Burton, a bit ahead of his stardom. We get various he-man functionaries of the day—Ray Danton, Steve Forrest, Tom Tryon, Jeffrey Hunter, Stuart Whitman. Even Henry Grace, the unknown playing General Eisenhower, adds to the suspension of belief, the feeling of garish color in the black and white, because (1) he looks *too* much like Eisenhower; and (2) he can't act. Halfway through the film's three hours, we're still spotting celebrities—Henry Fonda turns up, and there, in a bit on the Normandy beachhead, is Sean Connery, like Richard Burton not yet famous, his heavy Scots accent intact. We start to wonder if the French and German actors are as big in their nations as ours are at home. We lose sight of the film. We see only its poster.

Still, it is a compelling adventure, with extraordinarily convincing combat footage, especially a sweeping tracking shot from the air as the Germans strafe a beach mobbed by running, ducking, and dying soldiers. Zanuck hired three directors, perhaps to make it easier for us to remember who produced the film, yet the complex "you are there" among so many disparately motivated characters—from the day before the invasion right through the battle, from the points of view of soldiers, civilians, and the resistance, from our side to theirs—enjoys an amazing clarity. Zanuck's team works centripetally, gradually unifying the many elements into a narrative energy that pulls you into a single line, an unstoppable force. This isn't realism: this is opera. And by the nature of its subject, it is one of the few Big Films that did not seem, like *Cleopatra* or *The Fall of the Roman Empire* or *The Greatest Story Ever Told,* unnecessary.

In general, however, Big Film was the Bre'r Bear of the movies, big and dumb. It was not a director's or writer's medium, not even an actor's, for all the stars in sight. It was a producer's medium—as Grazzini says, "consumer product for the great international market." However, Stanley Kramer thought to bend the form to director power. To contain it even as he exploited its resources. To make it important through the use of an important topic. To give it the feel of New Cinema. Important was Kramer's trademark, the silly *It's a Mad Mad Mad Mad World* notwithstanding. He had tackled racism in *The Defiant Ones* (1958), nuclear holocaust in *On the Beach* (1959), the lunacy of fundamentalism in *Inherit the Wind* (1960). Now he would deal with Nazi war crimes in *Judgment at Nuremberg* (1961), with Spencer Tracy, Burt Lancaster, Richard Widmark, Marlene Dietrich, Maximilian Schell, Montgomery Clift, and Judy Garland.

This is a Solemn movie—in theme, in approach, and in the poster, a line of the stars' heads, grave and portentous in line drawings against a black background. This is Solemn casting, even, with a sense of bourgeois apocalypse in Tracy's playing one of the Allied judges in the trial of certain German magistrates. Tracy had logged his share of crooks and good-timers, and the teaming with Katharine Hepburn so lightened his style that he turned quasi-screwball. But by 1961, after *Father of the Bride, Bad Day at Black Rock, The Old Man and the Sea,* and his Clarence Darrow in *Inherit the Wind,* Tracy had become something of an American patriarch, and he underlines this at the movie's start when he refers to himself as a "rock-ribbed Republican who happened to admire Franklin Delano Roosevelt." That covers just about everyone between Ayn Rand and La Pasionaria, so Tracy is the Great American Father. He is Reason. "I want to understand," he tells Marlene Dietrich, everyone's second-favorite anti-Nazi German,* here playing the widow of a German war hero executed by Americans. "I *do* want to understand." Even: "I *have* to." He is Justice.

---

*Everyone's favorite, Lotte Lenya, would have been impractical, as she was busy launching her gallery of delicious grotesques in *The Roman Spring of Mrs. Stone* that same year.

Lonely at the Top. Spencer Tracy takes a troubled, pensive walk through the ruins of Hitler's twelve-year Reich in *Judgment at Nuremberg*.

Even more Solemn is Burt Lancaster, not only because he is one of the defendant judges, but because the others are vicious or reckless opportunists while Lancaster's Ernst Janning is a man of honor. Can anyone play tortured nobility better than Lancaster, especially when Abby Mann's script gives the character almost no lines? It is all uttered in Lancaster's eloquent gaze; so he is Justice, too. No. Lancaster is Guilt.

And Judy Garland is Suffering, in her first crack at a serious dramatic role* after two and a half decades of Trolley Songs. This in itself is Solemn, an automatic Oscar nomination, not least because Garland must portray the Aryan survivor of an exemplary case of "racial pollution," brought against an older Jewish man who platonically befriended her when she was in her teens. Will she testify for the prosecution, when all she wants is to put the terror behind her? Overweight yet terribly frail, Garland is

*Garland had played non-singing parts before, but nothing of this weight. For all that, it could be argued that her greatest acting part is that in *A Star Is Born* (1954), though by sheer weight of numbers it is also her most musical role.

very, very good—but Montgomery Clift is beyond discussion. Here, as in *The Misfits*, he doesn't seem to be acting as a victim of sterilization who is excruciatingly taken apart on the witness stand. This is worse than Solemn. This is history with a movie star's face.

Most Solemn is the turbulent Max Schell, as counsel for the defense, for this man thundering at—and at times tormenting—witnesses really *is* German. He's even mean to Judy Garland.

Whereupon, in the film's most Solemn moment of all, Lancaster suddenly rises, frozen in indignation, to ask, *"Are we going to do this again?"* The following day, he makes a long statement, inculpating all Germany, all Germans, his hard fury all but sweeping Schell from the courtroom. Now Lancaster is Righteousness, and he tells us, in a line that could serve as a watchword for the decade's movies as a whole, "It is not easy to tell the truth."

But then, as one of my favorite Bible characters says, "What is truth?" For Schell is not finished. How, he asks, replying to Lancaster's *J'accuse,* can only Germany be guilty? The Russians are guilty of signing a pact with Hitler. The Vatican is guilty. American industrialists are guilty. Winston Churchill is guilty. (Schell's reasoning gets a little absurd there.) If Germany is guilty, the whole world is guilty.

This is Kramer and Mann's truth: that it's not only hard to tell but hard, harder, to hear. The United States, it turns out, does not want to hear about Nazi war crimes, because the trials are sabotaging our relations with a post-Hitler Germany, needed to bolster free Europe against the Soviets. All these guilty verdicts may be good justice, but they're bad politics—and, as a final title card informs us, of all the defendants sentenced to life imprisonment in 1949, none was still serving in 1961.

The film is direct and tough and, yes, Solemn, but it is not simplistic or sentimental. And Kramer knows how to make a movie out of what is essentially a play set in a courtroom. His camera movements startle, as when he hurtles in for a close-up of Schell just as he jumps out of German into flawless English, or during Lancaster's big speech, when the camera slowly spins about the room of judges, prisoners, witnesses, and spectators, probing the site like a modern-day Macaulay, seeking the nature of the past in the character of its statesmen. Kramer is most sharp in tracking Tracy's walk through Nuremberg, following him into a ruined amphitheatre. As Tracy muses on the power of the Nazi rally, the sound track provides a German chorus in a rousing march. Kramer pulls curiously up to the empty rostrum. And we hear Hitler screaming.

Judgment at Nuremberg, for all its success, is not a key sixties film, mainly because opinion makers refuse to regard it as one. They don't like Kramer, perhaps because he's so solemn about being Solemn. He's Hollywood highbrow. So someone as silly as, say, Douglas Sirk, with his banal soap operas and *Taza, Son of Cochise,* comes off far better in the annals than the issue-conscious Kramer. Maybe there's something suspicious about a movie director who doesn't do soap operas. Andrew Sarris, grouping directors by talent, ranks Sirk as high as the second category, while Kramer doesn't place till the back of the book, in the ninth circle along with Roy del Ruth, Arch Oboler, and Jack Garfein. Richard Roud's *Cinema: A Critical Dictionary,* a huge encyclopedia of "the major filmmakers," doesn't include Kramer at all. No doubt Sarris and Roud like Kramer's *Ship of Fools* (1965) even less than they like *Judgment at Nuremberg.* This one, too, is about the difficulty of getting anyone to face the truth, but it lacks *Nuremberg*'s battling, worrying, and finally despairing quest for justice. *Ship of Fools* is *Grand Hotel* with a Message.

It counts more stars than there were in heaven, perhaps our most international jamboree yet: French Simone Signoret, German Oskar Werner and Heinz Ruehmann, English Vivien Leigh, Greek Lilia Skala, Scandinavian Alf Kjellin, Puerto Rican José Ferrer, and Americans Lee Marvin, Elizabeth Ashley, and George Segal, not to mention the José Greco dance troupe. The only one missing is Toshiro Mifune, though Kramer might argue that his polyglot cast was designed to advance the universalism of his allegory, for we are all on the ship, all fools.

So Michael Dunn tells us at the top of the film in one of those "all the stage's a world" prologue speeches. Kramer tips his hand a wee bit here (even more so later, when, in a costume-party scene, Nazi Ferrer dilates upon the extermination of inferior beings while wearing devil's horns), but he is only being faithful to his source, Katherine Anne Porter's vastly denounced best-seller of 1962. And let it be said that Kramer marshals his forces far better than Edmund Goulding, *Grand Hotel*'s director, marshaled his, what with the pre-Method Garbo facing off John Barrymore's velveteen ham and Crawford's all-American jazz sparring with Wallace Beery's phoney late Biedermeier. Kramer gets more of a blend, even with Signoret's moistly introspective *volupté* on one hand and Lee

Marvin on the other. And Kramer's trademark searching camera is as busy here as in *Nuremberg,* with its moody pans, its patient studies, its retreats in dismay, its stealing around the back of a head for a close-up. The camera is as shocked as we are by these characters' refusal, and inability, to see themselves fairly. "The stupid cruelties, the vanities!" Oskar Werner observes, not necessarily of Richard Roud's encyclopedia. Michael Dunn salutes us as we disembark: "I can hear you saying, What has this to do with us?" A pause. Then: "Nothing."

Moviegoers don't like to be told they're fools. If there must be New Cinema, let it be *Psycho* or *Hud,* wherein the fools are clearly demarcated, distinguished from *us.* Actually, the question is: Will Old Cinema survive, or will it become misfit, forced off the screen as the public gets used to New Cinema's penetrating grip on what is true as opposed to what is glamorous? Well, as Clark Gable tells Marilyn Monroe in *The Misfits,* "Nothing's forever." But "That's what I can't get used to," Monroe replies. "Everything keeps changing."

"It is not easy to tell the truth." It's hardly an original perception, but it is a permanently relevant one.

So what ever did happen to Bette Davis?

Changes, baby.

Five

The Acculturation
of the Monster

New Cinema loves evil. At the very least, it yearns to comprehend it, and at most it seems actively to delight in it. Once, movie plots surged toward the humiliation of the villain—in, say, the ferocious ride of the Klan to save the Cameron family to climax *The Birth of a Nation,* the mangling of Francis X. Bushman in *Ben-Hur*'s chariot race; the cut direct when an admiral praises Charles Laughton's astonishing survival in a *Bounty* lifeboat yet refuses to shake the sadist's hand; James Gleason's "The people—try and lick that" to Edward Arnold in *Meet John Doe*; or, more complexly, in *High Noon,* not Gary Cooper's eradication of the Miller gang but the moment just after, when he throws away his badge in rejection of a cowardly society that does not deserve protection from Miller gangs.

Scenes like these, and even the entire careers of such stars as Mary Pickford or Errol Flynn, helped define America's moral code at least partly because the villains always looked villainous. They snarled and bullied. They were sinister or greedy or Charles Laughton. But by the 1950s they were already being displaced by morally irresolute heroes, and the *Hud* effect of the 1960s densely compromised the characterological code. If a film's hero serves as its villain, whom are we to root for? This is opera without a soprano.

It was especially jarring when New Cinema gave leading roles to little-known actors, or went beyond *Hud* to limn not merely selfish or amoral charmers but despicable beasts. With Newman or McQueen, we can balance the less appealing characters with their finer sides—consider the Bullitt in the Hud, so to say. But whom are we to sympathize with, identify as the deputy of our better nature, in *Dr. Strangelove* (1964)? Everyone in it is a nut or a jerk. Where do we fit into the equivocating discoveries of *Blowup* (1966), which offers anti-reality instead of an anti-hero, or the joyriding lawlessness of *Bonnie and Clyde* (1967)? How are we to protect ourselves from the velvet brutality of the killers of *In Cold Blood* (1967) when they are played by newcomers, actors without a Bullitt in them, for all we know—and most persuasive actors at that?

In short, we are moving from the world of the scoundrel to that of the monster. A child-molester, for instance. Better: a child-molester who murders the mother to get to the kid. Yet this is no thriller, but a romantic comedy, Stanley Kubrick and Vladimir Nabokov's *Lolita* (1962). A dark comedy, I grant you; and what macabre romance! Yet—as Nabokov makes deliriously clear in his novel—it is love, the same pining, remorseful, relentless, physical, and emotional love that has energized popular art since when. *Lolita* is a love story. A love story disgusted with love. Or no: disgusted with these particular lovers. Or maybe: sympathetic to them but cynical about their possibilities. Kubrick keyed the casting most precisely—James Mason as Humbert Humbert; Shelley Winters as the widow who fancies him; Sue Lyon as the tot *he* fancies, doing baroque things with her bubble gum as Mason patiently wheedles and impatiently demands; and Peter Sellers as his shadow double.

But for Lyon's three or four years' advantage on the novel's nymphet, everyone is exactly right, and Kubrick goes to town. "How did they ever make a movie of *Lolita*?" the ads gasped. The answer is "Faithfully." Nothing is stinted, even this early in the 1960s, even in a tale so notorious that it turned Nabokov from a *New Yorker* spoke into a great international wheel, an author of major art. Some say the film cartoons the book; they can't have read it. Nabokov wrote the screenplay and liked the release print. And if it is not absurd to speak of Shelley Winters's greatest performance, this is it—loathsome and touching, unlikable yet lovable, a study of and attack on American motherhood in a way that no film had

Lolita. Shelley Winters has just discovered James Mason's diary, revealing his disgust for her and love for her daughter. Hell hath no fury like a woman scorned? All Winters does is get angry. Mason, scorned, commits murder.

yet dared present. Even *The Manchurian Candidate*'s terrifying Angela Lansbury was at least a villain to respect, vicious but formidable. Winters's Charlotte Haze is simply ridiculous. Between Nabokov's characterization and Winters's reading, the American petty-bourgeois woman is not only skewered but liquidated, especially in her pathetic cultural ambitions. Like Mason, Winters has chosen a uniquely inappropriate love object— Mason himself. He is Continental, urbane, replete with resonances. As Winters puts it, trimming her admiration with a fiasco of pretension and a toss of her hand, "Paris, France, ma dah." Love makes Mason paranoid; it makes Winters incoherent. And when the jealous Winters sends Lolita off to summer camp and, in a letter, orders her fascinating European boarder to assume a lover's duties or move out, Mason's incredulous, amused, and absolutely withering laughter marks something new in cinema, in romance, and in man's relationship to his mother.

Kubrick went to England to film *Lolita*. Sam Peckinpah made *Ride the High Country* (1962) in California—all over it, from Los Angeles's Griffith Park way up to Bishop in the north. Yet this western challenged Hollywood behavioral codes even more than *Lolita*. Nabokov's novel, after all, was elite material, promising elite cinema. The western is fundamental pop Americana, morally and emotionally the form least open to New Cinema. So, for starters, Peckinpah casts as his villain Joel McCrea, perhaps the sweetest of all western good guys. Against the background of an evolutionary, a self-modernizing West, Peckinpah will give McCrea a kind of Last Ride, reuniting him with his long-lost friend, straight-arrow lawman Randolph Scott. Scott will hire McCrea on as deputy in the guiding of a gold shipment to safety—but McCrea intends to hijack the gold and bushwhack his old pal Scott.

Somewhere early in production, Peckinpah, McCrea, and Scott realized that the two actors had better switch roles. McCrea was a little too sweet to be plausible as a faithless adventurer, and Scott always had a touch of the thug about him. Still, Scott was an unofficial hero of some three decades' standing by then. To introduce him, as Peckinpah does, shilling for a carnival sideshow in an outlandish Buffalo Bill wig and a ghastly red beard, is to trash the western's essential virtue: its self-esteem. To allow Scott to forge ahead with his skunk's plot against McCrea violates the western's emotions—and killing off McCrea in the closing frames as Scott (sadly, at least) rides off with the other survivors violates its morals.

Does New Cinema love evil? Does Peckinpah? Is he simply pointing out that sweetness doesn't survive and thugs do? We know what Peckinpah doesn't love—schmoos. Early in the film, McCrea shakes hands with a bank teller, a dreary fool, and Peckinpah closes in on the handshake, then examines the teller's reaction. He is befuddled, as if he never met a Real Man before, or even been in a Peckinpah movie, the best place to meet one. Still, he's luckier than the Hammond brothers, who are Real Men but—the only mortal sin in Peckinpah—lack style. The Hammond boys have disgusting personal habits and think rape is a hoot: so far, so good. But in the whole great pack of them there's not one with a commanding walk or a faraway stare. Peckinpah has nothing but contempt for them, though they fill *Ride the High Country* with plot when they make off with Mariette Hartley and the ever-decent McCrea rescues her. Naturally a gunfight ensues, but this most ancient of the western's

formal elements gets a thorough renovation in Peckinpah's caustic revisionism—this is not good guys versus bad guys (for Scott, one of the
"good guys," is a bad guy himself), but Real Men versus schmoos. One
thing a gunfighter needs is honor, but schmoos have none, and there is
a marvelous, terrifying, Peckinpavian moment illustrating this when a
Hammond is shot and one of his brothers calmly picks up his rifle. The
wounded man, his life slopping out of him, looks at his brother as if to
ask, Does your calmly picking up my rifle mean that I don't need it
anymore because I'm just about to die?

Yep. And down he goes.

Amid all the examinations of personal style, Peckinpah does not
have time to work in too many riffs on the theme of changing times and
the displacement of both good and bad guys of the older West. Still, it
makes itself felt, perhaps because we begin to suspect that all the great
sixties movies make at least some reference to the notion that we, the
audience in the theatres when these films were released, were living in a
new age—even, that we were going over into the future. And it doesn't
work. It doesn't work because it debases style and honor. It only likes
survivors. And isn't it the least admirable people who tend to survive,
the monsters? Yet Warren Beatty's most telling line in *All Fall Down* is
"I hate life." Even survival doesn't work. New Cinema doesn't love evil;
it is trying to explain it.

It is trying to explain, for instance, why Ann-Margret, the post-
beat baby-doll temptress of Douglas Heyes's *Kitten with a Whip* (1964),
longs for "serenity, security, and all that jazz" yet bursts into John Forsythe's serene, secure suburban home with two punks for the sheer fun
of trashing what Ann-Margret longs for. Does she hate what she loves
because she can't have it? Is she rotten because a rotten world corrupts
those with spirit? "Bookies and pushers," Ann-Margret sneers, "make
more than preachers."

Punks terrorizing the bourgeoisie was a favorite fifties trope, especially of the B movie, which accepted punks at face value as psychopaths.
Men are what they do: cobblers make shoes, gymnasts flip and tumble,
and psychopaths terrorize the bourgeoisie. But the 1960s wants to understand the psycho, from Anthony Perkins's Norman Bates on. The 1960s
wants to heal his wounds and develop preventive treatments for others.
Kitten wasn't born with a whip, was she? How did she acquire it?
Moreover, writer-director Heyes's film, despite its exploitative title, is not

a B, but a well-made Universal feature.* Heyes has an ear—one of the punks, James Ward, is a big, infantile surfer with a touch of North Beach bongo nerves and a scalpel in his pocket, and his partner, Peter Brown, is imaginatively articulate in a spiffy outfit; their verbal duets, half manic hedonism and half penis rivalry, yield a kind of non-physical violence that keeps the film suspenseful till the real violence starts. Heyes has an eye as well, giving us a *Tweety and Sylvester* cartoon on the television when Forsythe first realizes that the girl he took for a helpless waif is a predator—that he is playing the mild bird to her relentless cat. Like Tweety, Forsythe wins out in the end, but only because the secretly ambivalent Ann-Margret finally takes his side against her punk pals. The three terrors die in a car crash; Forsythe awakens in the hospital, ready to pull through. "Maybe it is a mistake to feel sorry for kids like that," says a police detective. "Then, maybe it's a mistake not to." Inside the psycho is a bourgeois dream struggling to come true—inside Ann-Margret, anyway. This is a rather fifties notion: that everyone wants to be like everyone else. But feeling sorry for dangerous people is a sixties remedy.

Indeed, feeling sorry for everyone becomes routine now, as monotonous as a household chore. It explains why moviemakers filled their screens with heroes who despise and sneer and cheat and rape, why we were expected not to hate them for their cruelty, not to dwell overmuch on how we would feel with Hud for a father or Jake Holman for a son— not sorry for them, probably. In *All Fall Down,* Eva Marie Saint is so crushed when Warren Beatty won't respond to her love (and the news that he has made her pregnant) that she crashes her car. Yet the film isn't her tragedy; it's his. When Beatty's formerly adoring younger brother Brandon de Wilde goes after Beatty with a gun, we know he'll end up feeling sorry for him and won't shoot. True, de Wilde's sorry takes in a good deal of disgust and sudden self-knowledge; if the tragedy is Beatty's, the anagnorisis is de Wilde's. Still, other people's compassion seems to dog the sixties anti-hero, so much so that a kind of monster class is built into an elite.

---

*The punks-on-a-rampage form was still throwing off unreconstructed B's late in the decade, as in MGM's *Hot Rods to Hell* (1967), a fifties quickie in all but the color photography: father Dana Andrews, mother Jeanne Crain, and two children menaced by two boys, a ghastly script, and Mimsy Farmer, the sixties answer to Yvonne Lime. Whenever the bad kids appear, the sound track erupts in rock So We Know They're Bad.

Thus even a sufferer of the Holocaust is treated almost as a villain because he doesn't feel sorry for anyone, in Sidney Lumet's *The Pawnbroker* (1965). Flashbacks to Rod Steiger's youth with his wife and children in the sunny European countryside contrast vividly with his present, deep in the dark inner city of Harlem, for Steiger has found his own Final Solution to the horror of the concentration camp and the loss of his family: the eradication of feeling. He, too, hates life, and has made the existential choice of denying it so fiercely that he has become the least compassionate man legally tolerated by society—a ghetto pawnbroker, trading in misery. Hoodlums and victims encircle his tiny domain, yet he is beyond caring. He takes no sides, believes in nothing, scarcely even in his own survival. Of course he has not lost the ability to care; he has simply, absolutely, denied it. Yet the film makes him a victim all over again, building up a series of atrocities to force Steiger to *feel*—torturing him, really, as vilely as the Nazis did. This is not an age to suffer ascetics gladly. Everyone has to feel.

Lumet feels, of course. One senses him caressing Steiger as he racks him. But New Cinema can also be "objective," as they were starting to call it then: unfeeling. Merely showing. Recounting. Perhaps—so delicately—observing. Actually, this was no novelty in Hollywood. Alfred Hitchcock had been working an objective camera for decades. He tells the story; you supply the feelings. Anyway, New Cinema wasn't as interested in unusual techniques as in subverting traditional moviemaking with new ways of telling old stories. *Lolita* and *The Pawnbroker* are undoubtedly new forms of film, both based on novels that would have been unfilmable a decade earlier simply because audiences would have found both protagonists unattractive. But *Ride the High Country* is an old form of film re-explained. What better place for the affirmation of a new sensibility than the western, a form concerned entirely with the old values of honor and morality? Marlon Brando thought so; his sole adventure as a director (as well as star) was *One-Eyed Jacks* (1961), a western, and in important ways a key manifestation of New Cinema.

Critics generally give it the faint-praise treatment—"interesting," say, but "confused." No. The film is clear. But it is slow, deliberate, as if Brando had wanted to commit an industry outrage. He did. Tripling the two-million-dollar budget and pushing a six-week shooting schedule into six months, Brando concluded work with a print lasting four hours and forty-two minutes, the Erich von Stroheim of the 1960s.* Paramount cut *One-Eyed Jacks* to two hours and twenty-one minutes, without the dimmest hope of recouping, but we of today look back on it as one of the first major anti-western westerns. In Brando's world, everyone's a crook. Brando's a crook. His erstwhile partner Karl Malden is now a sheriff; the sheriff's a crook. Malden wasn't even sound when he and Brando pulled off the big bank heist that opens the film. Pinned down by a posse in the mountains with one tired horse between the two of them, they agree that Malden will ride off to return with fresh mounts. He never does.

The bulk of *One-Eyed Jacks* surveys Brando's attempt to exact revenge after five years in prison. Crook that he is, Brando nevertheless must be the good guy, going by traditional western tropes, the valiant and shrewd warrior who confronts the corrupt lawman. But being in the right, Brando shows us, lacks point if everyone else is blithely in the wrong. Even Brando's new gang is a very mixed bag of the loyal and the sly. Frank Capra often showed us a comparably black world in which the American nation seemed composed of villains, cynical bystanders, and a reckless mob buying and selling the god of the moment. But Capra was keen to give his heroes an ally or two. How alone can you be if Jean Arthur's on your side?

No one's on Brando's side (except Malden's daughter, and she's no Jean Arthur). For that matter, Brando is a far cry from Capra's Gary Cooper or James Stewart. Brando's a crook. Movies of Capra's age loved life, not least for its verve and innocence, two qualities that New Cinema made disreputable. Brando, smoldering and snarling, "Git up, you scum-sucking pig" or "I'll tear your hands off," doesn't hate life, just the people living it. "You gob o' spit," he calls Malden henchman Slim Pickens, in flawless Method anger-calm. Why bother overselling the line? All men are gobs o' spit. It's not a discovery; it's a cliché.

On the other hand, Brando rouses himself for a considerable amount of violence, far more than even the soon to be brutally naturalistic Sam

---

*This is not to mention Brando's exhaustive pre-production period, which so alienated the engaged director, Stanley Kubrick, that he dropped out, and Brando asked himself, "Why not me?" In the future, everyone will direct a film for fifteen minutes; Brando took something like fifteen months, all told, and went on to another industry outrage when slowing the filming of *Mutiny on the Bounty* (1962).

Peckinpah allowed in *Ride the High Country. One-Eyed Jacks* counts beatings, shooting in cold blood, and Malden's awesome public whipping of Brando, capped by the breaking of the fingers in Brando's gun hand. Then, delighting in the perverse, Brando suddenly gets tasteful in the last reel, when he has to coldcock someone while making an escape from jail and knocks him out so primly we see the gun but not the man's head.

The sixties fascination with evil and violence and the impracticality of loving life grows so acute by mid-decade that one of the era's major films takes as its hero the nuclear device that destroys the world. Certainly it is the closest thing to a protagonist in *Dr. Strangelove; or, How I Learned to Stop Worrying and Love the Bomb* (1964), dominating Stanley Kubrick's high-concept truth-game cartoon as it spends the entire film steadily traveling toward Russia to the urging of drums and a male chorus humming "When Johnny Comes Marching Home." Certainly also this is a film—like Thackeray's *Vanity Fair*—without a hero, without even an anti-hero. Everyone in *One-Eyed Jacks* is a crook; everyone in *Dr. Strangelove* is a goon or a goblin. Consider the names Kubrick and his co-writers Terry Southern and Peter George gave their characters, as illustrative as Thackeray's Rebecca Sharp, Rawdon Crawley, and Lady Bareacres: General Jack D. Ripper (Sterling Hayden), the loony anti-Communist who launches the attack; General "Buck" Turgidson (George C. Scott), the oafish deputy in the War Room; the two Russians, glumly treacherous Ambassador de Sadesky (Peter Bull) and frantic Premier Kissov (unheard and unseen but a heavy presence on the phone); the idiot Colonel "Bat" Guano (Keenan Wynn), in charge of liberating Hayden's air base from Hayden; Major "King" Kong (Slim Pickens, a mouthful itself), head of Hayden's bombing mission; and of course Peter Sellers's three roles, as Hayden's British aide Group Captain Lionel Mandrake, as the pointlessly reasonable President Muffley, and as Dr. Strangelove, the only one of these characters who adds nothing to the plot but everything to Kubrick's atmosphere of capricious naturalism.

Religion is the expression of a people's self-belief. When religion is strong, the popular tales treat world creation and the exploits of heroes. When religion is weak—when a people's self-belief suffers doubt—the popular tales treat world's end and the exploits of monsters. Such films as *Psycho, The Manchurian Candidate, The Hustler,* and *Point Blank* have helped steer us to this point, but Kubrick makes a decisive breakaway in the sophistication of his tone: satire, horror, irony, and spoof, factored

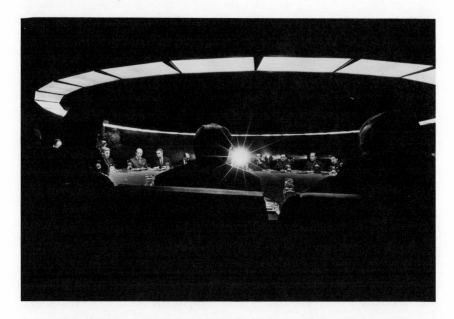

The Great American Movie Still of the Sixties: the War Room in *Dr. Strangelove*. Look for President Peter Sellers, left of center on the far side of the table.

together into a tidy epic on the capers of grotesques. No other comedy is as serious as this one, no thriller as amusing, and what fairy tale ever seemed so historical?

Some of *Dr. Strangelove* is topically allusive, as is Hayden's right-winger's obsession with the contamination of "our precious bodily fluids." Some of it is a keenly distilled black humor, as when Wynn's troops arrive and Hayden's men wonder why the supposedly Communist invaders look so authentic—uniforms, insignia, materiel. They could almost be Americans. Says one soldier, "Probably got them at Army surplus"—this, by the way, just before a battle so convincing it looks like documentary footage.

But most of *Dr. Strangelove* is various fun, chance hits falling out of the action—President Sellers's famous breaking up of a scuffle between the Russian Ambassador and General Scott, crying, "You can't fight in here—this is the War Room!" Or the opening pun, over the credits, of planes more or less balling and holding hands to the tune of "Try a Little Tenderness." Or Pickens's analysis—in the air, on his way to the nuking of Russia—of what the Army considers practical for the bombardier's survival kit, which, along with money, rations, chewing gum, and a combination Russian phrase book and Holy Bible, contains lipstick, condoms, and nylons. "Shoot," Pickens observes, "a fella could have a pretty good weekend in Vegas with all that stuff."

Perfectly true, and this is what is so striking about *Dr. Strangelove*—the realism with which Kubrick rams his fantasy home. All his types of comedy are one comedy, all the speculation is persuasive, all the parody is a report, an exposé, a Book of Revelation. Kubrick's source, Peter George's novel *Red Alert,* is serious, pure thriller. But when Kubrick started filming, he found the camera kept picking up on the absurdity of the situation, rendering it freakish. In substance, *Red Alert* is chilling; in effect, it was coming out chillingly silly. Gilbert Taylor's cinematography emphasizes this, with deranged, black-night lighting for the indoor scenes and an almost pre-talkie pastel gray for certain outdoor shots, as if trying to read from a children's storybook during an eclipse of the sun. Kubrick toys with this, filming close-ups in the confrontation between Hayden and Sellers head-on at Sellers but from below at Hayden, catching the craggy soldier who murders the world as an oracular bust, a fifth head for Gutzon Borglum's monument of crucial Americans in the Black Hills.

By far the film's most potent coupling of the real and the bizarre lies in the actors' performances. Searching through the most tightly fitted ensembles of the early 1960s—of *Splendor in the Grass, The Hustler, Breakfast at Tiffany's, To Kill a Mockingbird, All the Way Home*—one cannot find a parallel. Especially not for Sellers's tour de force of British dope, American fool (with the most faultless imitation of an American accent in the history of Anglo-American relations), and German Frankula, astonishing as he wheels into the film's last ten minutes, a virtual contraption of a man, part plastic, leather, and steel, constantly battling his Heil Hitler arm, manipulating his cigarette, balancing between cynicism and fury (like Kubrick), and giving a reading of the word "slaughtered" that captures the film's giddy ferocity in a moment.*

*Second Footnote on the Worthlessness of the Oscars: Sellers was nominated as Best Actor, as were legitimate competitors—Richard Burton and Peter O'Toole for *Becket* and Anthony Quinn for *Zorba the Greek.* Rex Harrison won for *My Fair Lady.* What tosh! *My Fair Lady* swept the prize night because Hollywood loves a winner. *My Fair Lady* also won Best Picture, Director, Color Cinematography, Color Art Direction, Sound, Adaptation Scoring, Color Costuming (not to mention unfulfilled nominations for Best Supporting Actor and Actress, Screenplay, and Editing).

The casting is superb throughout. Scott truly digs into the bumpkin stupidity of General Turgidson, a necktie away from the kind of man who leads a lynch mob, so enchanted by macho gamesmanship that he goes wild with delight in the War Room when describing the effect of Hayden's bomb—though by then everybody present knows that this bomb will set off Russia's doomsday machine. As for Hayden, *Dr. Strangelove* was one of the few times this curiously mishandled movie star manqué lucked into a first-rate picture. Kubrick's *The Killing* (1956), in which Hayden masterminds an intricate race-track heist, was one of the few other times. Apparently, Kubrick sees Hayden as a warrior gone rogue, a strong man on the wrong side. In *The Killing,* Hayden plays not only a leader but, in the developing of his scam, something of a genius except for one miscalculation, an unreliable suitcase that blows away his game. In *Dr. Strangelove,* however, Hayden is the worst kind of leader, not only fanatic but demented—and this is a man, Kubrick demonstrates, with the power to blast the planet.

Would Kubrick's very cautionary tale have had anywhere near as much force with an actor less apt than Hayden, immense and methodical, chain-smoking intensely phallic cigars as he outlines his theory of manly "essence," confusing women with Communists in his highly textured macho psychology? Women want to drain him of semen, Communists to purge him of beliefs; they all seek his essence. Maybe it took a victim of both Hollywood's star system and McCarthyism—which Hayden was— to put this paranoia together so beautifully. He is the ultimate Bad Father of the 1960s, a kind of Mrs. Bates, Lee Marvin, and Pat Hingle (in *Splendor in the Grass*) joined and raised to the level of mythopoeia, the worst monster in an age whose passion is the fearful worship of terrible gods.

Loving the bomb, idle joke that it seems, actually keys in one of Kubrick's most insidious running gags, on the theme that war is made by those who lack love. On one hand we have that wonderfully peaceful opening sequence of planes making love (to, remember, "Try a Little Tenderness"), on the other Hayden's joyless obsession with the loss of bodily fluids. Hell's demons make war because they don't know what affection is. Scott, turgid buck indeed, is called to the War Room in the midst of a sex date with his secretary, and Pickens treats the bombing of Russia as a combination Last Ride and Once in a Lifetime Lay. He climbs onto the bomb in the plane's bay and, in Kubrick's most dazzling shot, plunges with the bomb shouting "Ti-yo!" and waving a cowboy hat. It is literally fabulous—a picture for the new heathenism of monster love, what in political contexts was being referred to as "maximizing the contradictions." Apocalypse now.

For all its artistry, *Dr. Strangelove* would appear to be a rare sixties film that is fundamentally political—like *The Manchurian Candidate,* motivated by a social purpose. The theme is war preparedness and the message is, We're too prepared—in fact, some of us are disquietingly eager. A printed warning before the credits states that our armed forces claim that systemic safeguards will quash any Jack D. Ripper. However, just a few months after *Dr. Strangelove's* release, Sidney Lumet's *Fail-Safe* (1964) projected the nuclear destruction of New York and Moscow not by human intervention but by a technical kink such as we all know machine-age systems are subject to—maybe something as small as a defunct transistor. *Fail-Safe* seems even more grittingly political than *Dr. Strangelove,* for in place of Kubrick's *chiaroscuro* ontology of the monster world is a pure—a deadpan—naturalism without a note of sound-track music. Real life. Peter Sellers's American President is a marvelous study in comic possibilities; Lumet simply elects Henry Fonda as he is—"all of that compassion coming through," he explained later. Lumet does include a demented officer—Fritz Weaver, who melodramatically breaks down in the SAC War Room when the President orders the destruction of our own planes. But in general this is plain and very credible work—fiction-vérité?—not least when the War Room staff members let off whoops of joy when one of the attacking planes is shot down. A general shouts, "This isn't a football game!"

It *is*. Like *Dr. Strangelove, Fail-Safe* shows us statesmanship as a contest of two sides playing to win, with chance factors affecting their skills. Like *Dr. Strangelove, Fail-Safe* flashes its official note that the professional soldiers say it cannot happen. And like *Dr. Strangelove, Fail-Safe* nevertheless left its first audiences with the ghastly impression that, sooner or later, it will. Kubrick, a latter-day Bosch, fades out epically—yet in the black irony of the 1960s—on footage of mushroom clouds, to a voice-over of Vera Lynn's World War II ballad, "We'll Meet Again." Lumet holds to his You Are There realism as the bomber approaches Manhattan. The Empire State Building from overhead. A flock of pigeons leaping into flight. New Yorkers in freeze-frames. The screen goes white, then black.

The credits roll over a confused hubbub. Then a whine of white noise. It's over.

One thing about these two films: they don't hate life. On the contrary, they plead for Westerners to place a higher value on human survival than on brinkmanship statism. This is very sixties, of course: ban the bomb. But one notes a cynical tone in both the gleefully eerie *Dr. Strangelove* and the dead-on earnest *Fail-Safe,* a feeling that statism will endure. This is an age that crushes its own ideals, builds defeats into its purposes. It struggles for racial fairness yet tolerates—at times delights in—anti-Semitism. It explodes the hypocrisy of the leaders of American government, yet adopts hypocritical leaders of its own. It works against Amerika the Beast, yet cheers for some of the most terrifying slave states the world has known.

And it still is out looking for heroes, yet chooses inferior people. Bryan Forbes's *King Rat* (1965) puts the "cream and bastards rise" syndrome into the context of world war—more pungently, class war—and most exactly in the setting of a Japanese-run prisoner-of-war camp. A British film, based on James Clavell's novel (drawn from personal experience), it focuses on survival procedures of British soldiers in desperately adverse conditions. Who is the hero? The idealistic James Fox, upholder of traditional good-egg teamwork, noble, lovable, and ready to bond? Or the ideal-crusher, the King, George Segal, an American charm boy who manipulates, cajoles, bullies, and cheats? Or even our old sixties moralist, Tom Courtenay, skulking and crashing through the camp in a permanently hopeless mission to catch the King in *peccato* and, incidentally, strike a blow against the system of privilege that keeps the Courtenays down?

Whom does the film love? It doesn't love the King. But Fox does, taking him, in stubborn naïveté, for a misunderstood knight. Postwar American films were much less interested in American class structures than our films of the 1920s and '30s (and, somewhat, the very early '40s) were. But all English films—all things English, right down to Callard & Bowser's toffees—are about class, and it is notable that Fox can admire Segal precisely because smart Americans, especially a smart con man, aren't readily placeable. The King is by English judgments beyond class—but for the technicality that he virtually runs the camp: the King in truth.

King Rat, as the title implies, thinks Segal is the monster, but Fox thinks the defiantly yet ineffectually virtuous Courtenay is. There is no hero, even here in the alleged Hero City of men at war, and Forbes presses the point home at the end, when Courtenay lets loose with a proletarian tirade at Fox and the liberated Segal rides off in silent despair, abandoning Fox without a farewell. Even a monster has his sense of turf. The King's was the camp. Back home in the States he'll be just another street-corner deadbeat.

Foreign films like *King Rat* helped texture the home product's striving after a new morality, a behavioral code and an order of angels and devils fit for the time. The trouble with American cinema is that, on one level, everything's a western, a battle of good and evil in a wilderness innocent of social influences. Pure good, pure evil. Even Warner Brothers in the 1930s—a dead center of political moviemaking—is more concerned with personality than with the impact of culture. The 1960s is our classic revolutionary decade, yet how class-conscious was it? A foreign movie the 1960s loved was not *King Rat* but Michael Cacoyannis's *Zorba the Greek* (1964), which loves life so indiscriminately that it shrugs at brutal murder and dances in the face of failure. "Love" was the buzzword, remember?

American monsters of the 1960s are not King Rats, not sovereigns of a corrupt or beleaguered system, but the insensitive—those who, like the Pawnbroker and General Jack D. Ripper, have no feelings, no love. Lee Marvin in *Point Blank,* let's say. Perfect. But at least Marvin is good at whatever he does. When he shoots a bed, that bed is *killed,* and when he beds Angie Dickinson, she's in *bliss.*

So what about a loveless monster who can't even win the Oscar, though he does everything (including conspire to murder) to get it? This is Stephen Boyd in *The Oscar* (1966), another of Hollywood's I Hate Hollywood movies, this one much seedier, yet grander, than *Two Weeks in Another Town* or *Inside Daisy Clover. The Oscar* is a paragon of the "good bad movie," the terrible film that inadvertently gives delight—the magnificently idiotic *Rasputin and the Empress*; the deliciously muddled *Satan Met a Lady*; the terrifyingly stupid *Torch Song,* in which Joan Crawford thinks she's playing a dedicated yet put-upon actress but in fact reveals the frenzied megalomania of the movie star—she clanks into a table at El Morocco, calls a waiter over, and barks out, "Lobster Newburg and coffee!" And when a blind man takes a minute or two too long to answer her summons to cross town and pay her court, she asks, "What took you so long?," not kindly.

Hollywood, England. New British stars team up with classic and rising Americans. Above, Peter O'Toole confronts the Great Kate in full cry in *The Lion in Winter*. Below, George Segal schemes to save his ailing buddy James Fox in *King Rat*.

In the realm of the good bad movie, *The Oscar* may be the best of the worst, so high on its own drivel that it surprises, even enthralls. The fun begins as early as the credits—"with Tony Bennett as Hymie Kelly." (His mother was Jewish.) *The Oscar* is anything but New Cinema in its hoary rise-and-fall plot, its Elke Sommer, Jill St. John, and Ernest Borgnine, its robustly cheesy dialogue, its guest-star cameos. But, again, New Cinema's tenets are so pervasive that even a potboiler exposé takes on some of the bossy realism, the abrasive psychology that a Kubrick or Lumet would employ in more artistic films. Boyd's hustler who falls into acting and actually achieves a Best Actor nomination is no Hud or Berry-Berry. They are regrettable in many ways but—as Brandon de Wilde finds out both times—they do have feelings. Even Laurence Harvey's very epochal *Room at the Top* user does in some dim way try to find a little peace and a sense of emotional belonging in the midst of his ambitions.

Boyd's Oscar nominee is nothing—literally nothing—but ambition. Had the film been made of sterner stuff, it might have marked a milestone, for behind its stereotyped characters and giddy glitter lies a fascination with evil, with a sociopathic inability to feel, that epitomizes leading moviemakers' attitudes in the 1960s. *The Oscar* is something like the obverse of a Frank Capra film: instead of a fine man menaced by a society unworthy of him, we have a monster who somehow never lacks for friends. Everybody loves Boyd, though he treats his associates with contempt when they assist him and disgust when they balk. The man gives *nothing*. We are almost in the climate of *Dr. Strangelove*—its theme, not its tone—though here the moralistic figure is not good chap Captain Mandrake but Milton Berle, as an agent who finally washes his hands of Boyd. In a picture that includes a hopelessly unbelievable Walter Brennan playing a mid-American businessman considering Boyd as a commercial spokesperson and Peter Lawford, looking dazed, as a former star demoted to headwaiter, the addition of Berle sounds like more best-of-the-worst nonsense. Actually, Berle gives the film's central performance, even in a small part. He is the vestige of Old Cinema morality, the show-biz veteran who gives us just that much distance from the devouring Boyd—the John Wayne, you might say, who by Rights of Profession shoots Liberty Valance.

But here's something. What if some sharp, ultra-sixties director gives us nothing to distance us from the monster? What if we are dumped into the horror disarmed, even personally connected to the evil? In the past, Hollywood had made plenty of films on the exploits of monsters—

think of Universal's horror cycles; of the Dangerous Man and the Treacherous Woman of film noir; of *This Gun for Hire* (1942), which made Alan Ladd a star in the part of a sadistic killer, though Ladd does redeem himself by the end; of *The Lodger* (1944), who turns out to be Jack the Ripper (even worse, Laird Cregar); of *The Stranger* (1946), who turns out to be Orson Welles as a Nazi; of *Touch of Evil* (1958), Welles now a Fascist police detective. These films were released in times that believed in good-versus-evil standoffs, good invariably winning except in rare cases of tragedy. And these films also tend to include an adversary figure to distance us from the feelings of the monster and, by conquering the monster, to restore social order: Nazi hunter Edward G. Robinson in *The Stranger* or rival detective Charlton Heston in *Touch of Evil,* even stagey, tedious Edward Van Sloan in *Dracula.*

By the 1960s, monsters are proliferating rather than exceptional, and the adversary figure is often so weak that we have nothing to protect us from taking on the feelings of the monster. It is not enough to have someone opposed to evil. We must have someone actively pursuing it on our emotional behalf, someone we can side with out of affection or just respect—and someone with the power to destroy the evil. Captain Mandrake is simply ineffectual; we laugh at him, so there is nothing between us and the bomb.

Even worse, because she is so powerless, is the heroine of Roman Polanski's *Rosemary's Baby* (1968), who drives the public into crazes with her dithering and wondering. All praise to Mia Farrow for fulfilling the director's intentions—for he obviously does not want us to identify, even sympathize with, Rosemary, one of the film's very few characters who is not a full-fledged ghoul. Farrow winces, whines, and withers, but she can't stand up and say no. And look who is on the other side—dearly dotty Ruth Gordon, rock-of-ages Ralph Bellamy, savvy Patsy Kelly, even the young and very serious Charles Grodin, as an unaligned but crucially impedient doctor. All our favorites.

Polanski is rooting for the devil. A year before the infamous Rolling Stones concert at Altamont and the climax of rock-as-demonism, the director says, this is what the times favor; this is where we have landed. We like the darkness. We sing the monster. Polanski makes one miscalculation, in the casting of the unappealing John Cassavetes as Rosemary's husband and the man who "turns her out" as an unwitting member of the devil's band. The husband is supposed to be attractive and admirable—trusting him against her better judgment is how Rosemary is drawn inside the demon ring in the first place. It should have been someone tender, lighter, nicer—John Philip Law, Keir Dullea, Richard Benjamin, Michael Sarrazin, or so. Cassavetes looks too hungry to be trusted.

Without a pursuing agent to recodify our slipping morality, where are we but in hell? Like Captain Mandrake, Rosemary cannot stop the devil in time, and the world ends. At least, the world we know undergoes radical change. It not only revises its view of what constitutes a hero; it begins to value villains more than their victims, finds evil not just more interesting than innocence but more appealing. This is New Cinema at its newest, at its most revolutionary advance upon the Studio Age parables of the Capras and Vidors. This is cinema in which not James Stewart but Edward Arnold is the protagonist, and while Arnold may not exactly win, no one who gets the bulk of the screen time can be called a loser.

Richard Brooks's *In Cold Blood* (1967) is exemplary here, unthinkable before its day and very anticipatory of what we see fresh in theatres now. The absolute realism of setting, caught in black and white in low-key "natural" light, the briskly unenhanced vitality of the dialogue, and the frank treatment of the sole sexual episode—Scott Wilson's bout with a pickup in Mexico while Robert Blake, one bed away, glumly waits for them to finish—is very Contemporary American Cinema, dark beyond noir, honest beyond Production Code, and authentic beyond studio polish. Yet some of *In Cold Blood* is very sixties, such as the prudent use of the then unknown Wilson and Blake as the murderers, roles too touchy for established names, according to the beliefs of the time—nowadays these would be considered Oscar-baiting parts for major stars. There is, too, the almost total lack of editorial manipulation, unheard of (especially for a crime film) in the moralistic Studio Age and rare in the auteurist 1980s, when directors are expected to govern the action, as if making *hommages* to each movie even as they film it.

In Cold Blood was filmed in cold blood, as an uninflected narrative. What *does* Brooks think of his two principals, merrily practicing their back-alley scams, coolly killing the Clutter family, not for an imagined fortune in a nonexistent safe but for the fun, or the self-importance, or the sheer intensity of it, and never showing the slightest regard for the lives they have destroyed? More to the point, what does Brooks think of the Clutter family?

Today we take for granted films in which men kill for no apparent reason, not even for money, or in which coddled kids spy for the Russians, or in which the bored bourgeoisie turns to crime to enhance its sense of hip. But in 1967 cinema on the more or less unmotivated slaughter of four harmless people, even in the wake of Truman Capote's very popular book, was a frightening prospect.

Alfred Hitchcock's *Rope* (1948) preceded *In Cold Blood* on a similar theme, similarly taken from life (the Leopold-Loeb case, which was filmed eleven years later as *Compulsion*). It further preceded *In Cold Blood* in suggesting something of a homoerotic liaison in the two killers' relationship. However, Hitchcock experimentally filmed *Rope* in a single indoor set in a series of ten-minute takes, each capped by a close-up or blackout, which makes the whole remarkably theatrical—the close-ups look like posters. *Rope* is something like an old-fashioned three-act stage thriller put on film. It is never quite "real"—thrilling, certainly, but not as persuasive as some other films of its time, let alone sixties films, particularly *In Cold Blood*. Moreover, Hitchcock further distances us by making the pursuing adversary figure, James Stewart, the protagonist. *Rope,* then, is about Stewart's unmasking of two killers. *In Cold Blood* is about the killers themselves.

They are a mismatch, unlike the high-tech preppy Nietzscheans of *Rope*. Scott Wilson's Dick Hickock is a natural con man, most comfortable when least moral, whether "hanging paper" (passing worthless checks) on a clothing store or charming up a stranger with whom he and Blake have hitched a ride and whom they are planning to kill. "It's the national pastime," Wilson crows. "Stealing and cheating!"

Robert Blake's Perry Smith broodingly disagrees, but he goes along with it, all of it. The dark half of the pair, Blake is also the one withThe Motivation, for brooding if not murder: a father problem. Bad parents are not original with the 1960s, of course—James Cagney had a definitive Bad Father in 1931 in *The Public Enemy* (and his mother was no Auntie Mame, either). Still, from *Psycho* and *Splendor in the Grass* and *Lolita* on, this does register as a riff of the day. "It's us against them," Wilson tells Blake.

One wonders if it was the playing of these parts that kept Wilson and Blake from making it as movie stars,* for they are not only brilliant actors but compelling personalities, magnetic and unique. Should they

---

*Blake made it big in television, as Baretta, ironically a law-enforcement officer. But he was never a major name in film, and Wilson hung on in supporting roles, most notably as the pathetic killer of Robert Redford in Jack Clayton's *The Great Gatsby*.

be? Two wasters good for nothing but crime? Are we going to want to see more of men so believable as killers in cold blood? It could happen to you, boys and girls. Blake claims a murder in his past to humor Wilson. Why did he do it? "No special reason. Just for the hell of it." To which Wilson replies, "That's the best reason of all."

Capote found murderers fascinating. Perhaps Brooks's somewhat up-market casting simply respects the guiltily hero-worshipping spirit in which the novel might have been composed; perhaps a movie featuring two out-and-out creeps would have bombed. In any case, Wilson and Blake are well to this side of creep by the electricity of their naturalism, unusual in a Brooks film because he was not good at firing actors up in the style of Kazan or Schlesinger. As well, most of the small parts were assigned to amateurs—real people, rather, non-actors, residents of the mid-nation state where Capote's heroes went to kill and Brooks's company went to shoot.

Real is what it is, and Brooks spares us nothing, almost. He deleted an episode in Capote in which the two killers deliberately swerve their car to run down a stray dog trudging at the side of the road. Four people killed for the hell of it, the best reason of all, okay. But a murdered dog might deaden audience . . . what? *Sympathy* for the killers? And we can't help noting that Brooks's Clutter family is cast with considerably less glamour than Brooks's killers. Maybe this, too, honors Capote. But what sitting ducks. When a gas jockey spots guns in the back seat of Scott Wilson's car and takes them for pheasant-hunting gear, Wilson says, grinning, "Well, them birds don't know it, but this is their last day on earth!" Then, in the back-and-forth, criminal-victim cutting chronology that shapes the film, Brooks jumps to the Clutters, to Aaron Coplandesque heartland music. A pretty daughter. A son smoking on the sly. Mr. Clutter is strict but not without a sense of irony. He wryly warns his son that peppermints in the morning will stunt his growth.

One of the larger ironies of book and film is that the treasure hoard that supposedly attracts Wilson and Blake to the Clutters does not exist— as if the murder of four people for a substantial amount of money were, let's say, at least logical. What difference does it make how much money the Clutters had? It doesn't seem to make any difference to Wilson, though Blake is furious at being cheated. Wilson doesn't feel cheated: "We scored, didn't we? *Perfecto!*" The scoring is the killing.

As with *Rope*, *In Cold Blood*'s plot includes inculpatory detective work, but John Forsythe—the policeman who tracks down Wilson and Blake—does not dominate as James Stewart does *Rope*. Nor does Brooks feed out the suspense, as Hitchcock does. *In Cold Blood,* again, is about the crime more than the apprehension. It is about the people who commit murder. Are they willing monsters or helpless victims of an urgent demon? As a reporter asks, "How can a perfectly sane man commit an absolutely crazy act?" Yet nothing in Brooks's—or Capote's—Hickock and Smith seems crazy. Killing to them is like winning, like fucking: scoring. Here you score a phoney check, there you score a stray dog; here you score a Mexican bimbo, there you score the Clutters.

In Cold Blood is not a polemic. It's art, without question Brooks's most expert film and one of the most densely directed films of the time. The structure alone is a wonder: following Capote's bobbing and weaving around the crime, checking in on the Clutters, then the itinerant Wilson and Blake, then back to the Clutters; jumping ahead of the murder and sliding without transition into the deep past; not reaching the big set-piece murder scene till after Wilson and Blake have been arrested and interrogated in Las Vegas. Throughout, Brooks makes great use of echo texture, the visuals in one scene not playing out their full meaning till we see them repeated or developed in later scenes. This is one of those two-visit films, too rich to fall into place at one sitting, as when Brooks gives us a questionable close-up of the soles of Blake's shoes in an early shot, or when Gerald S. O'Laughlin as Mr. Clutter attends to his neck with loving detail in a shaving scene. (Blake's shoe soles provide the law with major evidence for the trial, and O'Laughlin will be the only Clutter to have his throat cut.)

Most impressive is Brooks's stable of father figures, which not only punctuates the narrative but unites the murderers and the victims in that Blake's vexed relationship with order, authority, and reason reflects a vexed relationship with his father, and Mr. Clutter—the only member of the family whose death is dwelled upon in book and film—excites both rage and sympathy in Blake. Wilson kills the other Clutters; it is Blake who kills Mr. Clutter, whom Brooks presents, at just that moment, as the double of Blake's father. The hangman Blake faces on the gallows similarly undergoes this psychological transformation, but then the story Capote wrote is loaded with information about fathers—for instance, the older man who picks up the hitchhiking Wilson and Blake and unwittingly staves off their attempt to murder him, with seconds to spare, by stopping his car for a serviceman, an act of fatherly kindness; or the feeble old fellow who survives with his grandson by collecting bottles on the highway for the deposit pennies, a kind of father-as-child. And is not John Forsythe, the detective who tracks Wilson and Blake down, a sort of father to the community, as protector and conservative moralist, and especially in his still-reverberant persona as the titleholder of the fifties television sitcom *Bachelor Father*? What else was Forsythe known for? His evocative association with the merrily contented household of the 1950s contrasts sharply with what we see of the Clutters, and was surely as much a part of Brooks's casting politics as was the choice of the unknown Wilson and Blake and the numerous Kansans who play—who were—the Clutters' neighbors.

Up to the closing sequence, detailing Wilson and Blake's execution, *In Cold Blood* represents one of the artistically exponential films of the 1960s. Its absolute realism of portrayal and setting and its sophistication of camera-narrative technique are utterly beyond what films of earlier eras were capable of, New Cinema in vigorous maturity. Suddenly, at the gallows, Brooks becomes argumentative. Polemical. A reporter we have not seen before weighs in with a harangue against capital punishment. The movie halts as this talking head holds forth on the horror of killing— not of killing the Clutters, but of killing Wilson and Blake. It is as if, having spent two hours showing us the very grin of evil, Brooks fears to encourage our natural distaste for it, and spends a final fifteen minutes wiping the grin away. *In Cold Blood* is a paradox; it fears its own discoveries.

In this, the film mirrors its time, and seems a document not only of sixties art but of sixties politics, of the rock generation's flirtation with anything "countercultural," but preferably the radical, the dangerous, the demonic. Mercy for demons, *In Cold Blood* pleads. *Mercy for demons!* As with Stanley Kubrick's delight in filling *Dr. Strangelove* with jerks and zanies, we wonder whose side the moviemakers are on. Sure, *Dr. Strangelove* is a cautionary work, serious at heart. But there is something disturbingly gleeful at the end, when the good doctor, suddenly realizing that he has left his wheelchair, screams, *"Mein Führer!* I can walk!" It's the devil's resurrection. The 1960s gave us reproachable messiahs.

Yet, in another part of the paradox, we are coming to admire evil without believing in it. This could be a difference of perspective: the Clutters believe in evil and Richard Brooks doesn't. It could be a difference of sociopolitical agendas: Lieutenant Calley is evil but Hickock and Smith are not. New Cinema, like some prominent "liberals" of the 1960s—who so discredited liberalism that the United States has been turning steadily to the right ever since—is trapped in its own insights. Artistically, it has the power to do anything it wants. Thematically, it is moving into doublespeak, tearing down the notion of heroism to replace it with the notion of the villain hero.

Evil is interesting. Even the Clutters would have to admit that. But evil was always interesting. D. W. Griffith, virtually the author of Hollywood's good-versus-evil hornbook, thought evil was interesting. But evil is becoming reputable, perhaps admirable, even beautiful. So hateful is the Bad Father now that artists are making saints of his Wicked Sons.

Six

Different Is
a Genre

By the second half of the decade, the cultural attitudes we now associate with the 1960s are actively enlightening or obscuring the canvas of American film. A very post-1950s "cool" has set in, the cool not of the elite city-tight coffee-bar cat but a demotic go-everywhere cool marketed on buttons and posters, the cool a high-school student can adopt after spending a daring afternoon strolling San Francisco's Haight-Ashbury or New York's East Village. The drug culture will make an appearance, mostly in "exploitation" films like Roger Corman's *The Trip* (1967), which is not about traveling. Monster-worship, egged on by the sometimes patently corrupt heroes of the left, continues. Film becomes overtly political here and there.

Nevertheless, the main strain continues to sound the note of un-aligned, apolitical independence first heard at the start of the decade, before the 1960s became its own legend. *Psycho* and *Breakfast at Tiffany's* and *Splendor in the Grass* sang a sturdy theme: that the liberty of movie-making is a purely artistic concern. Still, liberty is vast; it makes one restless. Writers and directors find it tempting to reflect the age, not unconsciously, by absorption, but deliberately, through mimicry. Not since Warner Brothers' working-class studies in the Depression, and all Hollywood's war effort in the 1940s, has the movie industry been so keen on tapping into the here and now.

We see this particularly in the adoption of renegade styles of all kinds. The anti-establishment viewpoint as a kind of all-purpose sixties aplomb enters upon every side, in leads and bits. Late-sixties movies are a theatre of hip. Irvin Kershner's comedy *A Fine Madness* (1966), from Elliott Baker's novel, offers as its protagonist Samson Shillitoe, a poet who is not only self-centered but recklessly sociopathic. Yet we are to see him as an attractively free spirit, an artist beyond bourgeois order, a man living out a mythology. Kershner couldn't have cast the film better, for the supporting players are New York actors or anti-star Hollywood people, human-scaled (Joanne Woodward, Jean Seberg, Colleen Dewhurst, Patrick O'Neal, Renee Taylor), while Shillitoe is the most mythological figure of the day, James Bond, in one of his early attempts to outtype 007 and establish himself as an actor. The film was not successful enough to do so, but Connery is in fact marvelous in an impossible part. Shillitoe is the kind of man jails were built for. Unleashed, he wrecks the world. Yet Connery endows him with such charm that by the end, when O'Neal, the doctor he has cuckolded, manages to subdue Connery long enough to perform a lobotomy on him, we are truly distressed at the prospect of a "fixed" Connery—at how the authorities not only need to fix all non-conformity but take, as O'Neal does, a briskly malevolent pleasure in doing so.

Even glistery movie stars get into the act. Elizabeth Taylor is an unmarried mother in *The Sandpiper* (1965), and though she sends her precocious son (he can quote *The Canterbury Tales* in Middle English) to an Episcopal private school, she at least involves the headmaster, Richard Burton, in an adulterous affair, and also poses nude for sculptor Charles Bronson. It's the free life. And it's everywhere, even in *Flare-Up* (1969), a cheesy thriller starring Raquel Welch, whose boyfriend James Stacy presents his credentials as a stand-up guy in the poster of Emiliano Zapata that hangs on his wall. For those who don't get the visual, Stacy captions his admiration in noting that Zapata was "a revolutionist." You know, one of us. Suaver, but similar, is an exchange between Julie Christie and George C. Scott in *Petulia* (1968). "You a Communist, Archie?" Christie asks, and Scott, smiling, says, "I hope so." A joke of some sort. Imagine joking on this topic in the Studio Age, or the 1950s, or even in the early 1960s, before hip became the all-encompassing American style.

Nonconformity can be as much a doom as a wow, however. How does it fit in with the responsibility to the social contract and the hard fact of earning one's living? If Samson Shillitoe's madness is fine—for him, not for others—some people were simply born to be square, like Robert Redford in *Barefoot in the Park* (1967), from Neil Simon's Broadway hit. Redford, a young lawyer just married to Jane Fonda, is "too" logical, sensible, proper. He leaves ties inside books to keep them pressed; so he must be put through the paces of a screwball comedy to learn how to have fun, which comes naturally to Jane Fonda. It's not unlike a thirties pairing—Cary Grant and Carole Lombard, say. But in thirties screwball, when Grant turns wild he becomes hot; in *Barefoot in the Park,* when Redford turns wild he becomes scary, at least to Fonda. He crawls around on the roof of a brownstone, defying death. He ignores the state of his ties. He goes barefoot in the park.

Of course, *Barefoot* was not a Hollywood creation, simply the filming of a stage hit, with two of the original leads (Redford and mother-in-law Mildred Natwick) and Simon adapting his text to open it up for film. It opens nicely, showing us places the play kept in the wings—the five-flight climb to Redford and Fonda's apartment, the weird Middle Eastern restaurant (on Staten Island) whither screwball neighbor Charles Boyer takes the young couple, to Fonda's delight and Redford's disgust, and of course the park, in Washington Square. Another Broadway comedy, Herb Gardner's *A Thousand Clowns,* came west in 1965 with some of its stage cast to be comparably opened up, but this time with a great deal of Manhattan location work, including a shot of the half-completed Lincoln Center. *Barefoot in the Park* could have happened anywhere, but *A Thousand Clowns* is very New York, not least in its mock-chilling prologue, before the credits, of Jason Robards and his twelve-year-old nephew Barry Gordon downtown awaiting a terrifying event—people going to work! To the beat of "The Union Forever (Hurrah, boys, hurrah!)," we see the ant colony of Manhattan spring to life, rushing, arriving, pouring into the workplace. Note the ironic use of a song whose chorus ends with the phrase, "the battle cry of freedom."

In *Barefoot in the Park,* "freedom" is a timely buzzword; in *A Thousand Clowns* freedom is survival, and must be fought for, especially by Robards, a professional unemployed madcap who has a habit of leaning out of the window to shout things like "Everybody on stage for the Hawaiian number, please," and, as an intelligent dropout, can articulate very precisely the unquiet desperation of the millions regimented by ties of labor and love. Freedom matters so much to him because there is nothing between it and slavery. But the Child Welfare Board is threatening to take his nephew from him if he doesn't find a job. And Robards wants to—needs to; because he *can* love, in fact. Yet he can't quite bring himself to compromise his battle cry of freedom. His wry wit is treasurable. Here's a man who knows how to have fun. But there's something pathetic in his never-say-die nonconformism. This is liberty without responsibility.

Even more influential—certainly better remembered, and an indispensable VCR title today, when *A Thousand Clowns* appears to be all but forgotten—is Stuart Rosenberg's *Cool Hand Luke* (1967). This is the tragic version of the nonconformist. This is what happens to the odd man when he is of the working class rather than the intelligentsia, when he cannot outwit the authorities because they're armed and he isn't.

Luke is another of the rebel heroes Hollywood had been treating since the 1950s, fully fledged in backstory (Luke is a much-decorated war veteran), latest rebellious incident (he is arrested because, drunk, he had been decapitating parking meters—i.e., murdering the rules for what can be allowed), and casting (Paul Newman, second only to Steve McQueen as head Hollywood rebel, arguably the first, except Newman looked presentable in a suit and McQueen didn't; that's *rebel*). As in certain of McQueen's roles, the sixties rebel cannot beat the system as did the Studio Age heroes like Clark Gable's newspaperman or Gary Cooper's cowboy. In those days, heroism belonged in the system, which is why James Stewart conquers entrenched corruption in *Mr. Smith Goes to Washington*. In *these* days, the system is so corrupt it cannot be mastered, and it breaks any would-be masters. *Cool Hand Luke* is no *Hud* or *Great Escape,* sifting the interior contradictions in the concept of heroism. *Cool Hand Luke* accepts the hero as flawed because even a compromised heroism is preferable to the system's murderous rage. We have reached the stage of the hero as his own victim. How else to describe a man who gets himself sent to a brutal work camp for a worthlessly destructive stunt?

Once in the camp, Newman seems virtually suicidal. His amiably fearless style outrages his jailers, and, fighting fellow prisoner George Kennedy, Newman is badly beaten but refuses to quit. "You're gonna have to kill me," he says—which turns out to be literally true. That night, at poker, Newman wins on a bluff. Kennedy, amazed, says, "Just

Three views of nonconformity. The Wild One is Sean Connery, above left, with Joanne Woodward in *A Fine Madness*. Connery is a poet, but Barry Gordon, left, with social workers William Daniels and Barbara Harris in *A Thousand Clowns,* is regarded as maladjusted, not a rebel but a loser. The worst mistake a sixties maverick could make was to underestimate the world's intolerance. Above, the tragic side of nonconformity as Paul Newman finally breaks and begs for mercy in *Cool Hand Luke.*

like today, when he kept comin' at me with nothin'." And Newman tells him, "Sometimes nothin' can be a real cool hand."

The words sound tasty but the sentiment is incorrect. Nothin' is the death hand. As Warden Strother Martin puts it, "What we got here is failure to communicate." It was a phrase of the age—but what we got here, really, is failure to calculate the odds. George Kennedy, like George Segal's King Rat, knows how to work within the rules without vexing his dignity. Newman doesn't. "Luke's got more guts than brains," observes another prisoner, Anthony Zerbe. But the prisoners admire Luke because, as Kennedy explains it, "You're an *original*, that's what you are!" Nevertheless, with the camp staff actively working to crush Newman, Newman breaks. He crawls. He grovels. He blubbers for mercy.

Now everyone hates him, for shattering the last illusion, that there is freedom within even the tightest corner of the system. Newman makes one last run, and is shot—but he smiles "his Luke smile," and director Rosenberg treats us to apotheosistic shots of Luke in better days so we can savor the tragedy. Nonconformism can kill you.

Ironically, the 1960s was Hollywood's most nonconformist decade, the one in which most of the good movies were not triumphs of their type but typeless, unlike all other movies. Moviemakers warned of the problems of originality while they enjoyed being originals. A slew of comedies apparently designed to be cult films pushed back the borders of what was deemed commercially acceptable, possibly just for the fun of it. So Paul Newman's stubbornly massive tragic hero of a Luke finds a kind of daffy reflection in the heroes of two films made in Britain, Richard Lester's *The Knack, and How to Get It* (1965) and Stanley Donen's *Bedazzled* (1967), both about a nerd who wants to become Lochinvar. Lester's rangy verbal patter and millimicron-tight editing and Donen's episodic fantasy, centered on the antics of devil Peter Cook and Faustian Dudley Moore, showed how exhausted the "well-made" American sex comedy had become, with its sensible Doris Day and naughty Tony Curtis. *The Knack* is so hectic in its hunger for a home run that its players race each other just to first base. It's in heat. *Bedazzled* is so rich in lunacy that the throwaway gags vie with the big set pieces, as when Cook, in the middle of a conversation with Moore, points at a woman carrying a grocery bag and the bottom magically tears and everything falls smashing to the ground. Just for the fun of it.

Luke's drive for independence destroys him; Lester and Donen got away with it. So did Mel Brooks, whose *The Producers* (1968) is obnoxious and tasteless, a visual position paper on how far sixties hip can go. Brooks's first full-length feature, *The Producers* suffered poor distribution and flopped, but a cult quickly gathered and it became legendary—mainly because it tests cultural limits on what is acceptable subject matter for comedy. *Everything,* says Brooks—not only the flaming queen and the drughead, established butt figures; and not only the panting, cooing, love-crazed crone, a relatively familiar type (what would Gilbert and Sullivan be without her?) taken into new realms of loathsomeness; but even Hitler. Charlie Chaplin's *The Great Dictator* and Ernst Lubitsch's *To Be or Not To Be* both treat Nazism comically, but both also make moral demarcations. Brooks takes no sides—everything is amusing because everything is contemptible. So *The Producers* works up to the opening night of a big Broadway musical called *Springtime for Hitler,* so atrocious that instead of disgusting the audience it first stuns but then, yes, *amuses* it. Because the victims of Hitler's twelve-year Reich of genocide and world war are contemptible? Most of Brooks's critics were stunned and not amused—but he did get away with it, for his films competed with Woody Allen's as reigning comic styles of the 1970s. Brooks even dared to return to the Nazi motif, remaking *To Be or Not To Be* in 1983.

George Axelrod did not get away with *Lord Love a Duck* (1966), the first film he directed as well as co-wrote. Set at a Southern California high school, *Lord Love a Duck* treats not only kids and parents but American culture in general. It's wide-ranging and indescribable. As Axelrod recalled to Richard Corliss, "This was the time of the Beatles movies [*A Hard Day's Night* and *Help!,* both directed by Richard Lester]. 'Different' had become a genre; there were musicals, and westerns, and 'different.'" Maybe *Lord Love a Duck* was too different, or—as many critics thought— too vulgar in its dissection of American vulgarity. The high school's Cashmere Sweaters Club is a nice touch—"All you need," says one of the gang, "is twelve cashmere sweaters"—but the gags are stupid, as when a Hollywood producer jumps into the sea to rescue a script, then cries, "Oh! I forgot I can't swim!" Bob Rafelson's *Head* (1968), planned to showcase the Monkees as Lester's films had framed the Beatles, was most different but least delightful, unlike *The Producers* a cult film without a cult. An absurdist gallimaufry, *Head*—note the boogying hip of the title—will do anything for a laugh, and gets none. The fun is, like, Frank Zappa leads in a cow that says, "Monkees is the craziest people."

Different had become a genre, and the 1960s was becoming a genre in its own time. Some of its films were not only commercially analytical but self-regarding in a way no other era's films had been. Many thirties movies were about the Depression, but no thirties movie was about how the Depression affects thirties movies. Thirties movies were not Movies of the Day. They were movies, period. Nor did the 1970s or '80s produce transparently self-advertising films. Pirandello isn't working in Hollywood anymore.

He would surely have appreciated *Barbarella* (1968), one of the most contemporary movies ever made, so up-to-the-minute, so sixties, that it was dated before it had hit the nabes. What producer Dino de Laurentiis, director Roger Vadim, and Vadim's co-writer Terry Southern seem to have had in mind was camp-"trippy" science fiction in a range of psychedelic Technicolors to mock the new rockadrugasex culture even as it exploits it. In the title part, Jane Fonda will be a *now* heroine—"Barbarella, psychedella," a chorus assures us over the credits—though the action is set in the forty-first century and the props include a Positronic Ray, a Tonguebox that transforms a speaker's language into any other language of his choice (very useful in a French-Italian production filmed in English), and a huge pipe organ that "plays" its victims, literally pleasures them, to death. Fonda takes a turn in it; she is so sensual that she breaks the machine.

There is a great deal of sex and death in *Barbarella,* and a great deal of Fonda wearing as little as possible while being menaced in piquantly sadistic ways—odd, as one of the many sixties creeds the film quotes is the disarmament movement. Odder yet is that Vadim was Fonda's husband at the time. What was running through his mind when he set up, for instance, the scene in which Fonda, bound and (of course) unclothed, is assaulted by windup razor-mouth biting dolls?

Unforgivably, the whole thing is slow-moving and, for all its excess, boring. It's six characters in search of an auteur, good guys Fonda, David Hemmings, Ugo Tognazzi, and the blind angel John Philip Law versus Black Queen Anita Pallenberg and her mad-scientist sidekick Milo O'Shea. So why does nothing happen? There's promise here, in a perverse way, something anticipating the explosion of porn in the 1970s and the development of big-budget sci-fi in the 1980s. Yet in the end the film's sole distinction is that it is probably the only sixties movie released by a major studio (Paramount) that is so replete with censors' nightmares that it cannot be shown on network television without losing its best scenes.

Different had become a genre; the 1960s was looking at itself. Some of this was, like *Barbarella,* smash-and-grab manipulation but some of it was commendably responsible, an attempt to use the screen as a public forum for issues that the age needed to investigate. Tolerance became an article of faith, partly in response to the civil-rights movement but also because American show business had long been a world of people of extractions—blacks and the Irish and Jewish found their first sense of celebrity acceptance in vaudeville and on Broadway, where Florenz Ziegfeld's headliners included black Bert Williams and Jewish Fanny Brice, where the Jewish Shubert brothers plotted to rule the world through their heavy theatre realty holdings, and where the flag was waved by the Irish-American George M. Cohan, whose co-producer was the Jewish Sam H. Harris. Show biz was sophisticated, and though actors' and directors' resentment of the largely Jewish movie moguls encouraged a strain of anti-Semitism in Studio Age Hollywood, still the moviemakers were almost as eager as Broadway people to preach the text of tolerance.

So we are not surprised to find Frank Sinatra, in the title role of *The Detective* (1968), crucially role-modeling sympathy for gays, though he is surrounded by some of the most energetic haters that an authoritarian, sexist, and racist organ like the police force is capable of producing. Hearing the term "fag," Sinatra replies, "Live and let live," and when cop Robert Duvall brutalizes gays at a rousting at "the trucks," Sinatra pastes him one right in the gut. "You think you're better than the rest of us," Ralph Meeker sneers. Wrong. Sinatra knows he's better. Al Freeman, Jr., gets the idea of interrogating prisoners while they're undressed, a tactic he picked up from a newsreel of the Nazi death camp. Nudity exacerbates the prisoner's helplessness. A disgusted Sinatra accuses Freeman of pushing for a promotion through the exploitation of prisoners, and when Freeman says "So what?" Sinatra explodes. "My old man was on the force twenty-five years and *he* never got a promotion! *That's* what!"

In other words, Sinatra has the credentials genetically and emotionally. He is better than his fellows because he came up the hard way yet maintained his ideals. He is telling the Ralph Meekers and the Al Freemans in the audience, Try to live up to my standard. If I can, you can.

A great deal of the sixties urging of tolerance feels more like a seasoning of the stew than the meat and potatoes: Elliot Silverstein's use of Nat King Cole (side by side with Stubby Kaye) as the balladeering narrators of *Cat Ballou* (1965); the black prostitute who bares her breasts in *The Pawnbroker*; or the deliberately provocative posing of Raquel Welch and Jim Brown on the posters of *100 Rifles* (1969). Even when tolerance floods the stew, the results might run to the likes of Stanley Kramer's *Guess Who's Coming to Dinner* (1967), with Spencer Tracy and Katharine Hepburn as the parents of a girl in love with Sonny Liston.

All right, no, it's Sidney Poitier. But isn't that the problem? Poitier's so reassuringly educated and smooth and polite, a bourgeois boulevardier, that the consent is an easy call. Hell, face it: Poitier was a better catch than most of the white men you knew. Put Tracy and Hepburn's daughter Katharine Houghton in the arms of the less, uh, chevaleresque Liston and we would have had an interesting film, suspenseful and troubling and controversial, a film really biting on a threat of the age. In the event, the only really worrisome scene in *Guess Who's Coming to Dinner,* the one moment when a public of liberals and bigots alike is truly unsure where the theme will take them, is when Hepburn's well-meaning friend and employee foolishly tries to sympathize with Hepburn over the calamity of her daughter's choice in men, and Hepburn coolly and utterly and without the slightest show of regret fires the woman from Hepburn's employ, bans the woman from Hepburn's life, and tells her—us—that she is a repulsive piece of junk.

Of course, this is high sixties, when the issues were sacred. Earlier in the decade, tolerance trod more gently, perhaps more realistically. There were no quick solutions because people are stubborn, even if—or especially because—Katharine Hepburn gives them a dressing-down. John Ford's *Sergeant Rutledge* (1960) and Robert Mulligan's *To Kill a Mockingbird* (1962) both deal with the trial of a black man for the rape of a white woman, both in tragic terms. In each case the man is innocent. *To Kill a Mockingbird,* set in the South, is a soft film, graying out its black and white, spreading sympathy among the contentious folk, and so nostalgic that despite its many sorrows one comes away thinking how lovely the past was. This film knows its black defendant can't get a fair trial, even with Gregory Peck, the most respected man in town, defending him. *Sergeant Rutledge,* placed in Ford's beloved cavalry background, outwits the bigots and unmasks the real culprit, a white man. It's a hard film, determined to prove that what it believes is what is true, and what anyone else believes is a pack of lies.

Still, both films look on American race relations as a no-win situation for the blacks. Brock Peters, *Mockingbird*'s defendant, is found guilty and is shot trying to escape. Woody Strode, Rutledge's defendant—and, I think strategically, the gladiator whose Fascist-defying death sparked the revolt in *Spartacus* that same year—is exonerated, but must face the knowledge that the corps he joined to find acceptance as a man will never truly accept him as anything.

Sergeant Rutledge had terrific impact when it was new but today, dating from Ford's final period of hasty, even clumsy films, it has faded from the perspective, while *To Kill a Mockingbird* seems stronger than ever for the powerful sense it evokes of time, place, and feeling, with its children caught between playtime and responsibility, its poignant look back at small-town culture, its sense of tribal hierarchies and seasonal celebrities, and its fabulous, sequestered boogeyman, Boo Radley, played by Robert Duvall. Is there anyone who grew up in the 1960s who didn't, at some point or other, joke about or analyze or simply mention this character? The name had magic. I named a German shepherd puppy after him. I was not intent on the issues; perhaps I should have named the dog after Brock Peters. But then this movie is a copious two hours, and parcels out its pleasures and wisdom with such opulence that outrage over Peters's fate is swallowed up in the wish that Gregory Peck were your father, that Peck's kids Philip Alford and Mary Badham were your siblings, even that Boo Radley were your neighbor. But one look at civic racialism does stay in the mind after all these years: after the trial, when all but the two opposing lawyers have left the courtroom, Gregory Peck starts out. Up in the gallery, the blacks get to their feet, and one pulls Peck's daughter up with him. "Rise, child," he tells her. "Your father's passing."

This sorrowful *kto kovo* just would not suit the actively politicizing late 1960s, so we get things like *Guess Who's Coming to Dinner,* which would be kitsch if it weren't already Socialist realism. More advocating yet is Norman Jewison's *In the Heat of the Night* (1967), suspenseful and characterful and admitting of irreconcilable differences but nevertheless posing an implausible unity of Southern redneck sheriff and black detective at work on a murder case in Mississippi. The detective is Sidney

Poitier again, so perfect you don't believe him for two seconds *as anything* (except a movie star); and the sheriff is Rod Steiger, which is a little too redneck to be true.

In the Heat of the Night is admirable storytelling, but Jewison and his writer Stirling Silliphant are running on the premise that movies can correct the world by describing it incorrectly. Yes, there's suspect Scott Wilson, noting Poitier's suit and tie and asking, "What you doing wearing white man's clothes?" And there are four hoodlums backing Poitier into an empty factory against a sign reading "Let us ALL be alert. We don't want ANYONE hurt." Poetic irony, right? But we also get the racist Steiger's very nearly immediate willingness to let the out-of-towner Poitier assist in a murder case, which almost as immediately turns to eagerness, and this seems wildly out of character for a lifelong racist and presider over a racist system. Even given that Steiger knows Poitier has the needed smarts, people are more usually locked into their ways, however self-destructive, than open to innovation. By the time Poitier and Steiger have developed that favorite Hollywood thing, conflicted camaraderie, we fall out of the story and into history. It's the age that is telling the tale, not the director, writer, and actors. The era is trying to hypnotize us with its imperatives.

At least the fade-out is naturalistically uncommitted. The murder solved, Steiger puts Poitier on his train north. Steiger says thank you. They shake hands. Then Steiger calls out, "Virgil! You take care, you hear?" A little something extra, not too warm, one of those empty Southern pleasantries from someone who'd as soon lynch you as tell you the time. Poitier says, "Yeah." Both smile. And that's all.

Another piece of sixties hip confronts us in a rash of films emphasizing youth as the fundamental thing in life, the place where the power lies. Kid Films of the 1950s saw kids as either the tortured victims of insensitive parents or as aimlessly rebellious cutups ready to sneer at anything—think of the delinquents smashing Richard Kiley's rare 78 jazz collection, because it's there, in *The Blackboard Jungle*. By the mid-1960s, youth is going to take over, because youth is beautiful, healthy, and uncorrupt, especially in California. We actively get a kind of documentary visual on this during the credits of Alexander Mackendrick's *Don't Make Waves* (1967): to the surfer-style title song, a cartoon shows Tony Curtis's red Volkswagen driving through the continent, out of the

East Meets West. New York nerd Tony Curtis scopes out exemplary
Californian Dave Draper in *Don't Make Waves*. As the film makes clear,
New York is glib and savvy and California is slow and stoopidd. But
who are we to argue with young and healthy? Hollywood moved west.

outdated power-structure urban Northeast on to the youth and beauty
and money and sex of Southern California. Go west, all men.

Don't Make Waves is a combination of American sex comedy (note
Curtis, a fixture of the genre) and the influential Italian sex comedy
(Claudia Cardinale is Curtis's love interest) bound up in a study of "life-
style"—beach culture, health culture, crackpot mind culture; and Curtis's
first sight of golden Sharon Tate dancing on a trampoline in the sun pre-
shadows the heterosexual mythmaking of Dudley Moore's first sight of
Bo Derek in *"10"*. This is the American Dream. In the Studio Age, the
national place to be was New York, or at least Chicago; most of the
countless gangster, backstage, newspaper, boxing, and even romantic films
took place in one or the other. By the mid-1960s, New York has the
wrong charms. It's outdated. So Easterner Tony Curtis falls asleep on the

beach on his first night in the West and wakes up to The New Phantas-
magoria—catamarans, surfers (including a dog), bodybuilders, acrobats,
motorcycle chicken races, a nut fishing in the shallows . . . and Sharon
Tate, a skydiver named Malibu who gives Curtis the rapture of artificial
respiration when he is clonked on the head by a flying surfboard.

Youth culture doesn't need California, however. You're supposed to
be young no matter where you live. *Wild in the Streets* (1968) begins in
California, where young rock star Christopher Jones endorses Hal Holbrook's senatorial campaign in exchange for Holbrook's pledge to lower
the voting age to fifteen. But the film's purview expands nationally as
Jones marshals American youth to his cause; as his team of debauched
groupies puts Diane Varsi into Congress, where she holds forth in a pirate
hat, beating a tambourine; as the Jones network spikes the D.C. water
supply with LSD; as Jones runs for President on the strength of his new
kid enfranchisement. Elected, Jones outlaws everyone over thirty. Oldsters
are to be herded into concentration camps where water coolers filled with,
yes, LSD, keep them pacified.

Is it the teenage dream of revenge, the parents' nightmare? Is it a
cautionary tale? *Don't?* Is it a pep rally for the adoption of legal rights
for adolescents? As the 1960s so often said, *Do it?* An American International feature, *Wild in the Streets* is too nasty and cheap to tell us
precisely what it's doing, other than dancing on the energy of the premise
Kids Rule the World. Now it's pure "fourth wall" action; now it's got a
"March of Time" narrator filling us in on the plot points director Barry
Shear didn't get to. Now Jones philosophizes on the system, with an eye
on Vietnam: "The only thing that blows your mind when you're thirty
is getting guys to kill other guys, only in another city, another country,
where you don't see it"; now he's just a luxuriating jughead. Now he's
tolerant, or just too lazy to get mad; now he's ordering the overdosing of
the entire population of Hawaii, the only state he didn't carry. Now we
are given a fix on grown-ups, when Jones's termagant mother, Shelley
Winters, slaps Jones without provocation and when the fair-minded Holbrook does the same thing to his son; now the film uses grown-ups not
as a threat but as a camp, when Winters attempts a reconciliation with
her estranged star of a son—"I'm a celebrity!" she screams, spotting him
on television—and, later, enjoys a mad scene in her "retirement camp."
Now we cut close to the bone of spectator comfort when one of Jones's
team, Kevin Coughlin, drops hints that he's gay; now Shear is afraid to

President Christopher Jones holds a press conference in *Wild in the Streets*.
Cheap set—but note the evocative blackshirts lining his study.

touch it. Now Richard Pryor, another of the Jones team, seems to be casually extemporizing his role; now Ed Begley, as a bigoted politico, is forcefully bubbling up like an Easter ham.

Wild in the Streets throws everything at you. Something will land— if not this minute, the next. By the film's extremely predictable ending (a bullied adolescent swears to do away with everyone over ten), a work with great potential for epochal analysis has petered out. Yet it remains the ultimate kid-rebellion film by the very size of its tale, by the honesty of its observations of the generation war, and by its sheer murderous ferocity. It is not a good film, not even a good bad one. But it's the one that went furthest in marking the weakened state of patriarchal totalitarianism. It counters Bad Fathers with Bad Sons. But isn't that logical? It's Bad Sons who grow up to be Bad Fathers.

What hurt *Wild in the Streets* is what hurt many of the youth movies, the lack of charismatic young actors. The rock-star-turned-President is a part James Dean was born to play—and in a way he did play it, for Christopher Jones is in looks, sound, and acting style a Dean mock-up.

Yet he has none of Dean's coiled-spring physicalization of his feelings, the sense that not just the man's soul but his tendons and muscles are caught up in his many dissatisfactions. Jones is characterized as a rock star—and sings a few numbers—strictly to give credentials to his role as a revolutionary.* Dean was so revolutionary as a human being that he was beyond rock, didn't need it. He raised up a cult without music. That's a revolution within revolution, and would have given *Wild in the Streets* a stature it otherwise seeks in the campy blustering of Shelley Winters or the superannuated boss-man thespianism of Ed Begley.

Lindsay Anderson's *If . . .* (1969) came from England with a more savage but deadly serious reading of the same situation, kids taking power. No tambourine girls here. No rock. No Shelley Winters. Just three senior students at a leadership-class public school who move from an innate distaste for the system, through an improvisationally calculated defiance of it, to, finally, a full-scale massacre of it. Anderson indulges in touches of fantasy and spoof—both at once when, on student-soldier maneuvers, an irritated student shoots the chaplain dead and he later turns up, hale and full of homily, in the headmaster's desk drawer. But where *Wild in the Streets* never truly believes in its perceptions, *If . . .* is intensely self-absorbed. Moreover, *Wild in the Streets*'s realism suffers from the endemic clumsiness of the quickie, that Cormanesque all-film-is-artifice-anyway syndrome, which, for some critics, makes a virtue out of expediency. The very lack of polish is seen as endearing; it makes movies less finished but somehow purer.

If . . . is quite polished even at its most experimental, as in a scene in which a student's violent flirtation with a coffee-bar waitress is filmed as a wrestling match with, literally, a wild animal. Anderson's illustrations of the power structure of the English public school are similarly bold, even in passing, as when the camera pans through a dorm of sleeping students to find a senior sharing a bed with a younger boy, or in the way one student, after a caning, tries to juggle his body parts to settle the pain.

Anderson has a sharp eye. As he is going for blood, he casts not Christopher Jones or Diane Varsi but young people with the character to

*And possibly because it had been tried the year before, in Peter Watkins's English movie *Privilege,* in which the establishment uses rock star Paul Jones as a kind of modern-day Christ, the Revolution co-opted by the Corporation.

suggest revolutionaries in the making. Malcolm McDowell, the rebel ringleader, is like a Tom Courtenay getting ready for the 1970s, enraged and nihilist where Courtenay was history's pathetic moralist. Indeed, Stanley Kubrick's *A Clockwork Orange* was waiting for McDowell just around the corner of the decade, and *If . . .*'s conclusion may be seen as preparation for it. Just because it's high school, Anderson warns us, doesn't mean it isn't war. With a campaign of repression smothering them, McDowell and his two comrades, joined by the waitress and a younger student—the very one, by the way, whom we saw in bed earlier, with one of the McDowell gang—arm themselves and take up positions on the roof. They have set fire to the chapel during end-of-term exercises, and students, faculty, and parents, forced out by the smoke, are mowed down as they appear.

Now, Anderson has clearly epitomized certain villains—the four head boys who tyrannize McDowell's house, the master who gave them free rein. But Anderson presents no shots of particular culprits going down to dust; it is the system entire—its victims as well as its stylists— that McDowell and his friends are making war on. Everyone not part of the solution is part of the problem—that very sixties phrase, loaded with the scattershot angers of the left. *If . . .* is disturbing not for what it shows but for how it feels. What it shows wouldn't likely happen. How it feels dramatizes a hatred that at times seemed to be the essential motivation of the Western left, a hatred for everything that was not specifically revolutionary—or, at any rate, wearing revolutionary clothes. Coming in 1969, *If . . .* has an apocalyptic air, but not because the revolution happened. The 1960s ended, at Altamont and Kent State, in despair and death. The revolution failed. *If . . .*'s sense of apocalypse lies in the furies it unleashes, and in its deliberately unequal sense of cause and effect. The cause is clear: the system *is* oppressive. All systems are. However, the effect is not a reformation of the system, a liberalization, but the slaughter of everyone in sight.

It was a bellicose time, yet it did support a powerful peace move-ment. Revolutionary is one strain of sixties hip; non-violence is another. We can follow the inculcation of pacifism in two films five years apart, from early 1960s to high 1960s. One film is American, with a starry cast, an instant hit and recurring favorite though not generally thought of as an especially sixties "kind" of work. The later film is European, cast without stars, and unpopular till a cult publicized it and growing audiences took it up as a classic of its age, ultra-sixties in outlook if timeless in appeal.

The American item is John Ford's *The Man Who Shot Liberty Valance* (1962), the one in which John Wayne calls James Stewart "Pilgrim." Hero Wayne and villain Lee Marvin represent the traditional Hollywood Wild West, the regime of the fast gun. Attorney Stewart, an émigré from the East and stubbornly unarmed, represents the coming tamed West, the regime of due process. The entire film is built on a series of confrontations between Marvin and Stewart, occasionally refereed by Wayne, and the first Marvin-Stewart meeting is gala, a stagecoach robbery during which Marvin savagely whips Stewart.* But the very center of the story finds all three leads in a restaurant, Marvin and his bullyboys terrorizing the place, goading Wayne to fight. And Wayne will; that's why he's there. Yet, even with the issues of who is good and who is evil clearly painted out for him, Stewart is as disgusted with Wayne as with Marvin for their readiness to draw and settle it. This, to Stewart, settles nothing. Well, it certainly settles whether Wayne's good or Marvin's evil will prevail. Why else would Marvin be named Liberty except to tell us that ideals do not conduce to freedom, but power does? Liberty's valence lies in the fear he inspires, as does Wayne's. Later in the decade, Stewart's beliefs would make him a New Hero. In Fordland, he is a fool.

Ford is all for Wayne's view of things, needless to say; Wayne is the essential Ford player.† Ford's is not a sixties consciousness—after all, he'd been making westerns since 1917. So Stewart must learn the efficacy of the gunfight as a solution to the problem of the world's Lee Marvins, and Stewart becomes The Man Who Shot Liberty Valance, facing Marvin in the street in the classic manner. But Stewart is no fast gun, and he's deep in the splendor of his cups—how else can a lawyer shoot a man down

*Typically early sixties, the setting for the robbery is a direly fake studio mock-up, and the camera setups allow Marvin to whip the air—Stewart is narratively assumed to be lying just out of the frame—so our Studio Age sensibilities, not yet liberated by late Peckinpah, can be spared the hard details.

†That is, essential to the familiar Ford of the talkie years. Counting all of Ford's films, including many silents that are probably lost, Ford's favorite leading man was Harry Carey, who appeared in twenty-five Ford features, to Wayne's fourteen. At that, supporting players J. Farrell McDonald and Ward Bond ace Wayne out in sheer number of performances, and George O'Brien takes the longevity prize: ten roles, in lead and support, from 1924 to 1964.

except on liquid courage? He can scarcely hold his weapon, and Marvin toys with him, shooting the pistol out of his hand, then shooting it away as Stewart tries to retrieve it. Finally, Stewart somehow gets himself into gear and the bullet flies true: Marvin is dead and everyone, including Stewart, is glad. As it happens, Wayne, watching over his buddy Stewart, is the one who took Marvin out. It's a very Fordian irony that it is Wayne, unsung, even unknown, who plays the film's title role. Because Ford's West is the West of Marvin and Wayne—Liberty Valance and the Man Who Shot Him—not of non-violent lawyers.

However, Ford was somewhat excrescent in the 1960s, always welcome but artistically and temperamentally a man in the fourth act of a three-act play. Jump across the Atlantic now to Philippe de Broca's *King of Hearts* (1967), which tosses the 1960s back into the 1910s. Instead of Vietnam, it's World War I. Instead of draft resisters and flower children, it's lunatics, escaped from their asylum in the chaos of the French town's evacuation. Instead of the eclectic, "far-out" costumes of the hippie generation, it's the eclectic, far-out costumes of the lunatics, who for some reason love to play theatre. Nothing is real to them, even war. An evacuated town serves as their stage. Yet we are not impressed with the apparently sane—at any rate, the functional—characters, all warmakers. The Brits are dolts, the Germans punctilious monsters—they have wired the town to explode at midnight, when the figure of the knight strikes in the municipal clock. The Brits send one of their men into the town to dismantle the bomb without telling him where it is or how to do it if he finds it. There is a kind of idiocy in everything the two sides do, a Lewis Carrollesque logician's nonsense, and if the enemy is idiots and our side is idiots, what are the idiots?

Blessed. *Now* is the time when James Stewart's ability to retain his ideals in the face of Liberty Valance's aggression would be seen as courageous—better, sensible. It was often said in the 1960s that in a crazy world it is the crazy who are sane, and the lunatics' observations on the actions of the military community point up their absurdity, not just the bloodthirsty horror of war but the warmakers' abysmal lack of judgment. Their incompetence. "What funny people," says lunatic Geneviève Bujold after a skirmish of Brits and Germans in which every man falls. All that death, yet nobody won.

The public had no trouble relating de Broca's World War I to American involvement in Vietnam, especially as the years passed and the film's

Vietnam Cinema. Above, the outmates of *King of Hearts'* Bedlam, saner than any warrior. Below, local resistance of the Pax Americana in *The Sand Pebbles*.

college-audience bookings increased and de Broca seemed to be giving us charades on the paradox of blindly following know-nothing commanders, or of treating peaceful inhabitants as belligerents, or of destroying a country in order to save it. *King of Hearts* did not start out as, but soon enough became, the first major Vietnam movie, for though it was not about the experience, it articulated and perhaps even shaped experiential reactions. What could be more Vietnamesque than de Broca's statement-response editing of, first, the execution of the German ordnance officer for his failure to blow up the town, and, a moment after his body falls, Bujold's telling soldier Alan Bates, the enlisted man chosen to save the town, "I want to make love." Make love—remember?—not war.

Bates is sound casting, his readily bemusable naïveté ceaselessly contrasting with the scheming warriors and the gleefully colorful lunatics. Bates is de Broca's Candide figure, alone in a world full of faulty deductions. Everyone else in the film is, to us, a foreigner; Bates, despite his English accent, is our deputy. One thing distances him slightly: his uniform. At length, he takes it off, takes everything off, in a famous early instance of total nudity, shot from the rear. Bates has spent the film haranguing and escaping from the lunatics, but at the fade-out Bates, the town's savior, deserts the Army and the world to apply for membership in the lunatic band at the gates of the asylum. Bringing with him nothing but a birdcage, he is like the bizarre totems of the old town clock—a hip knight for the 1960s, a dropout, naked and peaceful.

Yet more hip was the spy, suave and cynical, at times as ambivalent in his political views as his favorite haunt, cold-war Berlin of the East and West. Not since the patriotic cinema of World War II was the spy so popular, especially in films that countered the pyrotechnics of James Bond with intricate plotting, indecisive pacing, and, it was hoped, literate scriptwriting. The hip spy—such as Michael Caine's Harry Palmer in *The Ipcress File* (1965), *Funeral in Berlin* (1966), and *Billion Dollar Brain* (1967) or George Segal in *The Quiller Memorandum* (1966) or Laurence Harvey in *A Dandy in Aspic* (1968)—didn't trumpet his loyalties or drive a gimmicked Aston Martin as if it were a bumper car or get in a lot of pillowing between confrontations. The hip spy had, in fact, few confrontations at all. His enemy was all shadows—his own, possibly. "Our policies are peaceful, but our methods can't be less ruthless than those of the opposition," Control tells Richard Burton in Martin Ritt's *The Spy Who Came In from the Cold* (1965). "Occasionally we have to do wicked things, very wicked things indeed." Such as working with and protecting a former Nazi, "our" man in East Germany—for, in the world of John le Carré, author of the *Cold* novel and much of the worldview that permeates the hip spy film, official loyalties are not moral but political. Deals matter; people don't. Richard Burton tells Claire Bloom, "It's the innocents who get slaughtered."

This, le Carré teaches us, is the real spy versus spy behind James Bond's cartoon of good against evil. Our side is better than their side, but the two sides are alike in their methods, so Ritt begins and ends the film with shots of the Berlin Wall—at first a symbol of the heartless East but, at last, merely a sentinel separating a heartless East from a heartless West. For when Burton and Bloom are climbing over the Wall to freedom after the East German caper, Bloom is shot by her own side, because as a Communist sympathizer she could give the game away; and Burton, straggling back down to help her, is shot as well. Culprits get slaughtered, too.

Norman Jewison's *The Russians Are Coming The Russians Are Coming* (1966) is the comic alternative, though a warning to both sides not to let touchy situations explode into war through panic diplomacy. The atmosphere is frolicsome—a male Russian choir serenades us over the credits, and the action begins with a close-up of Soviet submarine commander Theodore Bikel's eye, as if in spoof of George Orwell's Big Brother. The sub, stealing into American waters, has run aground, and Russian Alan Arkin (in his first major screen role and fielding, by the way, a flawless Russian accent) leads a small band into a New England resort town to find a boat to haul the sub back to sea.

The frolic quickly cedes to outright farce. The very sight of the Russians terrifies the Americans, and a bunch of local crackpots led by Paul Ford, Jonathan Winters, Ben Blue (a cold-war Paul Revere, riding through town shouting the movie's title), and Sheriff Brian Keith muster themselves into a militia. There's a touch of romance for Russian John Philip Law and American teenager Andrea Dromm, who won't even take Law's gun when he offers it. "I'm not frightened," she explains quite brightly. But it is Jewison's point that frightened, and ignorant, is just what everyone is. With both sides acting hastily and desperately, the comedy turns black, halting only at the last moment, when an emergency forces both sides, on sudden humanitarian instincts, to work together.

Old Cinema made its case in the all-star, wide-screen, two-and-a-half-hour saboteur thriller *Ice Station Zebra* (1968), so military there are no women in the cast—it's all submarine interiors and North Pole ice. This is not a hip movie; on the contrary, it is retro, from the hash of acting styles to the almost scornfully phoney studio look of the final set at the Arctic outpost, where East and West have a showdown. Scenes between sharp, aggressively fey Brit Patrick McGoohan and Rock Hudson at his least two-fisted remind us how untextured fifties movie stars could seem when not goaded by a Kazan or a Frankenheimer. Ernest Borgnine gives a wonderful laff-a-minute performance as a Soviet defector, but the film is not a comedy. Who would have been more bumbly in the role? Frankie Avalon? Lilo? Jim Brown? Brown was unavailable, already signed on in another part, as a steel-balled, by-the-book officer. He, too, has a telling confrontation with McGoohan, leaving Brown's hopes for an Oscar in tatters.

Meanwhile, who is the saboteur? Who has inflicted damage upon the West? Is it McGoohan, of our team, but suspiciously screwy, perhaps morally pluralistic? Weren't all the great post–World War II traitors picturesque Brits? Or is it Brown, hiding behind the gung-ho façade? Is it Borgnine?—once a Soviet, always a Soviet? *Ice Station Zebra* is so unhip that it's Borgnine.

Clearly, the venerable Hollywood view of a moral universe is finished. We have taken too many monsters for granted, laughed at too much murder, sympathized with too many people who wouldn't think twice about ruining our lives. Film has begun to exist in a separate-but-equal cosmos that we accept as realistic but exempt from real-life considerations—such as, Do I approve of this character? or, Would I want him to marry my brother? We are so entertained by moviemakers that we buy their perceptions, or at least temporarily suspend our own. And, as we'll see in the next chapter, critics who denounced this ambiguous morality were swept aside along with Old Cinema, because madness was fine and one must be, above all, a king of hearts: of love, not judgment. Value judgments—remember?—were a put-down.

In such an atmosphere, films about the American Fascist impulse, about conspiracies and mind control, had more credibility than films treating the very active conspiracies and mind-control tactics of Eastern totalitarianism. Was this not why *The Manchurian Candidate* was not popular on its original release, why—as its writer George Axelrod put it—"it went from failure to classic without ever passing through success"?

More stars than there are in Russia: a PR shot for *Doctor Zhivago*. Note
real Russia in background. The 1940s popularized location shooting and
the 1950s developed it; but the 1960s made it mandatory.

To the mass audience, the truth is a nuisance. It doesn't entertain. Delusion entertains. *Le chic* entertains. A pose of independence synopsized in
an extravagant haircut or an irreverent T-shirt entertains. *In Cold Blood*
entertains because what happened to the Clutters didn't happen to you.

So a movie set in, let us say, the Soviet gulag system would have
been unappetizing. But John Frankenheimer's thriller *Seven Days in May*
(1964), on a foiled palace revolution—in the White House—was soup
of the day. Similarly, Theodore J. Flicker's satire *The President's Analyst*
(1967) sees the United States as a grid of thuggee networks and surveil-
lance screens; the phone company is run by robots. But then Russia-
hating was so fifties, so square, so Mrs. Bates. Bad Fathers like L. B.
Mayer had given it a bad name. The Vital Son does not emulate the Bad
Father. The Vital Son overthrows the Bad Father. But was the Vital Son
becoming decadent in his overwhelming belief in the code of hip? *Splendor
in the Grass* was good Vital Son art—or, hell, it was good art. But
entranced moviegoers were adapting to nearly anything that seemed to be
against whatever we used to be told we were for.

We should not be shocked, then, to find all-star Big Film taking up the Red flag, in David Lean's *Doctor Zhivago* (1965): revolution, romance, passion, terror, hit balalaika theme music, and a swarm of real actors, including Alec Guinness, Ralph Richardson, Julie Christie, Geraldine Chaplin, Siobhán McKenna, and Rita Tushingham! It's very Brit, though the good Doctor is Omar Sharif, so new that he is billed under the title amid a torrent of secondary names, curiously cautious billing after his international success in *Lawrence of Arabia,* three years earlier.

Lean is very forward in his presentation of oppression and uprising. That's thesis and antithesis, and the synthesis will be Tom Courtenay, inevitable as a first idealistic but then embittered revolutionary. "Feelings, insights, affections—it's suddenly trivial now," he tells Sharif. "The private life is dead for a man . . . with any manhood." Courtenay is so beyond feeling that he doesn't care that he is separated from his wife, Julie Christie, which clears the way for Sharif, who still has feelings. Just as well, for the Revolution is busily inventing its own repressions. We learn of villages caught between Reds and Whites, blackmailed by one side and leveled by the other. Courtenay shrugs this off. It's politics. "Your politics," Sharif fires back. *"Their* village."

The 1960s has principles after all, not least in the parallel between Russian villages and Vietnamese villages unable to pacify antagonisms in a no-front war. *In Cold Blood* happens to them. In fact, the 1960s happens to them, to judge by the large number of lines pointing up the judgments of the day, like Guinness's telling a youngster, "You're an impatient generation," or Christie's "Oh Lord, this is an awful time to be alive!" or, when she tells Courtenay, "They don't want a revolution," his "Yes, they do. They don't know it yet, but that's what they want." The key connection between Revolutionary Russia and revolutionary America is drawn by Courtenay after Tsarist dragoons brutally break up a peaceful demonstration: "There will be no more peaceful demonstrations." It is as if every movie made in the 1960s wants to be about the 1960s.

It is useful to compare *Doctor Zhivago* with *Spartacus,* Stanley Kubrick's similarly all-star spectacle of oppression and uprising, from the first year of the decade. A distinctly post-Studio feeling informs virtually every moment of *Spartacus,* a hostility toward unjust authority, from the grueling scenes of Kirk Douglas's slavery and training as a gladiator, through the backstage views of Roman politics as Laurence Olivier and Charles Laughton vie for the loyalty of John Gavin's Julius Caesar, and on to the formation of an army under Douglas's kindly eye. The film is rich but one-sided: all Roman power is oppressive and all rebellion against it is noble, as if Kubrick viewed the old moguls as Caesars and the independent directors as Spartacus. Of course, Roman power *was* oppressive, but history tells us that rebellions invariably become corrupt. Spartacus's rebellion never gets the chance. Outmaneuvered by mighty Rome, he and his army are destroyed, and the Romans decorate the Appian Way with crucified Spartacists. The attempt to correct Fascism with liberty, however tragic the outcome, is inspiring, but Kubrick's film won its great popularity not on its politics but on its art. This was 1960, remember— the "1960s," as such, had not yet happened. *Spartacus* is one of the age's coming-of-age films, like *Psycho* and *The Apartment* a movie of the Year Zero that proclaims the New Age by the force of its post-Studio honesty.

  Doctor Zhivago, much later in the decade, proclaims nothing. It doesn't have to; the era has been secured. Revolution needn't be kept pure and beautiful (and failed) now to be popularized. It is acceptable, even in mass-market Big Film. True, it reassures the complacent burgher with its look at the devouring barbarism of the Leninist state. But it is also very clear on the need for revolution in a Tsarist state. Did the same people who saw *The Greatest Story Ever Told* see *Doctor Zhivago?* Tom Courtenay is the Judas figure: he betrays the beauty of compassion. Julie Christie is Mary, both of them, the beatified and the sensual. Omar Sharif is one of the disciples, the one whose name you can never remember. And his balalaika is John the Baptist, because it always seems to know what's going to happen next, especially "Lara's Theme." *Doctor Zhivago,* in short, unites Hollywood's conservative and progressive strains, in a sort of Republican New Left. It shows how moviemaking—even MGM international moviemaking under Carlo Ponti—has caught up with the era's ability to dilate upon the tensions of the day while attracting the broadest of publics. *Doctor Zhivago* is not New Cinema precisely, but it is post-Old. It's a hip epic.

  Three English war films, like *Doctor Zhivago* in a historical setting, further outlined the new late-sixties view of warmaking as the state's most insidious act, of wartime as the clearest illustration of the greed, stupidity, and repressiveness of the master class, and of warriors as the class system laid bare, with the superintendents of power giving the orders well behind the lines, their dupes as the intermediaries who compose patriotic songs or write stirring editorials or serve as officers in the field, and the slave class going through the hell. Richard Lester's *How I Won the War* (1967), Tony Richardson's *The Charge of the Light Brigade* (1968), and Richard Attenborough's *Oh! What a Lovely War* (1969) are disparate in form, the first a surrealist black comedy set in the African desert of World War II, the second an all-star satiric romance on the Crimean War, and the third an adaptation of Joan Littlewood's avant-garde revue of World War I vignettes broken up by music-hall turns using the pop songs of the day. Yet all three films in their contrasting ways left the same impression, a politicized version of the all-impelling notion that initiated the sixties style in film: that we suffered from a terminal case of Bad Fathers, whether they be Hollywood producers or statesmen. When Lester's enlisted man John Lennon tells officer Michael Hordern, "I'm working-class," and Hordern replies, "I had a grandfather who was a miner . . . until he sold it"; and when Richardson's Whitehall pooh-bah John Gielgud reveals that he doesn't even know whom the British are fighting in the Crimea— "It's the French, isn't it? It's usually the French"; and when Attenborough's Maggie Smith sings "I'll Make a Man of You" to seduce young men into joining up, we take a lesson in how a superstructure of interlocking forces—social, legal, and cultural—sustains the power satrapy.

And while this is a true thing, this was also a hip thing. One did not have to be knowledgeable about history or feel passionately about politics to receive and endorse this message, because sixties moviegoing was in some ways a consumerism of ideology. One could enjoy the films and their lecture without changing one's life, without dropping out of the middle class and *its* role in the power structure. One could, like Raquel Welch's boyfriend in *Flare-Up,* casually admire the revolutionary stance, even adopt it—casually—because it's hot to be cool. As Pauline Kael remarked, on filmmakers' growing appetite for exaggeration and spoof, "To make sense would be to risk being square."

Patriotism had long been square; saluting the flag was something you did in second grade, at that only because they made you. Love of country had become such incorrect style that Vietnam was the first American military campaign since the movies took root in American life that did not inspire a rash of supportive cinema. Our entry into World War I was furiously encouraged by propaganda melodrama; the World War II years saw in a wave of films praising our Allies (including Russia, to Ayn Rand's profound chagrin) and our own courage, both of fighting men and waiting women; and the Korean years, early in the cold war, hosted numerous Communist espionage exposés as well as a flowering of battle-cry action pictures. Vietnam was virtually ignored. One could argue that most writers and directors were opposed to the war and therefore un-willing to support it in art—but they didn't make movies critical of the war at the time, either. Surely this wasn't a failure of will—not after *The Manchurian Candidate* or *Dr. Strangelove.* Could it possibly have been lack of interest? Hollywood had assaulted every received piety in the religion of Americanism. Why not this crucial one as well?

Vietnam not only didn't claim its cycle of morale-boosting or morale-questioning movies in the 1960s; Vietnam got *The Green Berets* (1968). What could affect morale less morally than this theme-park of a Vietnam, with a succession of riskless rides and thrills and its friendly natives, like the live Mickey Mouse and Goofy that stalk Disneyland to cavort at the snap of a camera? The orphan boy and his dog is always a popular attraction, especially when the dog is killed in combat. We even get a skeptical reporter (David Janssen), who has apparently been reading the newspapers, but John Wayne soon sets him straight.

The Green Berets, directed by Wayne and Ray Kellogg, was supposed to set the nation straight. It was well attended but, in the media, made into a laughingstock. And it was not Wayne's rigidly gung-ho politics that hurt the film as much as the cartoon characterizations and the kiddie-matinée-serial turns of plot in James Lee Barrett's screenplay, such as the Vietcong commander who is seen living in a mansion and dining on caviar as if he were Hugh Hefner. It sounds like *Terry and the Pirates,* but *Terry and the Pirates* was fun. *The Green Berets* is a bore. Wayne was an incorrigible, but one wonders what Janssen, Jim Hutton, Aldo Ray, Ray-mond St. Jacques, and Jack Soo were thinking while they were making it. Were they that hard up for work? So little thought went into depicting even the geography of the setting that, at the fade-out, as Wayne heartens the little orphan at the shore of the sea, the sun sinks behind them. However, Vietnam has but one coastline, along the South China Sea, to the east. The sun only rises there. It sinks in the west—over Cambodia.

As Michael Herr points out, "That wasn't really about Vietnam, it was about Santa Monica."

Seven

The Cult of the Director; or, The Intelligentsia Take Up the Movies

In the first years of the twentieth century, the movies were so disreputable that people with any dignity to protect scorned them. They were a miscreant novelty shown to a ragbag inner-city clientele of working-class families, immigrants, slumming sports, and sailors. Stage actors put their careers in jeopardy if they ventured in; it was unemployment rather than ambition that attracted D. W. Griffith, Mary Pickford, and the Gish sisters to the Biograph studio in a disused brownstone on New York's Fourteenth Street. But the development of the full-length feature, the widespread treatments of the classics, the daredevil participation of the prestigious opera star Geraldine Farrar, and the phenomenal success of Griffith's *The Birth of a Nation,* presented with orchestral accompaniment in "real" playhouses on a reserved-seat, top-dollar basis, all helped to broaden the movies' appeal.

Cinema killed vaudeville by drawing its audience away, but theatre, with its upmarket clientele, remained the nation's major performing art right to the start of the Depression. With the economy in ruins, everything based upon profit-and-loss accounting suffered, but the Hollywood studio structures were able to withstand the early 1930s while the theatre's more intimate, less fully capitalized managerial systems ran into trouble. Potential acting stars and arrived playwrights hotfooted it to Hollywood, the far-flung national network of touring companies imploded, and, on Broadway, after the record season of 1927–28, which hosted 264 productions, fewer plays were mounted each year, down to just 70 in 1960.

Meanwhile the movies flourished, less so in the late 1930s, more so during World War II, less so again in the television 1950s. All the same, theatre remained the prestigious art. Intellectuals had taken up the cause of film almost from the beginning—Vachel Lindsay, hymning the characterological mythopoeia of Mary Pickford, "the queen of my people," or James Agee, wryly ticking off Hollywood's vulgarities and good intentions and getting what can only be called hot for the young Elizabeth Taylor in *National Velvet.* But for most writers, movie criticism was a hack's arena, like the annual Ten Best lists a mere marshaling of good performances as opposed to poor ones, and entertaining or perhaps serious films as opposed to dull or trivial ones. Movie criticism was not important writing; it was consumer reports. Movies themselves were important enough to spark national controversies; they had been doing so since *The Birth of a Nation*'s racial depiction was called into question, and the numerous censorship battles of the 1950s proved how influential movies were thought to be. Interestingly, on Broadway, after a censors' last stand in the early–middle 1920s, the theatre seldom initiated controversy except among thespians. Theatre, though it didn't know it, was becoming less important.

In fact, the American stage had lost its monopoly as the admirable art by about 1960. Major directors and actors who might in earlier years have concentrated on Broadway were now only using the stage as a springboard, moving permanently to Hollywood as soon as they were invited. The movies had the money, the power, the fame. And New Cinema had something special to offer the writing moviegoer. Its fertile sense of independence was attractive. Its naturalistic acting rivaled anything on Broadway. Its nonconformist worldview begged for analysis. Above all, its originality stimulated both movie critics and their readers. One no longer read reviews in advance of a visit to find out if one might like a given film. One read reviews later, to compare one's reactions with those of the reviewer. One entered into a dialogue with cinema and its critique; one intellectualized the experience of moviegoing. There couldn't have been a

Pauline Kael in the Studio Age—moviegoing was experiential then, not reflective. Nor was there a body of classic film available for review and the gathering of perspective, as there was by the 1960s, in film societies, university screenings, and, especially, on television. It was as if the logistical and cultural apparatus for the intellectual conditioning of cinema occurred just as the movies became individual enough to need it. The intelligent moviegoer didn't just talk about the latest film; he talked about the latest film's reviews.

Federico Fellini's *8½* (1963) marks one of the first instances of this socializing of the filmgoing community, if you will. Foreign films had been giving critics a great deal to bite on since the early 1950s, but the early-Italian neo-realism of Roberto Rossellini and Vittorio de Sica or the dark allegory of Ingmar Bergman was not widely seen in the United States, and, besides, who read criticism in the 1950s? Moviegoers read ads. But Fellini's *La Dolce Vita* had enjoyed a broad distribution, and by *8½*, Fellini's next full-length feature, a mass of writers and readers stood ready. Sharp observers had been cataloguing Fellini's peculiar devices— the autobiographical elements, the poeticization of grotesquerie, the circus-like gaiety of Nino Rota's sound-track music, the tendency toward international casting (Americans had played leads in *La Strada* and *Il Bidone*, and *La Dolce Vita*'s cast included the Swedish Anita Ekberg, the American Lex Barker, and the French Alain Cuny in key roles). Still, this was extra fun; the films could be enjoyed as films, outside of any critical context.

But the astonishingly confessional *8½* seemed to have been conceived as a film that could not properly be seen until it had been explained. Even before a single frame ran by one, there was the puzzling title to consider.* There was the plot, or lack of it. There was the almost point-for-point revelation of Fellini's backstage world of producers and stars and reporters and fans, even his wife, all of them advising him on how to live, how to think, and what movies are, or should be. "So? What are

---

*Counting *The White Sheik, I Vitelloni, La Strada, Il Bidone, The Nights of Cabiria*, and *La Dolce Vita* as entirely Fellini's, the early, co-directed *Variety Lights* as "half a Fellini," and Fellini's contributions to the anthologies *Amore in Città* and *Boccaccio '70* similarly as halves, the director reckoned his oeuvre up to *8½* as seven and a half films—thus the title. It has no name because it is not Fellini's next film, but rather a gloss on the next film Fellini had been planning to make.

you working on now?" asks his doctor. "Another film without hope?" A floozy tells him, "You can't make a good love story." His writing collaborator wants out of the latest—this very—project: "The film is merely a series of completely senseless episodes." "Don't you take yourself a little too seriously?" yet another adviser puts in, and "Pagliaccio!" cries a detractor. Fellini himself puts in his oar, as Guido Anselmi (Marcello Mastroianni): "In my pictures, *everything* happens."

"I am Guido," Fellini told more than one interviewer, and though he had a habit of toying with interviewers, this must be true. There was his past, tipped into the action without any warning transition or the typical Hollywood memory haze. There were his dreams, psychodramas played as realistically as if they had happened, as in the first sequence, a traffic jam from which a suffocating Fellini escapes by rising into the air like a kite—and suddenly he is hovering over a beach, and someone is hauling him down by a rope tied to his foot and, in a dazzling process shot, he plummets to earth. There was even the set of the movie that *8½* apparently might otherwise have been (that is, if Fellini had made *it* instead of *this*), a huge spaceship moored upright in a field, as if ready to leap for freedom from Fellini's personal life, perhaps with Fellini inside.

Rich homework for the analyst, *8½* and the still-growing American interest in foreign films helped institute the movie column as something more than a guide to the best and the worst. The consumerist press did not fall out of fashion. But the magazine critic, with room to expatiate in and a connoisseur audience, became prominent. As yet another of Fellini's *8½* advisers tells him, "The audience has to understand the film."

Yet where were the American *8½*s to insure the critic's job security, the one-of-a-kind films beyond explicit narrative and Hollywood casting, movies as event and adventure? *Dr. Strangelove,* a year after *8½,* had the brilliance to excite discussion but also a clarity that neutralized it. *Dr. Strangelove* didn't need analysis, just praise. Then, too, the diabolical Kubrick was ingenious enough not to seem ingenious. There *is* much to analyze in *Dr. Strangelove*; critics have yet to catch up with it. But when it was new, it was only extraordinary, not difficult.

Arthur Penn's *Mickey One* (1965) was difficult, and had the nerve to intend to be. What is happening here? During the credits, we get views of Warren Beatty as lover and late-night boy, foolish, drunken, and a witness to something, something involving a man tied to a chair being beaten up. Then, in Beatty's voice-over, Alan Surgal's script begins: "The ride was over. I was trapped. And I find out I owe, suddenly, a fortune."

To whom, and how? And what is Beatty? A bad comic, it turns out. "I couldn't be funny if my life depended on it," Beatty tells us. "And it did." A bad comic "dies," in the hyperbole of show-biz argot, but Beatty's in trouble with a gangster and is on the lam. Still wondering about the details, we get a series of fascinating visuals from Penn: when Beatty, chased into a car dump, turns back to see himself walking away in a misty view of somewhere else; or when Beatty, now a full-fledged bum, sits in a soup kitchen as a stuttering man reads him the Bible; or when we catch on to Penn's majestic echo texture of trampolines and cymbals being crashed together. Ghislain Cloquet, a cinematographer active in the French New Wave, especially with Alain Resnais, gives Penn a camera beyond masterly, shooting things that couldn't be brought out on stage or in a book—or in color. *Mickey One* is possibly the most black-and-white movie ever shot, so dependent upon its shadows that one couldn't colorize it even if one wanted to. The sound-track score, too, goes beyond the usual, for while Eddie Sauter composed the main score, Stan Getz advanced upon it with, as the credits put it, "improvisations."

Shadows and jazz and no backstory: the whole film is on the run. Yet it is most calculated when most obscure. Alexandra Stewart, the girl Beatty takes up with, asks him what he's guilty of. "Of not bein' innocent," Beatty replies. Finally, Beatty is impaled on a spotlight beam and Penn pulls back to show Beatty on stage in a nightclub with the Chicago skyline lit behind him. "Am I comin' t'rough?" Beatty asks his audience. Coming through? Coming true?

We never learn what informs Beatty's fears. If the film is a study in paranoia, perhaps that's the point. Like *8½, Mickey One** is both naturalistic and fanciful, as reliant upon its techniques of narration as upon the narration itself. *Mickey One* is not "about" what it's about. It is about how it tries to tell us. Here was a party for the critics, but many refused the invitation. Was it too deep for them or too shallow? Was 1965 too soon for an all-out, everybody-has-to-join, national conversation

---

*We need another title explanation here. Early on, the fleeing and now anonymous Beatty watches a bum being rolled and grabs his Social Security card. We read the name: Miklos Wan . . . something long and Polish. This is immediately changed to "Mickey One," the name Beatty uses while on the run.

on a film? Or were the writers waiting for a film that the entire nation went to see?

Everybody saw *The Graduate* (1967), and it was two years later and perhaps high time for the club to open, and if the film wasn't deep it posed some fetching pictures. The critics declared a festival. Mike Nichols, director of Calder Willingham and Buck Henry's script (from Charles Webb's novel) left just enough ambiguity on view to cloud the absolute with fascinating doubts. Everyone understood *The Graduate* and everyone wanted to talk about it. Many of its lines became catchphrases: the one-word business lecture, "Plastics!" from an old gasbag to the copiously uncertain Dustin Hoffman; Anne Bancroft's peremptory "Waiter!" after Hoffman has impotently tried to get his attention—and the waiter immediately responds; or Bancroft's sumptuously frigid "Hello, Benjamin," every time she meets up with him—even the last time, when he breaks into the Robinsons' house and she coolly walks to a phone and calls the police. "Just a second, I'll ask him," she says into the phone, then, to Hoffman, "Are you armed?" It's amazing to think that Mrs. Robinson, the soigné Mrs. Bates of the late 1960s, was originally offered to Doris Day. Day wasn't ready for Cinema this New. "To each his own," she insisted in her autobiography. "I can't picture myself in bed with someone, all the crew around us, doing that which I consider so exciting and exalting when it is very personal and private." I wouldn't do it, either.

Some of *The Graduate*'s pictures became national puzzles. What did it mean when Hoffman crashes into his parents' swimming pool, in full scuba gear, as if he were trying to drown himself? Did you notice that Hoffman used a cross to lock the church doors when he ran off with Katharine Ross? And how about the oddly contented, or even vacuous, or maybe worried looks on the faces of Hoffman and Ross at the fade-out? As Hoffman says, to the "Plastics!" line, "Exactly how do you mean that?"

The Graduate was the climactic generation-war film of the 1960s, the one in which the parents are totally corrupt and the kids are spotless. Hoffman's folks (William Daniels and Elizabeth Wilson) are nagging jerks; Ross's father (Murray Hamilton) is a worthless nerd and her mother (Bancroft) a cold-blooded adulteress who deliberately punishes her lover Hoffman by marrying Ross off to a worthless nerd-in-the-making be-cause—well, that was another puzzle of the day. Because, having grown old and beyond happiness in a suburban California nowhere, she wanted to make her daughter just as miserable? This was the age that virtually invented the notion of the more or less infinitely screenable masterpiece, the film that not only can but must be seen several times before all its perceptions can be absorbed. Perhaps television's repertory airing of old classics—Astaire and Rogers, *Casablanca, The Wizard of Oz,* John Ford's westerns—had been paving the way for this view of great movies as endlessly self-illuminating, laying the groundwork deep in the 1950s. But it was not till certain titles of the 1960s that many people spoke of going back for a second or third viewing during the *original release,* perhaps after exchanging notes on them with friends or favored critics.

Certainly, Michelangelo Antonioni's *Blowup* (1966) defied the browser and encouraged the student. Here was something as direct as *The Graduate* yet as laden as *Mickey One,* a foreign film but a most contemporary document, at times rather grandly paced but almost savage in its eagerness to reveal. "Slowly, slowly," protagonist David Hemmings advises. "*Against the beat*": the punk clowns, and Hemmings shooting the model Verushka with his camera in such heat he seems to be screwing her, and the real shooting, to death, in the park (it *was* real, wasn't it?), and Vanessa Redgrave, against the beat, and Hemmings's blowups of his snapshots of the murder that never was, for the tennis game is *in fact* played without a ball and Hemmings can prove it because he bends over to pick up the "ball" and "throw" it back to the players, who are the punk clowns from the beginning.

It's a solid two-screening film—three if you're really with it— because sometimes you have to go with, not against, the beat, and *Blowup* was one of the times. More even than *The Graduate,* this was a critic's movie, an intellectual's movie, a status-defining movie, a movie for history. Anyone who couldn't get it was a yahoo, not a moviegoer; or a reviewer, not a critic. It was no longer simply a matter of I liked it or I didn't like it. What if you didn't like it and everyone else thought it was Total Cinema? Worse: what if you wrote a review saying it was pretentious and boring and all the heavy critics called it a masterpiece? What would that make you?

The 1960s made movies dangerous for the hack reviewer, the hack moviegoer as well. Movies had become intellectualized. You couldn't just know what you liked anymore; you had to know what was art. Say, for instance, that you attend a screening of the latest effort by a gifted

Crucial Sites of High Maestro Cinema. Saraghina's beach (in *8½*, top left), the surrealist tennis court (*Blowup*, bottom left, with David Hemmings), and the church (*The Graduate*), with mother Anne Bancroft, bride Katharine Ross, and just-about-to-be-lurched bridegroom Brian Avery.

director. As a well-connected critic, you have access to advance gossip
about the production, put together in great secrecy but said, by those
who have heard it from those who have heard, to be a highly original
proposition. You know no more than this. If it's original, you had better
be, too. On your way to the screening, you rehearse your terminology
and ten-dollar words. "The impact of . . ." "What sheer density of *hommage,* delicacy of *montage* . . ." "Reminiscent of Bergman's of Eisenstein's
of Truffaut's . . ." But the film turns out to be some two and a half
hours of excruciatingly paced parable on the destiny of humankind that
has more machines in it than humans. Technically, it dazzles. Emotionally,
it palls. Worried, you sense that this may be the director's intention, his
view of destiny as drawing us into an increasingly mechanized age fit only
for deadhearted survivors. Still, how do you praise a film that, in general,
bores you?

Few films have divided the intellectuals as fully as Stanley Kubrick's
2001: A Space Odyssey (1968), written by Kubrick and the distinguished
science-fiction novelist Arthur C. Clarke from Clarke's short story "The
Sentinel." In *The New Yorker,* Penelope Gilliatt led Kubrick's champions,
calling the piece "some sort of great film, and an unforgettable en-
deavor. . . . The film is not only hideously funny—like *Dr. Strangelove*—
about human speech and response at a point where they have begun to
seem computerized, and where more and more people sound like record-
ings left on while the soul is out; it is also a uniquely poetic piece of sci-
fi, made by a man who truly possesses the drives of both science and
fiction." Hollis Alpert, defining the middle ground in the *Saturday Review,*
found the film vexing yet worthy: "With all the sweep and spectacle,
there is a pervading aridity. . . . Nevertheless, Kubrick has, in one big
jump, discovered new possibilities for the screen image. He took on a
large challenge, and has met it commendably." In *Newsweek,* for the opposition, Joseph Morgenstern wrote that Kubrick's "potentially majestic
myth about man's first encounter with a higher life form than his own
dwindles into a whimsical space operetta, then frantically inflates itself
again for a surreal climax in which the imagery is just obscure enough
to be annoying, just precise enough to be banal."

Most of the big guns fired alongside Morgenstern. *The New Republic's*
Stanley Kauffmann called *2001* "a major disappointment" and, in the
New York Times, Renata Adler thought it "something between hypnotic
and immensely boring." By hindsight, we can say that *2001* revealed the

ecstasy available in science fiction, saw its potential for the metaphysical and the philosophical, and thus made an insignificant matinée genre into one of Hollywood's major forms. Yet it is notable that, when it was new, *all* writers found in the movie a wealth of material to sift for extrapolative deconstruction. Whether or not *2001* "worked" for them, whether they thought it a masterpiece, a curiosity, or a failure, it was a marvel of the day, to be inspected, discovered, and revealed. No book or play could have excited so much commentary, for books and plays did not command the audience that cinema did. Film had become the great American social medium, the national town meeting that everyone attends.

Directly after the film opened, Kubrick cut seventeen minutes from the running time to hasten the perhaps overly deliberate unfolding of his epic. Thus many people saw a more agreeable print than the critics had seen; meanwhile, the kids had taken up *2001* as one of "their" movies, something that gratified their sense of self mainly because so many adults couldn't get it. Not everyone attended *2001*—but just about everyone under thirty did, solemnizing the development of a youthful audience as the decisive element in a film's success and forcing a shift in producers' tactics that is felt yet today. The culmination of Kid Film was the Kid Audience, less concerned with the problems of humankind's destiny or even of Kubrick's masterly use, for the first time in its history, of Cinerama's artistic potential than with the right drugs to take before checking into the theatre. Ironically, the movies the kids most admired were often the same movies the intellectuals were most interested in—*Blowup* and *The Graduate* and *2001,* for instance, and, mainly, the work that inspired the greatest intellectual crisis in sixties moviegoing, *Bonnie and Clyde.*

You always knew when a film was important: Bosley Crowther would review it in the *New York Times* at least twice. *Dr. Strangelove* hit a triple off Crowther, mostly in considered but guilty yet impressed ponderation, which, to be sure, is a most highly ponderous consideration. Crowther knew *Dr. Strangelove* was a major film, but he didn't like it, and he knew it was a well-made film, yet it shouldn't have been because it was "a bit too contemptuous of our defense establishment for my comfort and taste." To offend Crowther, a moviemaker really ought to have no talent, certainly not genius. It's more symmetrical when only films that Crowther likes are major films, when gifted directors are soothing and not exasperating Crowther. Instead of this "devastating satire," why wasn't Kubrick making, say, *The Ox-Bow Incident* or *The Best Years of Our Lives,* art that a respectable *nomyenklatura* can respect? You have social analysis, you have sensitive acting, you have a literate screenplay, as sensible as an old woman's shoes, and You Stand on the Side of Fairness and Due Course.

Crowther was the *Times*'s moral custodian of film. If he approved a movie, it was good for you, and if he didn't it was detrimental for the nation. Crowther had been carrying this weight for decades. So when his multiple-review scan shielded *The Miracle* in 1951, the most imposingly positional American newspaper was in effect shielding it, too. "The whole future of the American screen," Crowther wrote at the time, "would seem to depend upon its freedom to handle subjects that heretofore have been taboo." A wider scope should be allowed, then. What worried Crowther was not the field of study but the approach, how moviemakers treated their subjects. Perhaps certain attitudes should not be allowed. While other critics rated *How to Murder Your Wife* for its humor and pacing, Crowther detected its mean spirit: "Never have I seen a movie, serious, comic, or otherwise, that so frankly, deliberately, and grossly belittled and ridiculed wives." Maybe the film's producer and writer George Axelrod was unconsciously airing something dark but universal about man's view of the practice of marriage. Maybe Axelrod meant not to affirm but to spoof the bachelor's reluctance. Maybe *How to Murder Your Wife* is an offensive piece of goods. Whatever it is, Crowther was less concerned with understanding art than with judging its attitude. In other words, we don't have to free ourselves of the concept of taboo; we simply revise the index of forbidden acts. *The Miracle* was a sincere, humanistic parable. *How to Murder Your Wife* was a misogynistic crypto-Gothic, snuff porn masquerading as farce.

And what was *Bonnie and Clyde*? A gangster thriller, a quickie rip-off. But—the nerve!—it was, sort of, in a maddening "now I am, now I'm not" manner, funny. A gangster movie is *funny!*

Crowther came down hard on *Bonnie and Clyde*. "This is the film that opened the Montreal International Festival!" he cried. Yet it was "a cheap piece of bald-faced slapstick comedy that treats the hideous depradations of that sleazy, moronic pair as though they were as full of fun and frolic as the jazz-age cutups in *Thoroughly Modern Millie*. . . . It has [Warren] Beatty clowning broadly as the killer who fondles various types of guns with as much nonchalance and dispassion as he airily twirls a big cigar, and it has [Faye] Dunaway squirming grossly as his thrill-seeking, sex-starved moll."

Forward forge adjectives till reels the mind, eh? Why the overkill? Doesn't Pauline Kael warn us that *"Only* good movies . . . provoke attacks?"* Certain other critics dismissed *Bonnie and Clyde* as the latest gangster chase-'em-up; they didn't know what they were seeing. Crowther knew. He had been over into the 1960s and it didn't work—for him. While he honored *Bonnie and Clyde* with repeated assaults ("a Crowther crusade," Andrew Sarris called it, "that makes the 100-Years-War look like a border incident"), *Time*'s and *Newsweek*'s critics published prudent retractions of their first negative opinions, and the country geared up for a *Bonnie and Clyde* vogue in fashion, attitude, and morals. Writers checked into the *Bonnie and Clyde* motel, dragging along their peculiar sociocultural baggage—John Howard Lawson, for instance, a Communist Party–lining playwright and critic of the 1920s and '30s who had moved west and become one of the Hollywood Ten. For Lawson, "There is no doubt that [*Bonnie and Clyde*] is an attack on American society, linking the evils of the thirties with the continuing predominance of oppression, corruption, and hypocrisy in the present." What does this have to do with a bunch of hedonistic bank robbers?

Like it or not, *Bonnie and Clyde* was the film of the era, and Crowther found himself virtually alone. Other critics who, like Crowther, had been offended or confused by it and who, like Crowther, had *not* written that it was offensive or confusing but that it was *badly made* (italics mine, because no one who is smart and honest can say that) had recanted. Indeed, like the men at *Time* and *Newsweek,* suddenly they weren't offended or confused; they were enlightened, not least by heavyweight critics who were able to appreciate *Bonnie and Clyde* at first sight. Convinced detractors were becoming notably thin on the ground. To find an ally, Crowther would have had to reach all the way down to *Films in Review,* a cult magazine run mainly on nostalgia pieces and given to calling anything it didn't approve of as "sociopathic." Listen to what *Films in Review* considered a publishable opinion: *"Bonnie and Clyde* is so incompetently written, acted, directed, and produced it would not be worth noticing were a claque not attempting to promote the idea that its sociopathology is art." As for Beatty, he "adds his own ignorance to the character-inconsistencies of the script." Director Arthur Penn's "artistic integrity is about on the level of Beatty's acting ability—i.e., close to zero." The writer, someone named Page Cook, was sufficiently confident to predict that "association with *dreck* like *Bonnie and Clyde"* would do Faye Dunaway and Michael J. Pollard "professional harm." Yes, that film really destroyed their careers, didn't it?

The problem is, you can only make a fool of yourself by pretending that a film is badly made because you don't like what it says. Only good movies provoke attacks. The Williams College professor Charles Thomas Samuels mounted a strong case against *Bonnie and Clyde* precisely because he saw, and admitted, how well made it was. That was why it was dangerous. Incompetent films don't change the world; excellent ones can. Samuels thought *Bonnie and Clyde* "a bunch of decayed cabbage leaves smeared with catsup," but also "well-acted, slickly paced, and brilliantly edited." As Samuels saw it, it was dangerous because "art initiates action . . . by reflecting contemporary attitudes and thus, through the power of reflection, confirming them." If the world is immoral, and you film the world as immoral *without reproaching its immorality,* you are condoning its immorality, and the world will become yet more immoral.

What threw nearly everyone but Samuels (and Pauline Kael, one of the film's earliest enthusiasts) was the genre question, New Cinema's ability to rehabilitate even the most primitive movie forms. Above all, *Bonnie and Clyde* veritably *is* a gangster chase-'em-up, even more than the western and backstage musical a film type born to be made quick and dirty for the delight of yahoos. Granted, we had *Bonnie and Clyde*–like films from Fritz Lang in *You Only Live Once* (1937) and from Nicholas Ray—his first and arguably his best—in *They Live by Night* (1949). But both Lang and Ray pictured couples more innocent than Penn's couple. The kind of film *Bonnie and Clyde* seemed to be, if you weren't discerning, was something like *The Bonnie Parker Story,* a dreary B of 1958 with Dorothy Provine as the steely heroine who leaves tacks on the floor to discourage nocturnal visits from her henchmen.

Bonnie and Clyde was clearly not made quick and dirty. The screenplay, by David Newman and Robert Benton, is expert, gobbling up goofy Texas vernacular the way Restoration comedies live on epigrams. The historical period is brought off with many a nicety, from the old black-and-white photographs under the credits that imperceptibly turn into likenesses of the two stars to the FDR poster we see as the car pulls away from the first robbery or the Eddie Cantor recording (of "One Hour with You") we hear during the gun battle at the motel. The editing (by Dede Allen) and the country-fiddle musical score work together to achieve the tempo of comedy, exhilarating till the Barrow gang commits its first murder—when, as Penn may or may not have intended, the gang's dare-devil charm twists into something desperate and vicious. If *Bonnie and Clyde* was a sixties demonstration piece, a test of one's sociopolitical credentials, this first murder was the key presentation. Penn sets it up with brutal wit, for while Bonnie and Clyde are busy robbing a bank, their doltish driver, Pollard, has parallel-parked the getaway car. Audiences scream with a glad surprise as Pollard effortfully backs and fills his way into the street with two bank robbers and the loot in the back seat, frantic to scram—but meanwhile a teller has run out and jumped on the car's running board, and Clyde blows his head off. It looks just the way the words sound, and audiences are suddenly very silent. Some of them make their peace with the film and go along for the rest of the ride, all the way on as far as it goes; others are permanently alienated.

Such artfully telling moments simply do not occur in quick and dirty movies. Genre film cranks out clichés; it doesn't offer its public the opportunity to join or deny the ethos of its age—to, in Charles Thomas Samuels's terms, accept or reject the reflection of contemporary attitudes. Slowly, slowly. *Against* the beat. Certainly, Penn regarded *Bonnie and Clyde* as a contemporary work, treating American repression and violence. In an interview, he recalled with approval that at one screening a group of black spectators strongly identified with Bonnie and Clyde as rebels; in another, Penn likened the Depression Southwest to "the south of the United States today: a church-going, highly moralistic, highly puritanical society, which has integrated and made a part of itself a kind of violence against other human beings which, viewed from the outside, seems absolutely intolerable."

So far, so good. But Penn also spoke of his version of Bonnie and Clyde as "obliged to fulfill some kind of role which put them in the position of being folk heroes—violators of the status quo. . . . We find ourselves confronted with the terrible irony that we root for somebody for a relatively good cause who is called upon to commit acts of violence which repel us."

Actually, we find ourselves confronted with bank robbers. Since when is robbing banks a good cause? The banks were seen as villainous in Bonnie and Clyde's Texas, yes. The banks were the Great American Foreclosers. But robbing them only made everybody poorer. Penn is at pains to show Clyde's acts of kindness to the helpless. "Is that your money or the bank's?" he asks a man during a robbery. It's the man's money. "Keep it," says Clyde. What magnanimity. But Clyde's no Robin Hood. The banks he robs are small-town savings-and-loan affairs, the banks poor people kept their money in. And remember, there was no deposit insurance in 1931, when Penn's folk heroes launched their spree. If a bank failed, you lost your savings. This is what Bonnie and Clyde are stealing. Not the fat off the plutocrat. The blood of the Texas poor. They robbed not for a good or even a bad cause, but for fun and profit. And, interestingly, for fame. In Newman and Benton's original script, Clyde was, as history tells, homosexual. However, let's be sensible, boys; and Clyde was reconstructed as impotent. But lo, his amazingly successful criminal life swells not only his head. Just before Beatty and Dunaway relax in a daisy field for their first successful coition, he tells her, "You made me somebody they're gonna remember." Fame is sexy.

Isn't this why *Bonnie and Clyde* had such impact? Neither for the comic skewing of a gangster thriller, nor for the fashionable "rebellion," but for the smashing bloody glamour of the two leads. In the film's first scene, their meeting, cinematographer Burnett Guffey revels in the pair— in her lips, his toothpick, the way she touches his gun as if she were handling his cock. That two such glorious love gods cannot copulate is Hollywood history in itself, and when they finally make it, the sense of beauty reaching not only climax but absolute completion—for the daisy field precedes their death by minutes—is terrifying. It says that stardom is its own morality, that good looks are the first virtue and glamour can do no wrong. Next, Penn should film *The Oliver North Story*, with Oliver North, for Penn knows the drill.

Bosley Crowther didn't, and he was quickly removed from the scene, because in fighting *Bonnie and Clyde* he was fighting the 1960s. He wasn't against the beat; he couldn't hear it. He didn't understand how divisive New Cinema was *supposed* to be—but then by 1967 New Cinema wasn't dividing segments of the public. The audience was one with the screen. Crowther was virtually the only person in the country who wasn't. He was making sense. He risked being square. And he misspoke himself. What he *meant* was that *Bonnie and Clyde* delights in crime. What he *wrote* was that the film is poorly made.

No film with two stars like Beatty and Dunaway, so superbly brought forth, is poorly made. They knew that much back in D. W. Griffith's day. Yet few writers in their dissertations on *Bonnie and Clyde* dealt with star charisma. Charles Thomas Samuels weighs his argument

Stardom as pure hotness: Faye Dunaway and Warren Beatty as Bonnie and Clyde. Take a look. Could such pretty people be guilty of anything but being fabulous?

as if the film were little more than a script and a worldview, as if the way the movie was conceived were more important than the way the stars' attractiveness certified their characters and got the audience to like them no matter what they did. As if writers and directors were all a movie-goer sees.

In fact, hit movies were increasingly being thought of, no matter what contribution the writer, cinematographer, composer, editor, and actors made, as the discreet triumph of the director. The 1960s had reached its reverence of the auteurist line, in which all films of all ages and climes are taken wholly as products of the man with the megaphone.

This theory, developed in the 1950s in Europe, recognized the uniquely generative power that European directors—as conceivers, co-writers, casters, coaches, and even directors of their films—commanded. It was less surely applicable to the American Studio Age movie, whose director might be assigned to a finished script, an assembled cast, and a corps of self-starting techies and autonomous shops. Of course the studio system had broken down by the 1960s, leaving the director, especially the hot director, and most especially the critics' idea of the latest hot director, almost entirely in charge, and a cult of reviewers and aficionados grew up around the notion of what we might call High Maestro Film.

This is the sort of movie that the connoisseur dines out on: New Cinema; very directed; artistically and culturally hip; an unusual, preferably an original, and ideally a unique work, appealing to the intelligentsia but generally popular as well, so the intellectuals have a major topic to address when they discuss it. Looking back on the 1960s, we find High Maestro candidates: *Psycho* and *Dr. Strangelove* absolutely; *Tom Jones* possibly; *Seconds* not quite, because almost nobody appreciated it; *Through a Glass Darkly* and *Winter Light* no, because Bergman appealed only to the most elite audience; *Lolita* and *The Misfits* yes, but then why was the writer as prominent as the director?

Besides, none of these could be approached in the terms I describe, for there was no pervasive cult of the director in the early 1960s. Foreign movies kept tugging at the idea; Fellini, in some ways the D. W. Griffith of modern film, made the High Maestro concept indispensable, not least because *8½* is about the problem of being a director with a cult. *Mickey One* missed out on a listing because it was not popular with intellectuals (or anyone), and *2001* suffered a major debunking. But *Bonnie and Clyde* was High Maestro Film by acclamation as Crowther rode off in his tumbril, and the union of the intelligentsia and the movies was complete.

Still, true High Maestro Film should come from a High Maestro, the kind of genius who, like Fellini, turns out not just a masterpiece but an oeuvre full of tropes and concepts, a richness of style but also of vision, something for the critic to write upon. For it was the critics, not the public, who decided who was maestro and who was not. The public can only make a hit; the writers make a reputation. The High Maestro is above all an important director, not merely popular, not merely successful, but written about as if everything he does matters. Cultural importance isn't innate; it is perceived—publicized, really. Thus, Jerry Lewis is important in France because critics write of his work as if it betokened greatness of tradition and influence. In the United States, Lewis is a man who does a telethon.

The problem with the selected High Maestros of the 1960s is that most of them could not seem to maintain a steady altitude. Arthur Penn never did anything to equal *Bonnie and Clyde,* Stanley Kubrick was almost dependably erratic, and even Fellini, it was generally agreed, was running on echoes, his track record, and empty after *Juliet of the Spirits* (1965), or possibly *Amarcord* (1974).

Richard Lester seemed a sound candidate, especially because he combined a contemporary zaniness with a highly personal technique. Lester was born in Philadelphia but came to us transmontanely, as the director of English movies. His style—a kind of surrealist, straight camp run on the exhilarating tempo of farce—was perfect for the Beatles films, *The Knack,* and *A Funny Thing Happened on the Way to the Forum* (1966). Though some found him slick, Lester was no formulator of aimless exercises. He varied his style with the projects, filling the episodic Beatles adventures with visual tricks (jump-cuts, weird-angle and off-focus shots), letting *The Knack* steam along largely on the jittery cool of its script, and staging *Forum*'s songs to spoof the very idea of musical comedy (for example, Michael Crawford needs to sing a love song, so he socks a tree and a harp falls into his hand).

Lester was unquestionably original, undoubtedly his own auteur. Another director, given the scripts and scores and casts of these films, would have come up with totally different results. Moreover, this was just about the most hip body of work in film—another reason why Lester appeared to be the emerging hero of High Maestro Film. After all, *The Knack* is virtually made of jokes about sex appeal, seduction, a rape; the two Beatles movies found the only workable format for sixties rock cinema in its interspersing of merry pranks with stand-and-deliver music breaks; and *Forum* mocked two of the decade's *bêtes noires,* parents and warmongers. All this suggested a master native to the era, someone inconceivable at any other time. In such a self-regarding age, a talent that seemed peculiarly empowered to explore it was vastly welcome.

Then came *How I Won the War* (1967), something like a Beatles film with death instead of music and politics instead of merriment. It was actively disliked, called self-indulgent. This is the "dog ate my homework" school of film criticism. What do you mean, self-indulgent? You mean you were bored by the picaresque structure? You mean you didn't enjoy the many touches of fantasy amid the naturalism, that you were confused because Lester conflated absurdism and realism? You mean you don't think Lester had anything to add to the body of anti-war film? You mean you got sick of those incomprehensible English accents? You mean you thought having the slain soldiers follow along with their squad but showing up on the screen in solid primary colors made a rather obvious effect? You mean that soldier Jack MacGowran doing a stand-up comic routine in baggy pants and a red putty nose with a pull-on wooden horse to canned laughter out in the desert was as awful as the last tour of *Blossom Time* presented by Messrs. Shubert, and even not dissimilar?

Look, the guy tried his best. Maybe the movie is not your cup of tea. Maybe it's a witless mess, style without content. But Lester wasn't *trying* to make a terrible movie. A film that doesn't work isn't self-indulgent any more than it is—to cite another all-purpose critic's assault word—manipulative. All art is manipulative; all art is self-indulgent. Any organization of narrative, every choice in characterization, is a manipulation. Novelists, composers, poets, painters, and other creators indulge themselves, liberate their fantasies in everything they create. *Der Ring des Nibelungen* is manipulative. *War and Peace* is self-indulgent. As far as that goes, what could be more manipulative and self-indulgent than watching a movie and writing one's personal opinion of it?

The opinions of Lester's next film, *Petulia* (1968), were respectful, laudatory but mixed. Here he retooled his style for a small piece of naturalism, so tightly wound that Lester's typical jump-cut flashbacks seem to encircle the story, bind it, strangle it. There are good bad movies, like *The Oscar*: poorly made yet entertaining. There are also bad good movies, and *Petulia* is one of them: brilliant but boring. It is love and obsession, American style, hauntingly precise in its evocations of the San Francisco *haut monde* and acted by a superb cast—George C. Scott, Julie Christie, Shirley Knight, Arthur Hill, Richard Chamberlain. But trying to understand it is very hard work and trying to enjoy it impossible.

This is the problem with High Maestro critique—the maestros are unpredictable. The only really dependable director is a dead director—Griffith, Ford, and Hitchcock are the American saints of High Maestro thought because it's already clear where the masterpieces come. Then, too, High Maestro critique can't exploit the current top directors, established but still in mid-career, because critics want to discover their idols, not inherit them. Perversely, some of the contemporary elect were much less likely candidates than Kubrick or Fellini—Franco Zeffirelli, for instance, who enjoyed a temporary (and controversial) High Maestro prestige for his two Shakespearean adaptations, *The Taming of the Shrew* (1967) and, especially, *Romeo and Juliet* (1968).

The two had much in common: largely English casts, striking location filming, and a picturesquely naturalized atmosphere. As with Lester, Zeffirelli's movies were original, his Shakespeare unlike any other's. And his *Romeo and Juliet* appeared to interpret the text in a distinctly sixties manner. The era was flattered. Casting teenagers in roles usually played by seasoned seniors inducted a classic into the youth culture—Romeo (Leonard Whiting) first appears dreamily strolling with a flower—and the morning after the lovers' wedding night finds them in the nude, so contemporary in its novelty that a shot of the scene was used as the film's logo. However, Shakespeare's kids mainly make war, not love, and the idyll of Romeo and Juliet naked together was undercut by Whiting's Brighton Pier tan line and the deft placement of arm and blanket to shield the breasts of Juliet (Olivia Hussey).

The Taming of the Shrew had already shown where Zeffirelli's strengths lay in the filming of Shakespeare—opulent designs, earthy realities, a caperingly majestic use of crowds and operatic passions. Indeed, Zeffirelli had got his start in opera (as designer, then director), which may explain his salient weakness, an often watery delivery of the poetry. *Romeo and Juliet* emphasized the strengths. It seemed all design, all crowd scenes, all passions made yet more operatic by the infusion of earthiness and violence. Some said that, as with Laurence Olivier's *Henry V*, Zeffirelli had brought us closer to the original in his renovation, had clarified Shakespeare through reinterpretation—yet, at the same time, he had followed Olivier in devising a way to lure drama out of the playhouse. In fact, Zeffirelli's *Romeo* was largely based on his famous 1960 Old Vic staging, the West End gone Italian. ("The director," Kenneth Tynan reported, "has even taught his English cast how to shrug.") Then, as here on screen, Zeffirelli edited Shakespeare for cinematic cuts, cast as young as was feasible (Judi Dench, the Juliet, was twenty-six, a chicken by thespian standards), saw Mercutio as grouchy rather than lyrical, and stunned with the ferocity of his swordplay. It must be said that the tragic confrontation of Tybalt and Mercutio, then of Romeo and Tybalt, was brilliant in the film, turbulent gallantry in the boiling piazzas as the lean and relentless Mercutio (John McEnery) faces off Tybalt (Michael York, in a strange cap whose horned brim makes him look like a devil) and Tybalt then stands to the avenging Romeo, their groups of partisans hysterically butting in, the two principals pounding each other with their fists when they lose their swords, the dirt and heat and sweat—and the

Ancient Verona in the 1960s: Zeffirelli's *Romeo and Juliet,* with (above) Juliet Olivia Hussey and Nurse Pat Heywood; and (below) flower children at war as Romeo Leonard Whiting (on top) whups Tybalt Michael York (on bottom).

blood—flying wildly in a scene so real as to seem beyond direction, without plan.

Such reportorial violence stood out especially in the United States, where fistfights, brawls, gunplay, manifestations of gangsterism, and the skirmishes and pitched battles of war were a part of the standard catalogue of movie scenes. Zeffirelli's *Taming of the Shrew* was a glitter of steeple and hose and stars—this was Elizabeth Taylor and Richard Burton's first decent film together—but *Romeo and Juliet*'s epic three-way duel was unlike anything one had encountered. An Italian director and an English cast had accomplished what the American western was never quite willing to do: to show what angry murder looks like.

Speaking of the western, and Italian directors, it was Sergio Leone who became the 1960s' first undisputed High Maestro, though it was the public more than the critics who first appreciated him. David Thomson calls Stanley Kubrick "a director who interests people who do not normally see movies"—tourists, in effect. Leone interested everyone else—all committed moviegoers, from the clued-in to the impulsive, and including intellectuals and oafs. Here was an American form brought to its climax by foreigners, the mythological aspect of the western redeveloped by European exaggeration and subtlety.

The very term "spaghetti western" suggests a quick and dirty version of the real thing. No, it was realer. It turned out that the American western—particularly the ubiquitous B—was the version of itself. Leone's work implied that there had not been a pure form to make a facsimile of in the first place. The form had never reached a climax because no American director had thought to style its parts as elementally as Leone. Obviously, an Italian would see the American western, already a favorite form of the *Cahiers du Cinéma* circle, with fresh—let's say disinterestedly fanatic—eyes. And perhaps only an Italian would cast his westerns with American actors (and bill himself under an "American" pseudonym as Bob Robertson, and pass off actor Gian Maria Volonté as John Wells, and list various techies under comparably atmospheric names) not only to authenticate his work but to scrutinize our easy-come approach to this ultra-American genre. Any American knows what a western is—and so doesn't understand it. Italians had to figure it out.

Leone starts from scratch—the deserts, the dirt towns, the come-as-you-are clothes, the quick-draw blood, the fast sex, the territoriality of men's shoving matches. The clans, the beliefs, the law. Leone builds an

America that never existed, even in its movies—an America, however, that its movies pretended to portray. Leone's advantage is that he doesn't have to pretend, and that he has no Production Code to honor. His tales are not meant morally. They are distillations of the American western, its characters idolized, its sites made into ceremonial haunts, and its clichés developed into holy text.

In the so-called *Dollars* trilogy—*A Fistful of Dollars* (1964; released here in 1967), *For a Few Dollars More* (1965; 1967), and *The Good, the Bad, and the Ugly* (1966; 1968), all with Clint Eastwood—Leone presented the first conscious ritualization of what American westerns had viewed simply as automatic activity: for instance, Karl Malden betrays fellow bandit Marlon Brando, Brando goes to prison, and Malden turns straight; but Brando shows up hot for vengeance. Or Joel McCrea is a good guy, so he saves Mariette Hartley from her loathsome bridegroom and his disgusting brothers; but the family will come after McCrea. Or John Wayne is good and Lee Marvin is bad and James Stewart is peaceful; but Stewart must learn what survival entails.

Leone's West is epic: historicized, allegorized, and above all mythologized. His plots are standard. *A Fistful of Dollars* finds Eastwood playing two rival factions against each other to purge a town of evil. *For a Few Dollars More* gives us Eastwood and Lee Van Cleef competitively chasing criminal Volonté, Eastwood for money and Van Cleef for revenge. *The Good, the Bad, and the Ugly* joins Eastwood and Van Cleef with Eli Wallach, all after a hidden gold shipment against a Civil War background. Thrice-told tales. But it is not Leone's plotting that dazzles; it is the way he imbues his tales with a Calvinist version of character-as-destiny. Leone's people have spiritual vocations; they are *called* to their lives. Better: they are called to Leone's movies, to exhale their personalities over the landscape so completely we don't know which came first, the land or the legends.

Leone is a purist, but the American western was impure, watered down; so Leone is a revisionist. American westerns tend to sidle around real violence in favor of colorful saloon brawls; Leone revels in blood, especially one-on-one snipings. American westerns center on Gary Cooper or Gene Autry; Leone's actors look like men who have been living on horseback. Leone has a sense of humor, too (of course a perverse one), and his composer Ennio Morricone devised a wholly new yet immediately self-authenticating sound style for the western, garish with a blaring mariachi trumpet or shrieking out a wordless choral backup, a noise as basic to Leone's westerns as Eastwood's dangling cigarillo.

All this is simply taking the western at its word, filming what America's stories told but were afraid, really, to show. That *A Fistful of Dollars* derives from Akira Kurosawa's *Yojimbo,* and that the spaghetti-western cycle as a whole bounced off of the phenomenal international success of *The Magnificent Seven* (derived from Kurosawa's *The Seven Samurai*), cannot lessen the impact of an Italian's revitalization of an American form. Sixties moviegoing shattered the notion of "the movies" as an almost entirely American product made for Americans. In the 1950s, *The Seventh Seal* and *La Strada* were "cinema," art film. But in the 1960s, *8½* was a movie; because everybody saw it. It wasn't that the intellectuals had taken up pop culture. It was that the whole country would go to art.

For all his distributors' fears that a truly Italian western wasn't quite a western, Leone didn't need Eastwood, Van Cleef, or Wallach to give his work ethnic credentials. (Anyway, none of them was a star when Leone hired them. Eastwood became a star in these very films, Van Cleef's movie career was moribund when Leone caught up with him, and Wallach was a stage actor who dabbled in film.) Leone himself gave the western credentials. He found in it a spiritual magnificence—and an intimacy— that even Ford had missed.

His details are bold—coyly Brechtian pastel rubrics flash on the screen in *The Good, the Bad, and the Ugly* as each of the title characters appears to tell us what he is, what role he will play. Of course Eastwood is The Good. Better, he's impassive. Everyone functions around him. Van Cleef is so much The Bad that he's neat and trim—always a worrisome sign in Leone. (How could anyone decent look trim in a mess like the frontier? The fair-minded have been blazing trails, not getting manicures.) But then Wallach is The Ugly because he's such an irritatingly *garrulous* mess. Leone loves Wallach's droll fatalism, however. A wronged man accosts Wallach in his bath, holds him at bay with a gun, gloats and moralizes. Suddenly Wallach shoots him from under the waterline—and tells the corpse, "When you goin' to shoot, don't talk. *Shoot!*" Later, an officer of the Northern side is taking Wallach to justice on a chain. Wallach jumps the train, pulling the officer with him, and, to free himself, lies next to the track so an oncoming train can cut through

Clint Eastwood without Sergio Leone. Suddenly he's neat
and trim, fit for a sock hop, in *Hang 'em High*.

the chains. The officer? He's lying in the trackbed, ready to turn into
. . . spaghetti.

It was the public more than the critics who made Leone a High
Maestro. His highbrow pop delighted the public while it fascinated the
intelligentsia. A rash of spaghetti westerns duly came over—something
like three hundred had been made from 1964 to 1968—but few had
Leone's grip and, sorry, none his genius. We appreciate Leone all the
more on viewing Ted Post's *Hang 'em High* (1968), an American attempt
to duplicate the spaghetti western. There's one paradox too many here.
The spaghetti western is already a duplicate. You can't twin a twin.

Hang 'em High is like any old American western. It has Clint Eastwood, the survivor of a lynching out to kill the seven men who strung
him up. Leone might have used the plot. And *Hang 'em High* has a touch
of Morricone, and a suggestion of Leone's wild-flying camera. But it's an
American film, a movie-star movie. It isn't willing to do what Leone

does. Just look at how Eastwood is groomed. He doesn't seem a mythic figure anymore, just a clean-cut western hero. The landscape, very Southern California, lacks the oppressive emptiness, the erupting dirt clouds and mangy greenery of the Spain that Leone used for his West. The plotting is direct-line-to-Hollywood: people speak their intentions, then carry them out. Yet ambiguous motivation is one of Leone's most telling observations, his main point of contact with the real world. Worst of all, *Hang 'em High* is rooted in traditional Hollywood morality, lawmen versus criminals—at its widest, a lynching judge (Pat Hingle, that essential Bad Father again) against a conflicted deputy (Eastwood). We're back to square one, to the unworldly, the *unwesternly* western, as if Leone had never existed.

On the contrary. Leone is one of the 1960s eminences, the High Maestro who remains *persona grata* on the weekend VCR circuit—the three *Dollar* westerns stand among the most popular "repeat" items in the repertory, the simple pleasure of the consumer and the elite discovery, and rediscovery, of the intellectual.

It was the 1960s that distinguished the separate movie publics, the *Hustler-* and *Children's Hour*–goers from the *Longest Day* people, the Cleopatrans from the Psychos. Yet it was the 1960s that increasingly harmonized them. It was an age of movies, because so much of the medium's history was being made in so brief a period—but also because American film was working harder than ever before to reflect a sense of the times. This, too, drew writers to film; it gave them the satisfaction of addressing multitudes on matters of consequence. However, taking in movies with such a sense of purpose tended to alienate writers from anything they couldn't use, anything that lacked the socializing, remoralizing spirit of New Cinema. And it must be said that once the art has crossed forbidden borders—over into, say, *The Manchurian Candidate* or *In Cold Blood*—it is hard to tolerate the innocuous.

At that, much of Hollywood's innocuous output had vanished, commercially exhausted or forced into retirement by dangerous competition. The woman's movie and the Saturday-matinée western, staples of the Studio Age, had simply died of old age. Died out, even: whole traditions were becoming extinct. The musical survived, but mainly in the form it had begun assuming in the 1950s, as faithful transcriptions of Broadway hits, especially—in the wake of the tremendous success of *My Fair Lady* (1964), the Hollywood original *Mary Poppins* (1964), and, particularly,

The Sound of Music (1965)—as Big Film, starry, expensive, and ubiquitous. By the late 1960s, everywhere one turned there was some vast musical playing a major theatre on a hard-ticket basis, complete with intermission, as if it were a play.

Most of the big musicals *were* plays. The practice of made-in-Hollywood song-and-dance had collapsed along with the studios, for most of them were put together by teams of experts, like ships in a shipyard. The Astaire-Rogers RKOs, the Warner Brothers backstagers, the Fox Betty Grable series, and the Freed Unit vehicles for Judy Garland, Gene Kelly, and Fred Astaire all flowered in the workshop environment. When the workshop closed down, so did the musical. There remained Elvis, but his were not great films. Richard Lester's two Beatles pieces came from England, and anyway were less musicals than zany comedies punctuated by songs. So the big studios, hoping to turn out more *Sounds of Music,* filmed a slew of Broadway shows.

Intellectuals find the musical vexing. First of all, it is generically based on the exploration of attitudes that many professional sophisticates can't get along with, such as innocence and the building of self-confidence. Why is everyone in a musical so *happy* all the time? Second, the musical has always been somewhat fantastical, naturalistically unreal. As one friend of mine explains it, "Just when you're getting into the story, they start singing." The musical isn't normalized, even for a movie—and it is, after all, a fundamentally *theatrical* form. It exists outside of time, even in Warner Brothers' politically aware Depression musicals, even when sixties directors amplified the fantasy with some earthy sensuality—Joshua Logan's orgiastic view of "The Merry Month of May," in *Camelot* (1967), or Francis Ford Coppola's oozingly erotic "Old Devil Moon," in *Finian's Rainbow* (1968). Third, there's all that singing and dancing. Not every critic has an ear for music or an eye for dance, and the ones who don't feel intimidated and defensive. They dismiss what they can't comprehend. Note that it took a *dance* critic (and an active theatregoer), Arlene Croce, to intellectualize Fred Astaire and Ginger Rogers—to make them, in fact, inviolable.

How many movie critics are on sure ground in this arena? When Renata Adler says that Julia Foster, the heroine of *Half a Sixpence* (1968), "looks like a girl who dreamed that she starred in a musical," the critic has caught exactly the performer's ability to suggest a chaste, somewhat narrow-minded young woman undergoing the musical's typical apotheosis of love through self-realization. But is Adler praising the casting or re-proving it? Is she musing upon this idyll or denouncing it?

Then, too, critics were navigating auteuristically by the late 1960s, and weren't quite certain where the director fit into the construction of a musical. Who films the songs, the dances? When we parse the Astaire and Rogers series, we don't think of directors Mark Sandrich or George Stevens as essential. It's the choreography (by Astaire, with Dave Gould and then Hermes Pan laying out the ensembles) that we count on, and the two stars' personalities, and the Kern or Berlin or Gershwin scores, or the RKO look, or even those blithering queens Edward Everett Horton and Eric Blore. George Cukor directed the film of *My Fair Lady,* but it seems much more like the Broadway *My Fair Lady* than like *Dinner at Eight, David Copperfield, The Women, The Philadelphia Story, A Star Is Born, Les Girls,* or any other Cukor film. So how does one speak of George Cukor's *My Fair Lady?*

How does one speak of *My Fair Lady* at all? It dates from 1956—and *Finian's Rainbow* was staged in 1947. Even given that *Finian's* anti-racist theme was still apropos in 1968, these projects weren't sixties enough to bear much discussion. Their music especially was out of synch with the age of rock. They might have served as solid family entertain-ment, but most of them did less well than they were supposed to, sug-gesting that the family market was closing down. Family moviegoing was for the 1950s, for *Cinerama* and *Ben-Hur.* In the divisive 1960s, kids and parents chose their movies separately.

True, there was that blockbuster *The Sound of Music,* one of the most profitable films ever made, a sound of money that surely, *surely* promised a lucrative cycle of adaptations of hit shows. But if *Camelot* can't draw with Richard Harris, Vanessa Redgrave, Franco Nero, and David Hem-mings, all highly contemporary names—with Redgrave, Hemmings, and the geography, you have half of *Blowup*—something is lacking in the notion of a family market. In the event, not all that many grown-ups made the visit, and the relative failure of Big Family Musicals like *Camelot* helped make a PG mentality routine in moguls' schedules. And musicals by their nature aren't PG material.

In fact, the 1960s saw the death of the Hollywood musical. Oathed to what had suddenly become the music of the past—Tin Pan Alley and the Broadway masters—and short of the enduring song-and-dance stars comparable to Astaire or Grable, the musical not only failed to advance upon or even recoup the insistently huge production costs it had instituted but often failed to please its devotees. The movie musical had lost its originality, its surprise, its uniqueness. Granted, many of the great series musicals of the past were formally organized genre pieces. Now, *42nd Street* was original. But *Gold Diggers of 1933, Dames, Footlight Parade,* and the other *42nd Street* retreads obviously were not. Nor could there be much genuine surprise running through the Astaire-and-Rogers or Grable films, since most of them were in a loose sense remakes. But they did abound in delight and charm, two qualities the 1960s generally could not seem to use. They were ingenious, too, in the way they discovered novelties within the fixed structure, as in Astaire's dances *over* Rogers in *Top Hat* ("I've appointed myself her official sandman"), with sailors in military drill in *Follow the Fleet,* in blackface in *Swing Time,* and with Rogers on roller skates in *Shall We Dance*; or in Busby Berkeley's big numbers, extravagant puns on Harry Warren and Al Dubin's songs (as in the rendition of the battle of the sexes literally as battle, in "All's Fair in Love and War" in *Gold Diggers of 1937*); or in the use of picturesque sidekicks to elate Grable's adventures.

With sixties musicals so dependent on Broadway hits, the movie theatre turned into a kind of museum. This did not deter audiences from, uh, screening *West Side Story, My Fair Lady,* and *The Sound of Music.* And no doubt it was convenient, for those not handy to Broadway or the big-city touring circuit, to take in *How to Succeed in Business Without Really Trying* (1967) in a duplicate of the original staging, right down to the casting of the minor parts, or to enjoy an elaborate opening up of the English show *Half a Sixpence* that retained the original's naïveté while giving the public the spectacular dimensions of design and choreography it expected of the Big Musical. Nevertheless, given the experimental mind of the films that were trying to define the era—*Dr. Strangelove,* say, or *Bonnie and Clyde*—the musical, by not adapting, was making itself superfluous, like *The Greatest Story Ever Told* the kind of thing you didn't expect to be seeing in a couple of years. These just weren't great stories, these musicals. And even when the scores were great, they were often sung by actors or dubbing studio ringers, like *Camelot.* Here was a fifteen-million-dollar production of a Broadway and West End smash; going to it was a little like ratifying a business deal. Jack Warner bags the property, tells his team to shoot the works, and everyone is supposed to see it because an event has been placed on their calendars. Or they go to *Funny Girl* (1968) because Barbra Streisand threatens to be the next big star.

On the other hand, hadn't sixties moviegoers come to mistrust events? How many *Cleopatra*s were they going to attend? The 1960s liked the unexpected, the stimulating. The intelligent spectator, supported by the critics, didn't accept his events as assignments by the industry; he or she liked to decide what was an event, learn by doing. Bosley Crowther didn't like the unexpected and resented the stimulating; look what happened to him. However fine the various Big Broadway Musical Movies may have been, they couldn't be events because they had already happened on stage. *Funny Girl,* in fact, made a dandy film, with an antic roller-skating number (deliciously wrecked by Streisand) that the original hadn't thought of and a marvelous "chase" version of "Don't Rain on My Parade," with Streisand charging after Omar Sharif on a tugboat in New York Harbor to close the first half of the road show on a very cinematic note. But *Funny Girl* didn't need to be a film the way that *Top Hat* or *Dames* or *The Wizard of Oz* or *Meet Me in St. Louis* did. Show us something new.

Thoroughly Modern Millie (1967) was the best the Big Musical could come up with as an original, at that with but two new songs (by James Van Heuṣen and Sammy Cahn) leading off a medley of old favorites like "Poor Butterfly" and "Baby Face." George Roy Hill directed, Joe Layton staged the dance numbers, and Richard Morris wrote the screenplay, but the auteur was whoever at Universal decided to do a twenties musical with Julie Andrews. The plot, mildly similar to that of the 1959 London show *Chrysanthemum,* comically treats the Chinatown enslaving of helpless young women, and the cast comes up rather a miscellany—Andrews, the 1960s' indicated empress of musical comedy, as Millie the "modern" (that is, the new style of independent woman—"Goodbye," Andrews exults in the title song, "good-goody girl!"); Mary Tyler Moore, from television, as an heiress so sheltered she pays for everything by check, even cab rides; John Gavin, a Universal contractee, as Moore's flame; James Fox, a *jeune premier* of New Cinema (in *The Servant* and *King Rat*), as Andrews's flame; Carol Channing, from Broadway, as a madcap socialite; and Beatrice Lillie, on hand as a sort of living show-biz legend to play the slaver and do Chinese shtick.

It's a stylish presentation, establishing a mock-antique feeling with iris outs, silent-movie thrill music here and there, title cards verbalizing

Andrews's mimed asides to the public, a Harold Lloyd–like tussle on the side of a skyscraper for Andrews and Fox, and the spoof treatment of Gavin's strongheart hero, handsome and stalwart and totally useless in a crisis. The film did well commercially. Still, viewing it today, we don't connect it with the 1960s, except for the implied feminism of Andrews's resourceful heroine—though this, too, is antiquing, an *hommage* to the serial heroines of the 1910s, who not only saved the day but their feckless boyfriends as well. *Millie* was entertaining enough but hardly modern, and that was the critics' problem: why did it have to be made?

Even the old-time, sure-thing genres found they had lost their audience—the musical bio, for instance. The form flowered in the 1940s, favoring the lives of Broadway composers because these would come with a catalogue of standards (one of them providing the title) ready to draw on: telling the George M. Cohan story, naturally you'd sing a great deal of Cohan. Jerome Kern, Cole Porter, Rodgers and Hart, and the Gershwins equipped similar outings. Running out of hot names, the studios reached Bert Kalmar and Harry Ruby (in *Three Little Words*), Gus Kahn (*I'll See You in My Dreams*), Sigmund Romberg (*Deep in My Heart*), and De Sylva, Brown, and Henderson (*The Best Things in Life Are Free*) before packing it in, thereby sparing us life-and-music sagas of Herbert Stothart, Silvio Hein, and the Lerner and Loewe of the 1910s, Pixley and Luders. (A ditty from their *The Prince of Pilsen* would have made a nice title, though: "Pictures in the Smoke.") The fifties bios preferred performers— Eddie Cantor, Blossom Seeley, Eddie Foy, Helen Morgan—and it must have seemed like a brainstorm when someone suggested that Julie Andrews take on the life of Gertrude Lawrence. Here you'd have the era's sole no-fail musical star (not counting Elvis, who didn't do Big Musicals) playing one of the great show-biz legends and singing Gershwin, Porter, Noël Coward, Kurt Weill, British music-hall, and "Limehouse Blues," not to mention another Van Heusen–Cahn title tune. This, of course, is *Star!* (1968), the bomb that more or less deposed Queen Julie and greatly hastened the end of the musical in general.

Perhaps *Star!* looked so bad because it followed so hard upon the epidemic success of *The Sound of Music*: same studio (Fox), same star, same director (Robert Wise), same art director (Boris Leven), same screen contour (Todd-AO). Perhaps *Star!* did so poorly because it was windy and putrid, interminably biographic yet never telling us anything we didn't already know about what show business means to people like Lawrence.

The songs are great and Andrews sings the hell out of them; the album is better than the film. But perhaps *Star!* did not persuade because Andrews is drastically miscast. A more authentic Lawrence bio might have been called *The Lady Is a Tramp*; Andrews is too classy, too reasonable, too nice. Worse yet, she is forced to carry the film almost *sola,* and, except for Daniel Massey's Noël and parents Bruce Forsyth and Beryl Reid in the early vaudeville scenes, she lacks vital support. Yet the bio used to be a cinch—and, the same year as *Star!*, *Funny Girl* proved that the bio still had a public. But *Funny Girl* has grip. It has drive, humor, talent, and passion, while *Star!* hasn't even a story. At twelve million dollars and nearly three hours, it played hard-ticket to empty houses, and a two-hour five-shows-a-day recutting, re-titled *Those Were the Happy Times,* drew even less well. Again, why was this movie made at all? And why were so many musicals about olden days and bygone ways of doing things? "Someone to Watch Over Me" and "Parisian Pierrot" and "Someday I'll Find You"— couldn't the musical accommodate the contemporary?

There was one attempt to contrive an up-to-date Big Musical—up-to-date in attitude rather than setting, and drawn from a Broadway title that dates back to 1951, Lerner and Loewe's *Paint Your Wagon* (1969). Fifties adaptations of Broadway shows made a point of bowdlerizing them—*Kiss Me, Kate, Kismet, Pal Joey. Paint Your Wagon* went out of its way to infuse a relatively innocent original with ribald situations. Lerner, who wrote the screenplay ("adapted" by Paddy Chayefsky, as the credits explain it), threw out his original story, on the doings of father, daughter, and her Mexican suitor in a California gold-rush town, keeping only the setting and eight songs. (Five new ones, by Lerner and André Previn, were added.) Now the tale concerned two friends whose relationship is challenged when one of them buys a wife from a Mormon,* and the three leads are those great song-and-dance talents, Lee Marvin, Clint Eastwood, and Jean Seberg. *Camelot* was opera compared with this.

All right, let's call it crossover casting. But it is somewhat illustrative of the decline of the Hollywood musical that seventeen million dollars'

---

*This was one of the few bits Lerner retained from the stage show, though it was originally more of a picturesque vignette than a crucial plot point. The only other surviving elements I can spot are the discovery of gold during a burial, with the speaker staking his claim during his eulogy, and the foreign lyrics to one section of "I'm on My Way," though, instead of the single Chinese verse heard on Broadway, the film raises up a veritable U.N. cantata.

Problems of the Sixties Musical. For one thing, they lacked voice (Lee Marvin and Jean Seberg in *Paint Your Wagon,* above). For another, they were too Broadway, heavy and painted (Carol Channing, opposite top left, reviving Marion Harris's 78 hit "Jazz Baby" in *Thoroughly Modern Millie*). Or the productions were overly elaborated (Walter Matthau and Barbra Streisand, opposite top right, in a rare intimate interlude in the overwhelming Fourteenth Street parade in *Hello, Dolly!*). Worst, the films were great but no one wanted to see them (Shirley MacLaine leads the corps in "I'm a Brass Band" in *Sweet Charity*).

worth of Oregon scenery and star salaries and director Joshua Logan's Beethoven's Ninth pacing doesn't contain, somewhere, *somehow,* a genuine musical voice. Worried, we scan the supporting cast to see if someone can carry a tune—Ray Walston, Tom Ligon, William O'Connell, Alan Dexter. What, Franco Nero wasn't available? We do get Harve Presnell in two numbers, but as his character isn't strongly connected to the plot, it doesn't help much. It's a little *too* somehow. Besides, Presnell seems alien in this company. When his lusty baritone rips into "They Call the Wind Maria," we become disoriented. We thought this was an all-talking, no-singing musical. Who let this guy in?

Yes, you can dub. They dubbed Natalie Wood, Richard Beymer, and Rita Moreno in *West Side Story,* Rosalind Russell in *Gypsy,* Audrey Hepburn and Jeremy Brett in *My Fair Lady,* Christopher Plummer and Peggy Wood in *The Sound of Music,* and of course *Camelot's* Franco Nero, the Jeanne Crain of the 1960s. But some actors aren't just non-singers; something in their personality resists music. Clint Eastwood's "I Still See Elisa" and "I Talk to the Trees," partly shot in extreme close-up, don't come off because the voice is pleasant but light, fragile, unformed. It sounds like Eastwood, but it doesn't give us the noise we expect his personality to raise. Dubious, we keep checking out Eastwood's synching technique. He handles it well, but he can't fool us because we know that Sergio Leone's Man with No Name has no music in him.

Marvin almost pulls it off (in his own voice), because he treats less lyrical material. His first number, "The Gospel of No Name City," is virtually rap, and "Wand'rin' Star" (sung on Broadway by James Barton, no Shalyapin himself) rolls out in a low, pensive growl that rather pleases. To his shock, Marvin got a hit single out of it.

To our shock, this all-basic sixties monster hero is, at the very height of the decade, re-endowed with humor and honor and even kindness. True, he's a rascal. He freely admits that he has broken all the Commandments—but he never cheated a partner. And Eastwood is an out-and-out good guy, moral and sweet. Even the difficulties of sharing one woman don't destroy the two men's relationship. The troublesome people in *Paint Your Wagon* are the righteous—the pioneer bourgeois families and the preacher who try to convert No Name City from a licentious but congenial outpost into a bastion of hypocritical civilization.

Here is the 1960s—the angry goons of the received pieties making war on what amounts to a primordial hippie commune. It is the preacher's haranguing that precipitates the apocalyptic climax in which No Name City collapses—buildings, people, and animals sinking into mud for a comic disaster finish. This, of course, is the "overproduction" that critics continually decried about the Big Musical; and the gala parade on a studio mock-up of Litle Old New York's Fourteenth Street in *Hello, Dolly!* (1969) was denounced as if the reviewers were being personally billed for it. Isn't it one of the movie musical's charms that it can show us what no stage production can?

It's doubtful that even enthusiastic critics would have helped the Big Musical hold its place in the era. There simply wasn't public enough to amortize these films' negative cost, distribution and publicity expenses, and the interest on the capital investment from contract signing to first royalty statement. The Big Musicals didn't flop, exactly—*Paint Your Wagon* took in the sixth highest receipts in Paramount's history to that time. But it turned out that there weren't any more *Sounds of Music* to make. The blockbuster musical was out of reach. The form itself had grown too Big for its public, and too tame. Moviegoers didn't want Lee Marvin creditably getting through "Wand'rin' Star." That's a party turn, not a musical. A musical is Astaire and Garland doing "A Couple of Swells." But that was over.

It must be said that the climate of opinion shaped by the critics made the musical generally unwelcome. Renata Adler, Bosley Crowther's successor at the *New York Times,* covered *Funny Girl* in a scandalously brief column and an unconcerned manner, as if implying that not only this film but all films of its kind were unworthy of intent discussion. Reading Adler, the younger moviegoer, raised on rock, would have no reason to investigate the more searching noises raised by Broadway composers like *Funny Girl*'s Jule Styne. That music, its singers, and this film were thus declared passé. As Adler noted, even the stardom that Broadway had represented to four decades of Hollywood musicals was finished. Streisand was one of the last really big musical stars to rise on Broadway: "There is something, too," Adler wrote, "about the poignance of a particular kind of ambition that is dated and almost nostalgic now."

The intellectualization of the movies partly encouraged the average intelligent person's distaste for certain traditional forms and enthusiasm for certain innovative ones, but also simply reflected the American moviegoer's casual loss of interest in some forms and discovery of others. The transaction really involved the movies and the moviegoer—but it appeared to involve the movies and the critics because New Cinema demanded New Critics to referee a dialogue between the art and its spectators. The reviews of the more discerning critics were like position papers for the culture, illuminating *8½,* moralizing *Blowup,* politicizing *Bonnie and Clyde.* This was what showed, what the buffs quoted, what the studios reckoned on. Perhaps never in American history was an art *and* its criticism so closely united with its audience.

Eight

Sex and Snuff

With freedom came excess; that is, to protect the artistic civil rights of *Psycho* and *Lolita,* we tolerate *Vixen!* and *Blood Feast.* The exploitation film is another of the 1960s' bequests to descendant generations, for there had been nothing like it before about 1966. Cheap and sensationalistic, exploitation purports to treat a theme of the day with some abandon—as *Wild in the Streets* treats the generation war or the so-called "blaxploitation" films of the early 1970s treated black power. In fact, exploitation deals less with the stated theme than with the public's direst wish-fulfillment or nightmare fantasies. Thus, *Wild in the Streets* isn't about the realities of a rejuvenated America, but the totalistic intolerance of teenage culture; the blaxploitation thrillers enthralled blacks and terrorized whites. Porn is, of course, an exploitation genre, as are horror films and, I think, the cartoon. Where the established social structure is meant to curb our Dionysian instincts for fear and delight, the exploitation film releases them.

We find a few instances of this ruthless art in the past—the notorious *Reefer Madness* (1936), on how puffs of marijuana drive you insane; or *City of Missing Girls* (1945), an exposé of the talent schools ("It's sensationally intimate," the posters whispered, "and boldly different!"); or, to an extent, the *I Led Three Lives* "Red" cycle of the early 1950s (though these were temperate because, unlike true exploitation films, they wanted society's approval rather than its guilty exhilaration). In all, the form didn't really create itself until the 1960s, because the decade offered two things exploitation needed in order to thrive—a strong economic base for the independent B film and a quiescent censorship. The 1950s prepared the advance: the withering away of the old studios left room for the underfinanced independent, and the censors were wearing down after losing too many battles.

Naturally, sex and violence were the elect points of exploitation; and why not, when the major directors supported by the big studio logos were making so free of blood and flesh as it was? *Cool Hand Luke* includes a scene in which the chain-gang prisoners watch a woman wash a car—not just a woman but the intensely enticing Joy Harmon, and not just watching but transfixed, the episode played as Harmon's deliberate teasing of the men. One shot shows her breasts rubbing soap on a car window. Then why shouldn't Terry Southern and Mason Hoffenberg's novel *Candy* (1968) be filmed, though it ends up as a chain of burlesque sketches in which various celebrities of the day—Richard Burton, Ringo Starr, Marlon Brando, Walter Matthau, James Coburn, and Charles Aznavour—seduce the unbearably willing Ewa Aulin?

Candy bombed. Perhaps the hot-sheets public, still gathering in preparation for the explosion of porn in the 1970s, resented the infusion of pop stars into what is best limited to pseudonymous players. Something like Russ Meyer's *Vixen!* (1968) was more to their taste, because it got right to the sex of the matter and avoided *Candy*'s occasional attempts to define its time and place with satire. Or possibly because Meyer's films, this one especially, cater to men's fantasy of women as unreasonable, vicious, and profoundly, undelimitedly sexual, coming on to nearly everyone who crosses their path, including blood relatives and the occasional other woman. As a sixties heroine, really a heroine of the X-rated movie scene, Vixen is a true pornucopia. But liberation has its price: caricature. With her emphatic eyebrows, flashy tongue, angry teeth, and superb figure—mature and Junoesque, as opposed to the tight-waisted *bébé* of *Candy*; not to mention Vixen's aggressive approach, more vital than Candy's adorably passive availability—Erica Gavin is the heterosexual man's bitter dream of womankind, desirable, faithless, and a castrater.

Vixen is a racist, too, in the film's bizarre attempt at a plot. The setting is southwestern Canada, where Vixen's husband runs a bush-league airline. After a series of sexual encounters, we're ready for some story, involving an American black man fleeing the draft and an Irish Communist with a ludicrous red beard who is planning to hijack the cast to Cuba. Everyone's down on the black man because everyone's a bigot. Vixen, at first, is the worst of them. But at a climactic moment the Communist arrogantly tells the black to shut up and the black, sensitive to racial nuance, senses that the sentence was unfinished. "Shut up, what?" he asks. "Shut up, *what?*" And the Communist obliges with "Shut up, NIGGER!"—which convinces the black that our own racists are better than hypocritical foreign lefty racists and precipitates a struggle for control of the plane, and our side wins.

This absurdly unadministered course in sex and politics—Gender Relations in the Age of Vietnam 101—would be a camp favorite if it had been in any way facetious, knowing, insouciant, Warholian. It would be A Famous Sixties Thing. But the Meyer "sexploitation" films (the preporn term for porn) were apparently on the level, not an attempt to forge a unique style out of elements of sleaze and spoof but a piece of very sexy, very stupid junk. As Winston Churchill once said of a pudding that didn't come off, it lacks a theme. Is *Vixen!* a cynical brand X hiding behind a fake piece of redeeming social value, or right-wing porn? Is *Vixen!* liberated in one way but not in another for a reason, or did a black man and a guy with a red beard happen onto the set just when a plane became available? Is *Vixen!*'s compounded "all partners are equal" sexuality meant to tease or enlighten us, or to found a handy convention for future porn idylls? What is the film saying?

This is a problem in assessing the B film in general but particularly the exploitative B: the movies are often so carelessly made that we aren't sure that the results reflect the intentions. *The Gay Deceivers* (1969) follows two young men (Kevin Coughlin and Lawrence Casey) who pose as gays to dodge the draft. It's a workable premise, twice timely: the draft was on every young man's mind, and the Stonewall Bar riots occurred just three months before *The Gay Deceivers* was released. The development is a bit farfetched, however. The draft-board colonel (Jack Starrett) whom the boys lied to turns out to be following them, presumably to check their story. Suddenly, Coughlin and Casey have to adopt a gay life-style— and not the chilled-out smooth of the clone but the ruthless fire of the queen, everything in pink and all their friends ravers.

There's the makings of sharp satire here—or, at least, an enjoyable farce—especially when Coughlin's parents take their look in; and Michael Greer, the then reigning divo of queen roles, brightens the otherwise typical B casting of goofs and ne'er-do-wells. So does a cinema vérité–like costume revel at Greer's apartment, a you-asked-for-it collection of the gay world's geeks and freaks, quite an advance on *Advise and Consent*'s oh so dignified after-hours bar. But Bruce Kessler's direction is so confused we never get a take on what is happening in the story. There's something odd in the linking of Coughlin as a nice middle-class boy and Casey as a debauched drifter. Isn't that a bit too E. M. Forster, a little too toff-and-trade for a modern American comedy set—of course—in California? This film is loaded with such contradictions, as when Coughlin's suspicious sister lures Casey into bed and Casey can't get it up, or when Casey storms away to drink off a sulk and ends up in a gay bar.

What is the film saying? Coughlin and Casey ultimately decide it's better to risk death in the jungles of Vietnam than defame their sense of manhood. But now the Army doesn't want them. They've been too persuasive, it would seem. At the fade-out, Kessler rests his view upon Colonel Starrett. "That's my job, Joe," he tells his assistant, "to weed out the undesirables." Now he's stroking Joe's ear. These two men are lovers! Whose side are we on?

"We don't want their kind in the Army," says the colonel, "do we, Joe?"

I want Vixen in the Army, because you know where she stands. She fucks everything. Who *are* the gay deceivers—Coughlin and Casey, the colonel and his Joe, or the people who made this movie? You thought you knew what exploitation entailed—sensory overloads on themes of the day. A lot of sex or a lot of violence, possibly both. *Zeitoper.* Instead, exploitation often appears to be simply inept film.

This is intrinsic in the concept of a B movie: the least able moviemakers are in charge of the operation. Or, rather, that had been true to about 1960 and the appearance of Roger Corman's *The Little Shop of Horrors.* In the primitive years of American film, to about 1910, everything was a B—quick and silly and cheap. As the big studios began to form—Universal, Paramount, Fox, Goldwyn, Metro, First National, Warner Brothers—the B became the cheapest film a major studio would release, or anything that came out of a small studio like Columbia or Monogram. They were cheap not only because little time, money, and talent was spent on them but because they fell into the ruts of genre, artistically cheap. They were the ground zero of business-as-usual, westerns or gangster shoot-'em-ups or a jungle-hero series so tied to cliché they virtually made themselves.

The insurgence of the independent production in the 1950s recreated the B movie. A B movie would still be quick and cheap, but it might also be something unusual, even artistic—isn't *The Night of the Hunter* (1955), by budget, style, and cast (Robert Mitchum, Shelley Winters, Lillian Gish, all unhot at the time; and Charles Laughton was the director, his only such credit in film), one of the purest B's ever made, and one of the great American films?

Then came Corman, and many other less well known dependents, often simply enthusiasts of the cinema who somehow got access to a camera, stock, a lab, and a bit of money and pulled it off. Like, say, George Romero, who made *Night of the Living Dead* (1968) in the outback of Pittsburgh using little more than a graveyard, a house, Carnegie Tech acting majors, and animal intestines provided by one of Romero's investors, a meat-packer. If *Vixen!* and *The Gay Deceivers* are exploitation films for the sexually prurient, *Night of the Living Dead* exploits violence. Or is it exploitative? Radioactivity has brought corpses to life,* intent on eating the rest of us. A platoon of the dead besieges a house of seven mortals; one man survives. As he greets the morning sun of the reprieved, the day of the living, zombie killers cleaning up the area take him for a ghoul and shoot him dead.

Obviously, there is rich potential for exploitative horror, and Romero does not stint himself, especially in the central set piece in which the mortals attempt a kind of jail break, and the ghouls tear two of them apart and feast, graphically and noisily, on the meat-packer's props. But there is as well the certain sense that a master is unfolding the tale, drawing the pictures, prompting the conclusions. *Living Dead* enthusiasts time the film's initiation point from a single shot in the film's third or fourth minute, very early for a horror movie to engage the imagination. A brother and sister visit a cemetery to pay respect to their father's remains. The brother teases the sister: "They're coming to get you, Barbara," he coos. And way in the distance, an old man—a father—can be

---

*In Romero's conception, there was no official explanation for the resurrection, but rather three theories. Two were cut from the release print, leaving the radiation story exegetic by default.

seen, staggering through the countryside. This is Romero's first ghoul, coming to get you.

The old man kills the brother and chases the sister; her flight, down a hill in a car and then on foot to the fatal house, sets the action into motion and it never pauses thereafter. And be it said that, just to even out the metaphors, when the ghouls finally clomp into the house, ravening and moaning, the creature who draws Barbara into their midst is her brother, his eyes hot on ice, as if, unlike the other ghouls, he actually knows what he's doing.

Many critics have pointed out that *Night of the Living Dead,* made in the fall of 1968, followed hard upon the worst year of violence in modern American history—the assassination of Martin Luther King, Jr., in April, succeeded by ghetto riots in a hundred and twenty-five cities, the assassination of Robert Kennedy in June, the troubles at Columbia University that same month, and the police riot during the Democratic Convention in Chicago, not to mention the Vietnam War, which entered a new phase in January of 1968, when the Vietcong mounted the Tet offensive, which lasted into spring in the siege of Khe Sanh and the occupation of and prolonged battle for Hue. Much of this was symptomatic of America's miserable race relations and the ultra-sixties generation war, but the received intelligence suggested a society breaking down in waves of hatred and murder, apparently in partisan clashes but possibly, at heart, in a barbarian free-for-all.

This is precisely what Romero shows us, in a miniature of a land gobbling itself up, and in a relatively symbolic group of mortals, a middle-aged couple and their little girl, a teenaged couple, the sister Barbara, and a black loner: parents and children, whites and black, sheep and a leader, the valiant and the awkward. We even get a picture of youth assaulting authority, so fundamental to sixties culture, when the little girl, turned ghoul, attacks her mother with a garden spade. Yet Romero says he had nothing in mind but a thriller, that the casting of black Duane Jones as the film's hero and martyr was a field expedient—that Jones was the best actor Romero could find. Given the presumably limited Pittsburgh acting pool (and the amateurish performances of the other men in the cast), this is undoubtedly true. Still, *Night of the Living Dead* seems an axiomatic sixties entry, not an artistically inductive film like *Splendor in the Grass* or *The Hustler* but a politically climactic film, one best appreciated in the aftermath. It was, in fact, seen only sporadically at first, not truly enjoyed till its cult began to gather in the early 1970s, when it became one of the first titles to popularize the "midnight screening."

A slew of *Living Dead* sequels of debased artistry has compromised the original's reputation, coarsened it with the dreary routine of the old B lots like Monogram—which only adds to the confusion over where the independent production ends and sheer exploitation begins. Then, too, *Night of the Living Dead* arrived when the king of goremasters, Herschell Gordon Lewis, was at his height: *Blood Feast* (1963), *Two Thousand Maniacs!* (1964), *Color Me Blood Red* (1965), *A Taste of Blood* (1967), *The Gruesome Twosome* (1967), and *She Devils on Wheels* (1968) pioneered exploitative violence in movies that dote on their own outrageousness. The scripts are inane, the acting thuggish, the verisimilitude halfhearted— yet we are never sure whether Lewis simply couldn't do better or whether, like Corman, he was using his limitations stylistically. When Jack Nicholson camps and parties as the masochistic dental patient in Corman's *The Little Shop of Horrors,* we know that he is bending sharp actor instincts into the movie's overall air of obtuse lunacy. The sci-fi premise of the man-eating plant from outer space impels not only the plot but the performers' orientation. Nicholson is as alien, and as silly, as the plant. But Lewis's gang are truculent gasbags. Is this a pose, a cheat, or Lewis's idea of acting?

It was the drive-in audience's idea of fun, and bluenoses were unable to censor Lewis, eager though they were to do so, because censorship legislation was founded on fear of sexual honesty, not of bloodletting. In Catholic countries, the swearwords are blasphemies; in puritan countries, the swearwords are scatological or sexual. American movie censorship was equipped to black out language and flesh, but lacked the apparatus to treat a grotesquerie of gore. And would not Lewis—when advertising "The worst film ever made!"—warn his public, "Shield your eyes!" and "Don't bring the kids!"?

A new age needs new weapons of restraint, and by 1969 even drive-ins, Lewis's haunt of choice, were closed to him. He tried to ease up, but Lewis curbed wasn't Lewis. Said he himself, "The gorehounds would be disappointed." And who would attend Lewis's art but a gorehound? Lewis abandoned the movies for the advertising world.

So censorship had adapted to the 1960s. Realizing that the in-house suppressions of the Production Code were intolerable to post-Studio moviemaking, the Motion Picture Association of America, under its new president, Jack Valenti,* devised a ratings system as a kind of consumer guide, usually based not on the reading of scripts but on the screening of finished films, with the possibility of negotiating a rating if certain lines or scenes were cut. Introduced in 1968, the ratings ran from G (acceptable for general audiences) through PG (parental guidance suggested) and R (restricted to those eighteen or older unless accompanied by their parents) to X (no one under eighteen admitted, even if accompanied by a Presbyterian elder). Clearly, this system was preferable to the autocratic procedures of the Hays Office, when a film fell under scrutiny—and enforced revision—during production. When, in fact, a film that did not accept these revisions virtually couldn't be released.

Nevertheless, critics of the ratings called it a disguised censorship when a serious, artistically intent title like *Medium Cool* got an X as if it were porn, or when a likely PG got an R because of the single use of a no-no word. It was an aberrant censorship, too, in its strict view of sex and leniency toward violence. *Midnight Cowboy*'s candid view of prostitution won it an X, whereas *The Wild Bunch,* the most bloody, even sadistic film of the decade, got off with an R. Furthermore, the system could be manipulated when producers deliberately wrote in a halfway wicked scene or two to get a PG for what would have been a G film, a rating considered commercially self-destructive for anything above the maturity level of *Thoroughly Modern Millie.*

Valenti's ratings have stayed in force, with some variation, ever

---

*Valenti was not a Hollywood veteran but an outsider, at the time of his hiring a special assistant to President Lyndon Johnson. This is an old Hollywood trick: disarming the Comstocks by putting its own censorship under the direction of a presumably untainted soul, and getting the extra benefit of his contacts and influence in D.C. Similarly, when Hollywood first set up such an office, in 1922, the head man was Will Hays, a Presbyterian elder of Indiana, chief of the Republican National Committee at the time of the 1920 election, and President Warren Harding's first Postmaster General (and one of the few members of Harding's cabinet to escape indictment in the Teapot Dome and Elk Hills oil-land scandals, Harding's Watergate). Hays had to be pure; he looked like an austere rabbit. But as he began to outline his plans to reform the movies, someone asked blithe, commentative Elinor Glyn for her view from the center of Hollywood (as novelist, scenarist, sometime performer, and coiner of the term "it," meaning charisma but taken to mean sex appeal). Glyn didn't know from Postmaster Generals, but she knew Hollywood. "Whatever will bring in the most money," she said, "will happen."

since—another of the sixties innovations that have become instituted as features of American moviegoing. Whether or not the system is an effective guide for the less venturesome spectator, it does mark the end of six decades of harassment by state boards, local police action, and the movie industry itself. Even if an X can hurt a film's business (some say the X works as an attraction), or at any rate kill the participation of the important mid-teen market, the MPAA ratings solemnize the collapse of movie censorship. Interested parties can picket a film and try to run a boycott, but a director who has total control of his work (that is, including the decisive "final cut") totally controls its contents.

Another lasting effect of the ratings system was its treatment of all films as "equal," whether they were clearly of artistic, mid-cult commercial, or exploitative origin. The ratings guidelines apply no more judgmentally to Herschell Gordon Lewis than to Federico Fellini. At various times, the ratings people have been more friendly to certain applicants, perhaps, more open about the rating process. But not more partial. Because the ratings are so visible to the public, they offset the implied status of a big-studio feature as opposed to an independent entry. We still note the presence of stars, the appeal of a money production, the prestige of the High Maestro. But the class system of the Studio Age, with its big house and "poverty row" outlets, its distinct A and B films, its *Grand Hotel*–implied ratings system of major names, and its exclusionary Oscar nominations, has been overturned. It isn't always easy to know what constitutes a major production anymore, or what an alternative major production of the film we are seeing might have been like. In short, the enormous potential of the B movie affected all Hollywood, and all its public.

The rise of the B marked yet another of the sixties post-Studio breakaways. The intellectualization of the American movie tended, like the best sixties movie*makers,* to dissociate itself as much as possible from Studio Age thinking, which held that story and personal charisma were the basic—and the most intelligible—components of a "good" film. Thus the emphasis on straightforward narrative flow and a stable of familiar and beloved stars. Thus, *Gone With the Wind*: something fabulous, but nothing special—the same kind of movie everyone was making, just bigger, grander, fuller. But sixties moviemakers found that there were many ways to tell a story, and advantages in casting unknowns (as in *In*

Cold Blood or *The Graduate* or *Wild in the Streets*); and sixties critics often discovered more in an *objet trouvé* than in the latest big-cheese show, especially something like *Hotel* (1967).

This is largely because of the redevelopment of the very concept of the B film, and the foremost developer of the B was Roger Corman, an extraordinarily influential figure in sixties Hollywood. One wouldn't have thought so from his beginnings in the 1950s, as already outlined in these pages, a mash of genre and cliché and shock material and your budget is three cents and the shooting schedule is already over—*The Little Shop of Horrors*, Corman himself admitted, was made in two days and a night. This is wildcat stuff. However, necessity breeding invention, wildcat stuff can concoct its peculiar fancies. Do it enough, and it becomes a style. Succeed enough, and the style becomes coin of the realm: borrowed, *hommage*'d, imitated, stolen, banked; choose your word.

Corman's dossier is compromised by his long association with American International Pictures, a combination of Monogram and *Dracula* founded in 1954 by James Nicholson and Samuel Z. Arkoff, who once said, "I look upon my movies as being merchandise." (What Hollywood producer didn't? Except you weren't supposed to say it.) As an independent, Corman let AIP distribute most of his films till he gave up directing in the early 1970s and formed New World Pictures, his own distributing firm—curiously, an art-oriented outfit, taking in Ingmar Bergman and the Stephen Sondheim musical *A Little Night Music* (if that's not tautological) rather than *House of Usher* (1960), *The Pit and the Pendulum* (1961), or *Tales of Terror* (1962), the typical Corman feature when he was with AIP.

Starting an Edgar Allan Poe cycle in films that could be shot inside a week, built around the lugubriously Poeish Vincent Price, and placed within a standard design frame was a brainstorm. There was cultural cachet. There was a triptych of sets—the austere main hall of the mansion, the grim park, the slimy cellar—that could be used with little variation right through the series, give or take a coffin. There was a general menace of people buried alive or tortured to death that exploitation doted on.

And, to the average eye, pure exploitation is what Corman's Poe cycle seemed to be. The art direction was not only limited in scope but banal—not a creepy mansion, not a maniacal park, not a bloodcurdling cellar: just a mansion, a park, and a cellar. Simply the sight of the Bates house in *Psycho,* balefully looking down on the motel, told more story

Here's a good look at a B, in the Poe-Corman *The Raven.* Left to right, Blackie the raven, Jack Nicholson, Olive Sturgess, Hazel Court, Vincent Price.

than any of Corman's Poes entire. Nor was the acting pool helpful, with people like John Kerr and Hazel Court in Price's support. And while the advertisements were far more salaciously gruesome than the films themselves, there was nevertheless an overriding air of sadism and meanness, as if, say, Corman was ham-and-egging his way through *The Pit and the Pendulum* just for the sake of the final sequence, in which Price straps Kerr to a table and sets in motion a gigantic scythe that slowly and inexorably swings down to meet Kerr. . . .

To the more sophisticated spectator, to whom a B is cheaper but not intrinsically less worthy than an A, Corman's Poes appeared to dabble, on and off, in a new style of horror, a style as teasing as serious, a kind of self-referential put-on—something between *It Conquered the World* and *The Little Shop of Horrors,* between the drearily legitimate and the penetratingly absurd. Was the style developed specifically to frame Vincent Price's gargantuan portrayals, something like a provincial Richard III imitating Sir Henry Irving? Was the style pitched to texture Price with eclectic faux pas, to apologize for him by making his surroundings even

worse than he is? In *The Terror* (1963), apparently improvised on the sets
just used in *The Raven* (1963) because shooting ended two or three days
ahead of schedule, Corman and his team (Francis Ford Coppola, Monte
Hellman, and Jack Nicholson—possibly among others—each directed a
different segment) brought the style into its prime without Price: Boris
Karloff, subtler than Price and of course a magisterial figure of horror by
sheer rights of history, took the lead as an eighteenth-century baron obsessed with his typically Poeish dead young bride.

   The Terror is no masterpiece. Its truculent surprises and merry disdain
for period sense front for an almost total lack of plot. But that's the point.
Plot, formerly the *sine qua non* of the B, has become less interesting than
style—and Corman, by now, is rich in style. With his abundant tracking
shots, his inflamed color sense, his sly *hommages* to the masters (and to
himself), and his laissez-faire use of his players' wildly unaligned acting
habits and their English, transatlantic, and downright urban-American
accents, Corman has devised something new in horror, movies we enjoy
not to see what happens but to see *how it is done.*

   This is the High Maestro reading of the B, locked into the traditional not enough time and money and still riding the standard rolling
stock of horror, crime, sci-fi thriller, and generation-war genres, but turning the meaning of the B inside out, from storytelling to demonstration
of technique. Thus, *The Masque of the Red Death* (1964) doesn't bother to
build any narrative on the premise that satanist Vincent Price holds court
while plague rages about his castle. Who needs narrative? The film is
structured like a ballet, a series of *entrées* and *pas d'action,* farandoles,
sarabandes, and plenty of variations for the soloists. Color is strategic—
the black countryside of the dying, always in night; the scarlet cloak of
a Bergmanesque death figure; the grotesque red-brown makeup of the
plague victims; the riot of blue, white, and green of the courtiers. Price's
clock has a pendulum made in a precise miniature of the one with which
he terrorized John Kerr in the pit, and *en soirée* Price gets his sycophants
to imitate animals. "How like a pig you are," he tells a man. "Be one."
A woman is ordered to play a donkey, another man to "ride that ass to
market" for instant *dolce vita.* The camera constantly shadows the principals from semi close-up, as if not filming but staring at them. The
movie is wildly active, yet there is no action. Everything is Corman's tour
de force, his elaboration of movie stylistics into a pageant of demonstration.

Corman's motto is Reach the Ultimate, as here when Broadway's Eugene O'Neill stylist Jason Robards essays the role of Al Capone in *The St. Valentine's Day Massacre.* The still is more subtle than the entire portrayal.

Though the bulk of Corman's work through the 1960s was closely associated with AIP, he made *The St. Valentine's Day Massacre* (1967) for Twentieth Century–Fox, moving out of the world of three-day shooting schedules, seventy-five-minute running times, pawnbroker budgets, and "saturation" releases for the yahoo market. *Massacre* is 100 minutes long, somewhat carefully art-directed, and boasts a cast of actors you've heard of, led by Jason Robards as Al Capone and Ralph Meeker as Bugs Moran. This is television's *The Untouchables* without Eliot Ness, Chicago in the 1920s amid a war for total power between the Capones and the Morans. Yet Corman tackles it—big names, tall budget, and all—as if he were still shooting for AIP, guying us with the facetious gravity peculiar to the Corman style. We get the "March of Time" narrator popularized in Warner Brothers' *The Roaring Twenties,* Mark Hellinger's films, and of course *The Untouchables*—it even sounds like the same man. But there's a hint of the roguish in his tone, as if he's waiting for a chance to emend his script with bizarre annotation. The money we see is not only the fake cash Hollywood always used but extra fake, as oversized as *lire*. Robards, the master of underplaying, gives a performance so over-the-top he might have coached with Vincent Price; he actually indulges in a mad scene— in Italian!—in a succession of crazed-gangster faces, his skin pulled so taut it could be a CAT scan.

And surely Corman goes to work on the violence, makes some state- ment—or, at least, styles it for us—as a sixties interpretation of a thirties version of the 1920s, from life to Cagney-Robinson to television to Cor- man? No. For a film that came out the year of *Bonnie and Clyde, The St. Valentine's Day Massacre* is nearly bloodless. Capone does his baseball-bat number, on a pair of inadequate henchmen, but all we see is Robards advancing and the victims, unbelievably, just kneeling there. Wouldn't you run? This isn't convincing moviemaking, especially now that we've seen Martin Scorsese handle the moment with tactless opulence. And when Robards cuts an enemy throat, Corman gives us no visual, not even a scream to tell us someone was there.

In fact, the film is a little stately for Corman, till George Segal and his girlfriend Jean Hale fight over her purchase of a three-thousand-dollar mink coat. Now Corman gets on the program, with his signature pushy camera, the odd angles, the tight editing, and an *hommage* to Cagney when Segal mashes a sandwich in Hale's face. She brains him with a radio. They reach the bed, and suddenly Segal is turned on. *That* old chestnut? Just as the scene threatens to go trite on us, Hale knees Segal in the groin, and Corman is Corman once more.

He really wakes up for the closing sequence of the massacre: the Capones liquidating the Morans in a garage. The atmosphere is Brechtian, for we already know what will happen and need only watch prudently for the auteur's unique illumination, like Athenians on Sophocles day at the Dionysia. Corman plays on the suspense, his narrator grimly reminding us over and over that each Moran is "on the last day of his life." We see them, variously heading for the fatal garage, Segal making plans to dump Hale—and at last the narrator goes for it. "There's plenty more," he intones, "where *she* came from."

By the late 1960s, Corman's style had infused the B in general. His air of precarious spontaneity, his creative camera movement and editing, his eagerness to test taboo, and his casual agglomeration of the natural and the fake—as in the garish concatenation of acting styles or the startling use of vérité footage—were adapted throughout the sub-industry, betokening a graduation from quick and dirty into lean and nervy. The B had been liberated. It became a kind of sixties devil, film without rules. Best of all, it was unpredictable, as television had been in the 1950s, when everything except the movie screenings was live. A B might be pure exploitation, or pure art, or, perhaps most frequently, a combination of the two, a director's bold talent overwhelming a genre's dingy intentions. The low budget kept the B locked as tight as a sonnet, but its new maverick impulse gave its makers development room, freedom of theme.

Of course, Corman's field of influence counted the usual hacks and fakers, so tracing the evolution of a given B cycle uncovers the banal as well as the ingenious. Consider the biker-gang genre—a Corman invention, for the sole earlier instance, *The Wild One,* is really something of a western on wheels, while Corman's *The Wild Angels* (1966) sucks up the youth thing, the California thing, the anti-bourgeois thing, the entropy thing, and the desolation-of-the-outlaw's-liberty thing into a schematic of conflicted contemporaneity, now crashing out on the heebie-jeebies and the helter-skelters, now dead still, listening for something. Corman has been widely credited with guessing what thing or combination of things was ready to go over with the youth and thrills market, and certainly *The Wild Angels* was a smash, not only at home but abroad. Here was America: motorcycles and anger and the highway and the leather, cops to the left of them and solid citizens to the right of them. Yet Corman left his imitators very little to work with, for nothing happens in *The Wild Angels* except that a major sixties cycle is launched. Pack leader Peter Fonda (as Heavenly Blues, after his eyes; or is he God? Corman is capable of anything) and his "mama," Nancy Sinatra, preside over gang rituals, an orgy, a funeral, and miscellaneous alienation. No plot, just episodes and the ever-winding road. Finally there's a confrontation between the gang and the middle class. A straight throws a rock, a battle ensues, and to alarums of police sirens everybody scrams. Then the film abruptly ends, on this exchange, *d'après* Samuel Beckett:

SINATRA (*to Fonda*) Let's go.

FONDA There's nowhere to go.

As usual producing as well as directing, Corman must take the blame for the atrocious script and the typical but here rather debased Corman acting crew of the vital and the squalid. Apparently the cast includes some real Hell's Angels, but the hand-held, improvise-it Corman style is so close to naturalism that it's hard to tell the Angels from the actors. (Except Bruce Dern, but then it's relatively easy to tell Bruce Dern from anybody.) Corman is also the man who took the romance out of the cycle life before it derived any, unless one counts *The Wild One*. There's nowhere to go because these people haven't come from anywhere. The movie has no story because the *gang* has no story, beyond birth, sex, and death. This is an innate defect of the B: not enough infinity. Corman was technically unlimited. But like all directors he was dependent on his writers, and when he didn't have Bogdanovich or Coppola dashing off a redo of a key scene, Corman's vision scarcely reached the next hill.

The Wild Angels is poor Corman, but it was all his followers in the motorcycle-gang series had to work with, so the biker cycle became the blind and the halt of the sixties B. Corman's founding infusion of existential gee-whiz disappears in the smoke of mere action films, all-talking, all-riding, all-fighting gang wars manned by such actors as Dennis Hopper, Adam Roarke, and Jeremy Slate, along with mamas Diane McBain, Sherry Jackson, and Sabrina Scharf. It's not exactly the Old Vic. Even as orgies of sex, violence, and gratuitous meanness, these films give the least. *The Mini-Skirt Mob* (1968) offers the novelty of mamas taking the lead, *The Glory Stompers* (1968) makes a timely crossing of borders when one of the Black Souls (the bad gang) teases a Glory Stomper (of the good gang) by mouthing, "I love you" at him and licking his lips in mock-ecstasy, and *Hell's Belles* (1969) rephrases the biker *Angst*—as if there were any left at this point—in middle-class terms, viewing the biker world as one of weekend clubs rather than till-death-do-us-die outlaws and thus banning that crucial element of the biker cycle, the disgusting behemoth in a leather jacket.

The behemoths are all over *Run, Angel, Run!* (1969), the sole entry in the cycle that fixes its characters in some kind of reality. Its titular hero even takes on some tragic weight. A biker who tells all to a national magazine (for money with which to start a new life, off the eternal road), he spends the film fleeing his former fellows, who want to kill him. "Have you seen this guy?" they continually ask of strangers, holding up what looks like an imitation of *Life* as they roar through California. Director Jack Starrett* treats Angel's run momentously, involving us in a way the series' earlier plot macguffins—a stolen bike, a thwarted love affair—never do.

Angel himself is fascinating, hostile and suspicious and trigger-tempered, but possessed of a certain diabolic charm and a sound man to have on your side in a fight. One of the distinctions of the sixties B is the high caliber of some of its players—Jack Nicholson being the outstanding example. William Smith, who plays Angel—superbly—never quite broke out of the B factory, perhaps because his smoldering-hulk physique typed him as the psychopathic villain that B's could never get enough of (whereas Nicholson could play almost anything; paradoxically, this made him less necessary to the B, as a protean man in a world ruled by the invariability of genre). Most of Smith's work in biker films found him playing sadistic gang leaders, not, as here, the rebel within the rebel organization. Unlike any other biker hero, Angel has the energy and vision to seek a life outside the rules and the resourcefulness to outride his enemies. He is like a western outlaw trying to bluff his way around what everyone who frequented westerns knew was the outlaw's certain destiny—and, indeed, in a scene reminiscent of countless westerns, Smith is trapped in a railroad yard and escapes (on his bike) by a spectacular leap onto a moving train.

The film's highlight catches Angel and his girlfriend (Valerie Starrett) hitching a ride in a train's empty baggage car. They are alone when they get in, but after troubled sleep awake to find company—a grisly thug, a bizarrely semi-intellectual nerd, and a giggly black man. The camera takes in an air of wonderfully undertoned menace, in that erratic but robust B naturalism we remarked in *Wild in the Streets,* as Smith warily tries to disconnect the electricity attendant upon the three strangers' awareness of the opportunity for disorderly conduct. The thug shares some wine and sausage with Smith in a territorial rite, like wild animals doing something instinctual with urine and feces. Then comes the violence as Smith battles with the thug while the black man crawls toward Smith's girlfriend and the nerd screams out, *"Get away from that white woman!"*

The scene has no counterpart in any movie of the day, a taste of

---

*The draft-board colonel from *The Gay Deceivers*. As we have seen with Corman's atelier, sixties B personnel were versatile.

Elements of the Biker Cycle. First, The Showing of the Colors (above) as the gang hits the road in *Angels Die Hard!* Then, Battling the Bourgeoisie (below), in *The Wild Angels,* as the outlaws defy the straights. Wouldn't you?

Non-violent defiance involves Going Around as Disgusting Brutal Oiks (above), in *Run, Angel, Run!*, and, last, we have The Biker's Tender Side (below), again in *Run, Angel, Run!*, with Valerie Starrett and William Smith.

outlaw life so fiercely nuanced it redeems the B movie's improvisational carelessness with a spontaneity that is honest, precise, and documentary. This is the sort of art that B-watchers dine out on, the off-Hollywood directness that transcends movie starism and production values and made the B unique, an exploitation not of headline sensationalism but of life among the savages.

It was *Easy Rider* (1969) that capped the biker cycle, though generically it marked a breakaway. Biker films were action thrillers emphasizing the hero's isolation within the biker system. From Heavenly Blues to Angel, the protagonist was caught between the uncomprehending and sometimes hostile outside world and the riotous but aimless ("There's nowhere to go") and even treacherous ("Have you seen this guy?") gang culture. *Easy Rider* both tightened the view of the biker and expanded the background canvas, doing away with the club scene entirely to propose its two principals as not enervated goblins but harmless loners in quest of something American to believe in. Like so many earlier movie heroes in search of self-realization, they pack up and hit the road—but where to? James Stewart, The Man Who (Was Thought To Have) Shot Liberty Valance, can go west. Bonnie and Clyde can tour the banks of the Southwest. The heroines of *Thoroughly Modern Millie* can come to the big city. Even Tony Curtis, an Eastern nerd, can find self-confidence and career success along the Malibu strand. Where does a biker go?

Wyatt (Peter Fonda) and Billy (Dennis Hopper) decide to try for New Orleans during Mardi Gras, but this is nominal, a frame for the panorama of America that writers Fonda, Hopper, and Terry Southern and director Hopper episodically unfurl. In fact, these two outdated cowboys have nowhere to go; simply that they bear the names of two mythological figures of the vanished West, Wyatt Earp and Billy the Kid, reminds us that present-day America cannot host any such quest. As with Arthur Miller and John Huston's misfits, their rightful place lies in the past, when bikers rode horses and saved towns from the black hats.

No question, Wyatt and Billy are good guys, completely reversing the terms of *The Wild Angels* and its successors. Most important, where all other biker characters (except Angel) rejected any possibility of reaching beyond their renegade cult, the unattached easy riders yearn to be a part of a vision of a greater America, something all-cultural, so big it has no horizons, no end. This is why New Orleans as the destination of their quest is no more than a name, something to shoot for in default of anything else. In the event, they aren't impressed by what they see there. Mardi Gras is bad America, not the delightful revel they had imagined but a rampage of commercialism. This quest needs not discoveries and surprise but a reaffirmation of what was always supposed to be there in the first place—innocence, independence, welcome. Fonda dubs himself "Captain America"; he wants the mythical to come clean with him, be purified. Mardi Gras is complicated, conflicted.

More affecting, affirming, is the dinner the two riders share with a rancher's family, and the hippie commune they visit. These are pure experiences, good America. The hippies are city kids trying the land. As farmers, they are in the apprentice stage, but they have the right spirit. They pray over their sowing, for "simple food for our simple taste." They may lack agrarian expertise (they are even short of food and water), but they do have innocence; in the atmosphere of the late 1960s, this is like having ukuleles, or high button shoes, or halos. It stands out. "They're going to make it," Fonda observes—to which *Newsweek*'s Joseph Morgenstern snapped, "Who does he think he is, Luther Burbank?"

Morgenstern wanted "to reach out and shake" Fonda and Hopper "until they stopped their damn-fool pompous politicizing on the subject of doing your own thing and being your own man." These were the clichés of the 1960s, along with the biker as a cowboy figure and a shattered vision of lost innocence and a fear that the American heartland was a lying, nosy, intolerant wasteland—Cluttered, so to say, with lurid, boring bigots. And who appointed the woodenly trippy Fonda and the relentlessly beat Hopper as our men of mission? "To my astonishment, then," Morgenstern admitted, "the movie reached out and profoundly shook me."

It shook many, not only the mass-cult oiks and college students, who were its indicated audience, but the intellectuals as well. *Easy Rider* is not artistically great, despite Laszlo Kovacs's cinematography, which caught far better than the screenplay the sense of national majesty and potential sabotaged by pettiness and ignorance; and despite a brilliant turn by Jack Nicholson, breaking through to fame for his portrayal of an alcoholic black-sheep-aristocrat lawyer wigging out on fantasies of aliens taking over the country. The irony is that aliens *have* taken over, that a murderous redneck repression foreign to stated American ideals is in power everywhere one goes. "We blew it," says Fonda, in a classic sixties line. They didn't blow it; we did.

The film concludes its view of America with the destruction of all three principals, murdered by strangers because they're "different." This used to be a right, if not a virtue. Now it's a folk crime. "They're gonna talk to you, and talk to you, and talk to you about individual freedom," Nicholson warns the other two not long before he is killed. "But they see a free individual, it's gonna scare 'em. . . . It makes 'em dangerous." *Easy Rider,* then, is tragic as *The Misfits* is tragic, as an elegy on the death of independence, rather than as *Bonnie and Clyde* is tragic, as an elegy on the death of beauty. Wyatt and Billy may annoy us with their idiot jargon, so replete with buzz terms and doper kvetch that they can go on for pages without saying more than the "getting my thing together, man," and the "Dig me, man," and the "Let's rap, man." And it must be said that, of all the people in Hollywood at the time, Peter Fonda is probably the second most irritating speaker of such lines and Hopper is beyond question the first. Shake them? *Muzzle* them.

Still, they are harmless people, hippies on motorcycles doing individual freedom. Some critics wondered if Wyatt and Billy's cocaine-smuggling episode that opens the film was meant to supply a character debt to be paid off at the end when some good ole boys blast the pair off the road—as if an involvement in drug culture were a fatal flaw. Surely Hopper, Fonda, and Southern didn't see it that way. Captain America's flaw is that he believes his land is noble, something the 1960s, from Port Huron to Charles Manson, decisively disproved. As Fonda said in an interview, " 'Easy rider' is a southern term for a whore's old man—not a pimp, but the dude who lives with a chick. Because he's got the easy ride. Well, that's what happened to America, man. Liberty's become a whore, and we're all taking the easy ride."

Time called *Easy Rider* "the little film that killed the big film." But though it was made cheaply, *Easy Rider* was not a little film. Unlike the biker series proper, it was produced not by a B factory but by Columbia, and it won the attention a true B never gets, including two Oscar nominations, for Nicholson and the screenplay. That's fair. The negative cost may have been a piddling $375,000, but the worldwide gross was $60,000,000, and that's big. *Easy Rider* had a "little" feeling in the three leads, all veterans of the B circuit, in a Cormanesque looseness of style, in a semi-amateur (or let's say, "hand-held") ease of direction, and in the many real-life characters playing bit parts, including some uncomfortably authentic backwoods rowdies. Still, in Hollywood, big and little have less to do with the size of your budget than the size of your profits, and the size of your profits dictates how you are perceived. Little is drive-in fodder, what your kids go to. Big is what you go to.

Easy Rider was big also because it was epochal, a work that extrapolated as it exploited. Even as it said that the 1960s didn't work, that America was the country that never happened, or had somehow corrupted itself, *Easy Rider* conjured up a vision of that wished-for America in this time. It exists somewhere, the movie seemed to say. The tragedy is that Wyatt and Billy couldn't find it. This is why the film hasn't dated, for all the atrocious sixties jive Fonda and Hopper emit. Idealists still hope to locate this America, or to revive it, and the film ceaselessly reflects their belief.

Above all, *Easy Rider* was big because it became prominent. Little films didn't, as a rule, which obscures the history of the B in its time of highest development. Some of the 1960s' least impressive B's have become celebrated for their sheer trashy vitality—*Wild in the Streets,* for example, or Corman's Poe series, which for all its influential creativity is nowhere near as artistically fulfilled as *Bloody Mama* (1970), one of the last films Corman directed before he reorganized his outfit for producing and distributing. *Bloody Mama,* on the criminal exploits of Ma Barker and her heinous brood, sounds like absolute exploitation, and it stars Shelley Winters, always a sign that someone in charge of production is dabbling in facetia. But under the madcap violence and non-sequitur dialogue lies an extraordinary alternative to *Bonnie and Clyde*: a joyride through hell led by a kind of camp Virgil who reads sociopathic violence not as some artificial political statement but as a megalomaniacal assault upon the social contract. *Bonnie and Clyde* says beauty deserves fame. *Bloody Mama* says depravity needs power.

That in itself is a kind of capsule review of the rise of the B in the 1960s, as a degenerate offshoot of the real Hollywood, hungry for notice, acclaim, assimilation into the mainstream, where the big profits lie and the critics consider. Depravity—whether in the blood feasts of Herschell Gordon Lewis, the sexuality of Russ Meyer, or the demonology of the biker cycle—made the B notorious. This somewhat displaced the striving of the B to redeem the curse of genre, to invent an elite version of itself— a contradiction in terms, as the B was, from the first, marketed for an undiscerning audience.

Whom, then, was Monte Hellman's *The Shooting* (1967) marketed for? This is sophisticated art, nominally a B western but in form a "quest" parable as cloudy as *Mickey One* yet as pointed as Sergio Leone. "What do you think we're following, after all?" says one character, and unfortunately Hellman and his expert writer Adrien Joyce (Carol Eastman) never tell us. Four people make a trek into the desert: the ambiguous Millie Perkins, the hero Warren Oates, his simpleminded friend Will Hutchins, and the villain Jack Nicholson. There are startling lines, somewhat in the Corman manner, as in Perkins's insistently repeated address of Oates as "Mr. Gashade," which becomes a kind of open sesame, like "Mr. Allegory" or "Mr. B Movie as Breakthrough Art." Hellman's eye, too, startles, as when Hutchins hears a gunshot and tearasses for cover while carrying a sack of flour, the white dust spilling out a fog about him as he runs. There are traditional western touches, especially in Nicholson's unutterably sadistic bad man. Leaving Hutchins helpless in the desert, he says with a grin, "Your brain gonna fry out here, you know that?" However, most of the picture is beyond genre—and thus beyond the B, so rooted in format that B titles were summoning terms, designed to lure customers who would get what they wanted. *Rock All Night* calls to the youth audience. *I Was a Teenage Frankenstein* brings in the youth and horror audiences. *The Wild Angels* then creates an audience instantaneously, the biker crowd.

As a title, *The Shooting* could pertain to a number of genres; it could refer to a number of the film's key incidents, for the story comes off as a sort of symbolical procession punctuated at regular intervals by gunfire. What do you think they're following, after all? But then the sixties love of film for film's sake, especially fostered by young entry-level idealists of the B units, weren't as concerned with plot and character as with technique. Again, the manner of narration was becoming, for some people, more important than narration itself.

Thus, Hellman's wonderfully devious shuffling and reshuffling of loyalties among his four principals overwhelms our bewilderment at their actions; and Nicholson's sadist and Hutchins's innocent so absorb us as a conflict of humors that we don't really need the definitive backstory—or conclusive ending—that the movie fails to supply. The B has undertaken important experimental work; the industry's toy store is selling to adults now. The B has turned *cinéaste,* as self-creating and ontological as François Truffaut. In the Studio Age, a B was like other movies, but cheap. Now, a B is not like other movies. Its evolution is so intent on self-definition that at times the B looks back at itself, as if the camera were commenting existentially on the concept of the B movie even as it turns.

For instance, there's a gifted assistant director waiting for his chance to sign his own picture. Opportunity knocks—but hark to the overtones in this ditty of an offer: a producer has some completed footage he wants to use and a star with two days left on his contract. The footage is outtakes of a horror movie and the star a very old, very dignified Brit who worked almost exclusively in horror. If the budding director can assemble something out of this, he's got a deal.

So Peter Bogdanovich concocts a script in which Boris Karloff can play a horror star planning to retire after the premiere of his last film, which is outtakes from *The Terror,* and since Bogdanovich has the use of Karloff for but two days, he balances the old man's story with that of an all-American boy who (like the "Texas tower sniper," Charles Whitman) suddenly and inexplicably goes on a killing rampage, the two stories to collide at the film's end, when the horror star and the gunman confront each other at the premiere of, naturally, *The Terror*—held, also naturally, at a drive-in.

And Roger Corman tells Bogdanovich, "Make it."

There are so many "movies" going on inside Bogdanovich's *Targets* (1968) that the film is more a state-of-the-art insertion into cinema history than an act of entertainment-enlightenment. What *Barbarella* was to the era itself, *Targets* was to the development of the movies in that era: a demonstration piece. There is, first, the simple challenge of Bogdanovich's integrating of spare parts and imagination into a whole, like some daredevil Henry Ford. There is, second, the vérité factor, so sixties and so Corman, in which everyone plays himself. Thus, Boris Karloff (as Byron Orlok) is in fact the star of the movie that he stars in in *Targets,* and Karloff is planning to retire after *Targets,* just as Orlok will—Karloff "the mandarin of horror," as David Thomson wrote, "eighty years old, leaning on a stick and a lovely Asiatic secretary, his skin a blend of Californian tan, jaundice, and the old parchments of Gothic castles." Bogdanovich plays what *he* is, a writer-director, and joins Karloff to watch an old Karloff movie, *The Criminal Code,* and, admiring Howard Hawks's story-telling, to announce, "All the good movies have been made"—as if *Targets* must be, perforce, a poor movie or a remake. Charles Whitman was unavailable to play the killer, so Bogdanovich found Tim O'Kelly, the embodiment of the patriotic, parent-honoring, wife-respecting nerd who suddenly becomes, for a day or two, the most lurid man in America.

There are the puns in the titles of the films invoked: *The Criminal Code* in a film that begins with a series of rhetorical questions asking why we have no gun-control to protect us from murderous loonies; *The Terror* as a caption for the mild-mannered (but monstrous) O'Kelly rather than for the "monstrous" (but mild-mannered) Karloff; and *Targets* as a warning that it is not only Bogdanovich's characters who are targets but we ourselves. There is the showboating structural design: two separate stories playing against each other scene by scene like parallel lines, to be twisted together at the end. There is the film's title on a sign on a gun-shop wall. There is the "dark and stormy night" opening typical of a Corman Poe. Floods and murder. Then . . . "The End," in antique lettering, and lights up on Karloff and company in a screening room, film-within-film. There is the feeling that the entire movie is a public-service commercial (for the control of firearms), which Bogdanovich can then turn about by calling *Targets* apolitical, a film for film's sake. That it is: a B that redefines the B's power, a film reassessing the nature of certain film categories—"exploitation," "real-life," "horror." *Targets* is the *real* terror, *The Terror* just a movie. But then so is *Targets*.

Haskell Wexler's *Medium Cool* (1969) pushes this one step further. This isn't just a movie; it's a weapon. The whole thing is about the shooting of cameras and the shooting of guns, and about the feelings of those shot and those shooting. Has a cameraman only history on his mind when he catches poverty, violence, terror, death? "Jesus, I love to shoot film," says *Medium Cool*'s protagonist, Robert Forster, a Johnny-on-the-spot cameraman in Chicago in 1968. In the pre-credit sequence, he and his sound man (Peter Bonerz) happen upon a car accident, calmly shoot it, call for an ambulance, and take off. They are not utterly callous, just devoted to the work. Forster's girlfriend recalls that scene in the Italian anthology film *Mondo Cane* (1963) in which giant sea turtles are filmed crawling the wrong way to lay their eggs and dying in bewilderment. Did the cameraman save the turtles after shooting them? asks Forster's girlfriend accusingly. Should they have? "The typewriter doesn't really care what's being typed on it," Bonerz remarks at a party when he is accused of lacking a conscience. The cameraman is a typewriter. He's not supposed to have a conscience; he's a machine. Like *Blowup*, *Medium Cool* is looking at a society that itself does too much looking and not enough seeing.

Wexler made *Medium Cool* as a statement of conscience, the machine's *J'accuse. Medium Cool* is, on the surface, very cool vérité footage (of an Army riot-control dress rehearsal, ghetto life, workers at a Robert Kennedy boosting office, the Democratic Convention, the police riot) mixed in with what could easily be improvised scenes by actors so natural looking and acting (Verna Bloom, Charles Geary, Peter Boyle) they might as well be vérité themselves. That's cool. But what *Medium Cool* tells of is hot stuff, all the feelings that came clashing together in the late 1960s and particularly in 1968 and mainly in Chicago. "The whole world is watching!" the students chant at the police. "The whole world is watching!" Someone calls out, "Don't forget Czechoslovakia! Don't forget Budapest!"—and, seeing the Army tanks roll into Chicago to defend the Bad Fathers from their dismayed children, indeed one remembers Czechoslovakia and Budapest. The film is made of antagonisms—generation war, class war, race war, the Vietnam War, even the war of the moral free-lancer against the reckless Corporation, and of course the war of the camera and its subject. "Is that thing loaded?" interviewee Peter Boyle asks Bonerz, looking at his high-tech mike.

Medium Cool is loaded, as a film about filmmaking ought to be. It has its moments of wit: when Bonerz says, "Did you know that for every man in Washington, D.C., there are four and a half women?" director Wexler gives us shots of four women walking along the street—and one pair of legs. It has its touches of sympathy, mostly involving Forster's befriending of a Southern woman and her thirteen-year-old son. But it is for the most part an irate Pirandellian slice of life—life because the Chicago cops are no actors (though one of them gives a quite impressive reading of the line "You stinkin' Commie!" as he bashes some kid's head in) and Pirandellian because the enacted scenes are every bit as naturalistic.

There's a fine sequence in a ghetto apartment, where Forster speaks to a black cabdriver who found a wallet containing ten thousand dollars, turned it in, and got into a peck of trouble. On Forster's way out, the door is physically blocked by a black woman who says she's an actress and wants Forster to put her on television. A black man assists her, the two of them haranguing Forster with chauvinist cant and pointed fingers and the stupid self-righteous class-action egomania that was as much a part

Medium hot, medium truth, medium sex. Robert Forster takes a medium view of Marianna Hill in *Medium Cool*. Photography, we learn, is
penetration. The film's last line is "And people are really being hit."

of the political scene in 1968 as Vietnam and the Chicago police were.
Forster tries to reason his way out, fails, and is finally bailed out by yet
another black man, who shoos the two idiots away, starts to let Forster
out, and then bars the door himself for more harangue. It's a trenchant
scene, film that tries to see how real film can get but also film that
reminds us that film makes everything unreal. "The [television] tube,"
one character observes, "is life." But life doesn't have an audience, or such
symmetry that a car accident up front before the credits is balanced by a
car accident at the end, as Wexler gives us. It is Forster's accident, with
the Southern woman, head-on into a tree—and as a passing car slows to
gape, someone leans out and snaps a picture.

If *Targets* is film for film's sake, *Medium Cool* is life for film's sake,
as close as anyone has come, short of out-and-out documentary, to putting
the world into the camera. It is arranged. It has an author—Wexler not
only directed but wrote and (of course) photographed it. Yet its realism
makes everything else in the decade look like *The Wizard of Oz*. "Look

out, Haskell," someone shouts as the cops deploy tear gas, right there in Chicago in 1968. "It's real!"

Looking back on the general run of films released exactly ten years before *Medium Cool*—*A Summer Place, Pillow Talk, Rio Bravo, On the Beach, The Diary of Anne Frank, The Nun's Story, Imitation of Life, Career, The Five Pennies, Say One for Me, The Best of Everything, A Hole in the Head, They Came to Cordura, Gidget, Don't Give Up the Ship, Anatomy of a Murder,* and *Ben-Hur*—we can see at once what a fine, broad, and busy road we have traveled in the 1960s. No other era in movie history saw such development in the cultural content of the material, such a powerful socialization of the moviegoing population; and only one other era saw more technical innovations, the transition from silents to talkies in 1927–29. By the late 1960s, movies spoke intimately yet pandemically to their various publics. Film no longer regarded itself as a church, an enforcer of the received social values, normative above all, but as an agent of transformation, often defiant of the ruling interests.

This marked not merely a separation of church and state, but a reformation that broke the church up into many sects, each free to challenge or support the relevant wisdoms. For instance, to pick just one example, a film about the generation war might excoriate parental tyranny (*Splendor in the Grass*), love the kids and forgivingly ridicule the grown-ups (the *Beach Party* series), worry over the hidden sensitivities of youthful criminals (*The Young Savages, Kitten with a Whip*), spoof the whole idea because essentially every parent-child relationship is a loving war (*Bye Bye Birdie*), expose with a kind of larky dismay the vicious hypocrisy of parents (*The Graduate*), or warn of the murderous hatreds a young ruling class would unleash (*Wild in the Streets, If . . .*).

There was, apparently, a film available for every interest, a line read out for each party. The next logical step would be films made not by pros but by intrigued amateurs—by members of the audience. And so we got what might have been the climax of the sixties revolution in filmmaking, the underground. The word is vague and rich at once: a circle of rundown theatres in various metropolitan centers; a number of game directors and their friends the actors; a small, venturesome public drawn from the back-street bohemian scene; patronizing and outraged reviews from the established critics—all this was the underground. But what was an underground film?

Here was the independent filmmaker at his apex, a homemade avant-garde not only heedless of commercial sensibility but signally opposed to it. The underground was satire, poetry, mood pieces, put-ons, high-concept what have you, and camp apocalypse in 35, 16, and even 8 millimeter. Taking over disused or abandoned old theatres, from the Charles and the Gate on New York's Lower East Side to the Cinema in West Hollywood, a movement that had its roots in the mid-1950s flow-ered in the early 1960s in the public exhibition—really, the flaunting—of the works of Bruce Conner, Ken Jacobs, Shirley Clarke, Gregory Mar-kopoulos, Ron Rice, Robert Breer, Bruce Baillie, Kenneth Anger, Jack Smith, James Broughton, Robert Nelson, Stan Brakhage, Jonas Mekas, and George and Mike Kuchar, among others. In place of the essentials of the Hollywood movie, narrative and characterization, the underground, sometimes called "the new American cinema," exploited image and the merest embodiment. In *Guns of the Trees* (1961), "a film by Jonas Mekas assisted by Adolfas Mekas," we get disconnected vignettes on the lives of a number of New Yorkers suffering incoherent problems and liberal anx-ieties, framed by shots of two crazies in suits and clown-white faces wailing miserably as they walk through a field of cabbages. The Mekases, who both appear in the film (a characteristic auteurism of the underground in general), shot the entire film silent, then added music and voice-overs, mainly remote comments like "Everybody in the Bronx is ugly" and "Every time I see a pregnant woman, I want to greet her as a friend, a conspirator" and "Sooner or later, everybody gives up." Allen Ginsberg reads his poetry from time to time. Some dialogue is post-synched, quite badly, and the lighting often lapses into the obscure. There are vérité shots of the police breaking up a demonstration in Washington Square Park. It's a boring film, but it's supposed to be—or it's *not* supposed *not* to be. Whether enigmatic or direct, the early underground was something other than entertaining, except for the bourgeois-clobbering spoofs like Jack Smith's *Flaming Creatures* (1963) or the Kuchars' *Sins of the Fleshapoids* (1964).

Even camp could become a drag, however, as in Ron Rice's *The Queen of Sheba Meets the Atom Man* (1963), another silent, this one accom-panied rather miscellaneously by Chopin preludes, snatches of symphonies, "Mexico Joe," and so on. Little happens. Parish favorite Taylor Mead awakens, does a number with heroin in a giant bucket, washes his hands with Vaseline, mugs and twinkles and dangles his tongue out of his mouth, and at length calls on Winifred Bryan, a huge black woman.

Separately, they tour New York, Bryan trudging through Central Park and Mead passing through an art museum to imitate and otherwise relate to the work on view. In the film's most famous shot, Mead capers along a length of window in a high-rise at night, the million lights of New York burning behind him.

Some of the underground compelled simply by the turbulence of the images it vomited up, as in Kenneth Anger's *Scorpio Rising* (1964), a homoerotic look at the biker world, crosscut with references to such icons as James Dean, Hitler, and Christ. The underground was almost all pictures, though Shirley Clarke's *Portrait of Jason* (1967) took the form of a spontaneous interview with a young gay black man who talks about his life, joking until, suddenly, he breaks into sobs. Norman Mailer's *Wild 90* (1968) was also improvised, on the premise that Mailer, Buzz Farbar, and Mickey Knox are gangsters hiding from other gangsters, passing the time in drink, the receiving of an occasional visitor, and, mainly, attempting to out-macho each other. Mailer even tries to out-vicious a police dog, barking at the animal—in fact bullying it, as Mailer has the advantage of running around unleashed.

"Unleashed" was the word for the underground generally. The abandonment of form and what most people think of as content led to a focus on personality. Not impersonation, but natural identity. The underground personalities took in cutups, hashheads, back-street stars, and holy terrors, not *rendered,* in the Studio manner, but simply presented. The camera turns and you are there. The ultra-independent new American cinema, rather than liberating the concept of film, confined it. Underground personalities were either too unpleasant or too vacuous to give pleasure when unleashed. For all its surprise and burlesque, most of the underground was diluted, enervated, stupefied. "Straight out of the most bloodless element of the New York underground," Renata Adler called Gregory Markopoulos's *The Iliac Passion* (1968), a Greek kind of thing with Jack Smith, Gerard Malanga, Andy Warhol, Markopoulos himself, and the indispensable Taylor Mead. Commenting on Markopoulos's "toneless, regionally accented" voice-over narration of pseudo (I guess)–pretentious amphigory, Aeschylus transposed by Gertrude Stein, Adler diagnosed "a case of being so alienated from language, not knowing how to use it or speak it, that there is a delusion of mastery to the point of poetry." The visuals were comparably primitive, not an advance on Hollywood technique but a sullen, spiritless reduction of it. "The camera, which hardly ever moves from side to side, for the most part zooms in and out in a kind of sucking motion." We see "people with boneless, uninteresting faces; naked bodies (mostly male) photographed with a remarkable infelicity of line; a few lovely Oriental landscapes; a number of superimpositions of one shot upon another, a kind of heaped, agglomerate photography." The underground went against the beat all right; everyone knew it was going to. That's why it was called "underground" more than "independent." It was secrets spilling out. Yet it was astonishingly unexuberant, so self-absorbed it became the one thing no one could have expected: dreary. Where was the *rebellion* of independence?

It lay entirely in the quality of the actors—the participants, rather, as they seldom played roles as such—and that "sucking motion" that aped at a dead-zero level the inhalation of stardom typical of traditional Hollywood technique. The camera "loves" the stars, soaks up the potent personality, ingests the glamour. So we worship. But the Hollywood star was prepared, developed, and expounded. Fame was administered. The underground star was merely placed on view. Fame was a goof; why work for it? Speaking of his work with the Andy Warhol stable of so-dubbed "superstars," including Viva, Edie Sedgwick, pokey, quirky Taylor Mead, Mario Montez, Eric Emerson, and Joe Dallesandro, director Paul Morrissey commented, "When they leave the theatre, people don't say, That was a great movie; they say, Those were great people."

But they weren't—that was the rebellion. "The Warhol 'superstars,'" wrote Pauline Kael, "generally did the sort of caricature imitations of Hollywood sex goddesses that female impersonators do in night clubs for homosexuals and slumming tourists, and added a backstage view of their own lives, so that one got not only grotesque comedy but the fullest sordidness they could dredge up." Kael found Warhol's underground "lethargic" and "depressing," "an ambiance of exhibitionism and degradation." All this it was. But it wasn't a failed attempt to entertain Kael; it was a successful attempt to humiliate her idea of entertainment.

The underground at its most potent concocted a film version of the off-off-Broadway "Theatre of the Ridiculous" movement that came into prominence with the work of Charles Ludlam: garish burlesques of everything, predicated on the notion that straights are vulgar idiots. In the Theatre of the Ridiculous, the second joke is that straights are like humans only much, much less so; the first joke is that straights don't get the joke.

Pauline Kael doesn't. The underground wasn't fun—and why was it filled with either gays or Norman Mailer? "What is the beautiful?" Oscar Wilde asked. "What the bourgeois call the ugly." Warhol's people weren't superstars as much as anti-stars, put-on stars, acting out a parody of fame—so laughable (because of their penetrating lack of appeal) yet so *invested* (because of the casual arrogance with which they failed to do anything to defend their presence on screen) that the escapade became something like a style.

So it was Warhol who put the underground into the mainstream, in the early 1970s, when his films (by then only produced by Warhol, directed by Paul Morrissey) were picked up by distributors for release in uptown theatres. Oddly, Warhol's beginnings, when he was, at least in title, the "director" of his films, were steeped in the sensory underloads of the underground aesthetic. Warhol represented the underground at its dead level: a man with a camera, no script, no editor, and no public. The notorious *Empire* (1964) was eight hours of the Empire State Building, caught from a single setup, as the light changed from day to night. *Eat* (1964) was Robert Indiana eating a mushroom, for longer than you'd think. *Blow Job* (1964) was a close-up of a man's face while he was being sucked off.

Anything you film is a movie. "Friends would stop by," said Warhol, "and they'd wind up in front of the camera, the star of that afternoon's reel." Anyone you film is a star; anywhere you film is a studio—Warhol's so-called Factory, for instance. Moving into talkies, Warhol made a stir with *My Hustler* (1966), perhaps the first prominent motion picture to treat gay life straight-on, without explication, euphemism, or apology. There is no plot. Set on Fire Island, *My Hustler* is a series of dialogues concerning a prostitute (Paul America) whom everyone else in the film is after. What matters is that, for the first time, Warhol's static-cling camera has begun to wander, even inquire; and Warhol's "friends would stop by" has given way to character casting; and Warhol's laissez-faire action has at last become situational.

The Chelsea Girls (1966) was Warhol's breakout piece, nearly four hours of talk (screened two reels at a time) featuring his "superstars" of the moment at their capers, so successful that it played engagements in virtually every major American city and a great many university cinema clubs. *The Chelsea Girls* is interminable, funny at times, and picturesque to say the least, queens and druggies raving, flaming, colliding. After

My Hustler's rather tightly centered conversations, *The Chelsea Girls* marked a return to the freewheeling Warholian improvisation of freaks. The film's underground power obtains less in Warhol's technique than in his use of lower-depths people—real-life ones, surely—doing the unmentionable and saying the unrepeatable not because that is on the filmmaker's agenda but because that is what they do. *My Hustler*'s characters were not less flamboyant but less exotic. The bitchy men and their woman friend scheming to entertain the hired boy were people anyone might encounter in different circumstances, the men in business suits, perhaps, temporarily closeted, walking the line. Even Paul America was believable—castable— as a hustler.

Later, Warhol did away with all this, rooting (if that isn't too spirited a concept) through the sex-and-drugs underworld for people who would hang out and just be. Warhol did personally direct one last situational film—almost, even, a plotted film, though the dialogue observes the characteristic Warholian off-the-cuff quality. There is, at any rate, a scenario: a band of cowboys rides into a western town, threatens a haughty cowgirl and her nurse, parties around, then breaks up as some elect to stay on and others head for the road of adventure. Roughly (very, very, *very* roughly) based on *Romeo and Juliet, Lonesome Cowboys* (1968) was the ultimate Warholian goof, all his most piquant New York creatures plunked into one of Hollywood's most traditional settings. Lean, moody Viva plays Juliet in jodhpurs and a whip, increasingly dubious about the sexuality of the cowboys when they fail to rape her. Irrepressible Taylor Mead is her nurse, one of his most successful portrayals. Louis Waldon (Viva's husband) is the leader of the cowboy brotherhood—they constantly refer to themselves as "brothers"—and his cohort includes ballerino Eric Emerson, who uses the hitching post as a barre for his exercises; Tom Hompertz, with whom Viva has graphic sex; Julian Burroughs; and the usual Joe Dallesandro, who at one point goes into a lively bump-and-grind cowboy folk dance, his sole moment in the entire Warhol oeuvre in which he shows some energy. Local color is provided by Francis Francine as the Sheriff, who can't keep the peace because he's too busy getting into drag.

Home, home on the range. Like a "real" movie, *Lonesome Cowboys* went on location, to Arizona, though Warhol secured an underground atmosphere in his merrily erratic lighting and jump-cut shooting, whereby

The resolutely unnerving underground. Louis Waldon has a somewhat less than secret yen for Tom Hompertz in *Lonesome Cowboys*.

the camera stops turning in the middle of a scene and starts up again a bit later, when the performers have changed their position or even moved to a different part of the set, which makes them look like the English toy-theatre cutouts mounted on metal braces and makes an obnoxious explosion on the sound track. Warhol was like a child with his camera, delighting in its use and features for the sport of it, inviting his pals over to pass an afternoon in hobby craft.

This contrasts vividly with the character of his gang, of course. But the inappropriate figures they cut in Arizona—even admitting the paradoxically supportive Christopher Street fantasy look of their cowboy outfits—only emphasizes the dire nature of the personalities Warhol chose for his films, his alien "great people," his superstars. Warhol, says David Thomson, "is not doctrinaire; he is so open to behaviour that he has disposed of deviation." Or no: he has disposed of normality. Yet by now Warhol's underground had surfaced. *Lonesome Cowboys'* Manhattan run took place at the New York Theatre, at the time an art house, the place you would go to see an important new foreign film or elite Hollywood classics like F. W. Murnau's *Sunrise.* The hot stuff. And *Flesh* (1968) premiered in legitimate first-run theatres, though this was in certain ways the most underground film of all.

Warhol notoriously spoke of a future in which everyone would be famous for fifteen minutes. Valerie Solanas, one of Warhol's Factory regulars, got her fifteen by shooting Warhol. It was a close call; at the hospital, the doctor attending Warhol apparently thought the situation hopeless till Warhol's friends told him Warhol was famous and the doctor got *his* fifteen by saving Warhol's life. While the captain of the underground recuperated, Paul Morrissey took over as director of Warhol's cinema, blending Warhol's "I don't care" technique with more traditional storytelling.

So *Flesh* is by Hollywood standards very nearly a movie. Again, there is no story, just episodes in the lives of Joe Dallesandro and his wife (Geraldine Smith): Joe and Geraldine *en ménage,* Joe out hustling, Joe having sex with a friend of the family, Jackie Curtis reading an antique movie magazine. Some of it is droll, especially a sequence in which Joe goes home with an old pedant (Maurice Barddell) for a "modeling session" (in fact, modeling as a discus thrower is all Joe ends up doing) and endures with unnuanced passivity the man's windy lecture. Some of it is simply uneventful, as when Joe and two less knowing hustlers discuss street technique. Some of it is dutiful underground *non serviam,* like the first six minutes, in which the camera just stands there and watches Joe sleep. Yet some of it is reasonable, like Morrissey's location work, which—for the first time in Warhol's cinema—actually does what location shooting does in the Hollywood product, establish locale. All Warhol's talkies are New York by the very sound of them, but this one pictures New York— the hustlers' meat rack at Fifty-third Street and Third Avenue, with the grim old subway dock, the all-night newsstand, Clancy's bar, and the Riker's on the corner, all pulled down in the 1980s.

The casting is totally underground, terminal Warhol. It is in effect an application of the fifteen-minute-fame theory, because, for all the kinkiness and desire and seedy human waste on view, these are hopelessly humdrum people. They are never as witty or wiggy or touching as you expect they'll be; they are not even particularly repellent, even at their worst. They are a kind of middle-class squalid, like the pedant who so earnestly, yet so vaguely, so pointlessly harangues Joe with scholarly trivia. Even Dallesandro, vividly on display throughout the Warhol oeuvre into the mid-1970s, and clearly chosen to be the central Warhol superstar as a kind of beveled mirror of Hollywood's hunger for beauty, is spectacular but dull. He has neither rhyme nor reason, just availability. Even there, he doesn't connect; for such sexual films there is remarkably little sexiness. In *Lonesome Cowboys,* Tom Hompertz is willing to pillow (in a woodsy setting) with Viva, but is so uncommitted to the act that she is forced to arrange and direct him as if he were a great rubber toy; in *Flesh,* when Dallesandro's wife, lolling with him in bed, asks him what he wants her to do for him, he says, "My laundry"; and in *Trash* (1970) Dallesandro is so drugged that he can't manage an erection.* Warhol's films are indeed exhibitionistic, as everyone noted, but Gable and Harlow, circa 1933, could show less and give more. Sex is energy.

Energy is what the underground largely lacked. True, much of its vitality was sapped by police harassment, for the authorities treated the early underground not as cinema but as porn, and they went after the downtown theatres as they never would have done the mainstream houses. In the 1970s, when the porn industry expanded and challenged court prosecution, censorship became sporadic, even, after a last gasp of active persecution of pornmakers and a few prominent porn actors, desultory. But by then the underground movement had collapsed, its leaders in retirement or, like Warhol, gone aboveground.

Nevertheless, it was the underground's emphasis on how pictures feel rather than on what stories tell that doomed it. It was dead opera, seizing upon something only to hold it interminably. The movement as a whole was very sixties in many ways—in its rebellious post-fifties attitude, its avoidance of imitation-real sets, its unen(Production)coded view of sex, its use in principal roles of "minority" people who in Studio Age Hollywood played supporting bits like sideshow freaks patronizingly admitted under the big top, and especially in its intense notion of experimentalistic mission, its belief that the method matters more than the material.

These are aspects of sixties moviemaking in general, especially of New Cinema. But the underground marked a kind of climax, a saturation

---

*By the time of *Andy Warhol's Frankenstein* (1974), Dallesandro is reconstructed, taking his friend Srdjan Zelenovic to a whorehouse and relatively enjoying a heavy bed session with Monique Van Vooren. But by then the Warhol-Morrissey outfit had abandoned the underground for the commercial marketing of fancy exploitation features, what one might call "B's with a patina of uptown suave."

point—in fact, a dead end. Almost everything that was valid about the new American cinema could be found in movies that the greater population attended; the revolution had already happened in plain New Cinema. Roger Corman did more to liberate repressed sensibilities than the underground could because Corman's perceptions were framed by a defining strength of action. At his worst, his forms dictated content: genre is destiny. But at his best his characters stimulated revelation. When, in *Bloody Mama,* one of Shelley Winters's brood, Robert Walden, goes to prison, we are not surprised that Corman hooks in a look at homosexual rape, even when Walden is chickened by the ever-disquieting Bruce Dern. After all, the scene *is* prison and the medium is exploitation film. A rape is logical, typical. But the scene itself, revolving around Dern's penchant for spanking foreplay, as Walden tries to calm his terror by singing a hymn, is brilliant, utterly off-the-wall and totally plausible, the kind of like-it-or-not naturalism that other prominent directors and writers would seize upon and absorb.

Thus it was the B film that enhanced the movies' honesty about brutal truths, not the underground. For all its vérité, it had no perspective; and without perspective, what's the point? "We can think of Warhol," says David Thomson, "as a primitive, as an extreme modernist, as the satirist or apologist of old Hollywood, or as the anthropological mythmaker of our metropolis. He is all of these, yet, pale and withdrawn, he tells us that the camera is more powerful than any purpose handling it."

That sounds good. It's even true. Yet one thing the 1960s needed more than anything else was new data, more about the world; and style doesn't equal knowledge. Style discovers knowledge. The underground was veils. It was *less* about the world. It was unnecessary. Next to new data, the 1960s loves virtuosity of technique above all—so that, say, *The Misfits* (new data) and *Bonnie and Clyde* (virtuosity of technique) are great epochal films and *Dr. Strangelove* (data *and* technique) is *the* epochal film. The underground gave no data and prided itself on innocence of technique. So in the end it was as wrong for the age as it had been inevitably born of it, like the unwanted child of sexy parents. Of all the cheap, the independent forms of movie that rose up or thrived in the 1960s, exploitation, porn, gore (they call it "splatter" now), and horror are still very much with us. Only the underground is gone.

Nine

1969; or, Ten Guidelines for the Future Making of Movies

If someone like Richard Lester were directing a movie on the history of the movies, and he wanted to treat the 1960s in rapid-fire montage, one might expect renderings of such key shots as *Psycho*'s murder of Janet Leigh in the shower, Clark Gable's landing of the *Misfits* mustangs, Audrey Hepburn's singing of "Moon River" to her own guitar on a fire escape, Bette Davis's singing of "I've Written a Letter to Daddy" as Baby Jane, Anne Bancroft's cradling of Patty Duke at the fade-out of *The Miracle Worker, Goldfinger*'s laser beam heading toward Sean Connery's treasure pouch, Lee Marvin's murder of the bed in *Point Blank,* the uncharted face of Dustin Hoffman in *The Graduate,* the death of Bonnie and Clyde, the soaring of Stanley Kubrick's spaceship to Johann Strauss's "On the Beautiful Blue Danube," and Newman and Redford's leaping off a cliff into a stream to escape the superposse. There would be sly, bemused references to Kid Film; the independent feature; all-star Big Film, so vast and so inane; the *Beach Party,* Poe, blood feast, and biker cycles; the roadshow musical. Clips of the concert documentary *Woodstock* (1970) would highlight the countercultural schism, especially in the interview footage with the mostly outraged locals, one of whom irately cries, "They're hot on pot!" We would see flecks of Natalie Wood, Warren Beatty, the young Ann-Margret, the late Bette Davis, Peter O'Toole, Marcello Mastroianni, and Julie Andrews, Peter Sellers trying to reason with General Jack D. Ripper, Jane Fonda performing her floating-in-a-spaceship striptease at the start of *Barbarella,* Peter Fonda experiencing a trip, and Henry Fonda playing Presidents. There would have to be historical pinpoints as well— Gene Shuftan lighting *The Hustler,* Henry Mancini scoring *Breakfast at Tiffany's,* Richard Brooks realizing that he could film *In Cold Blood* just as it had been written, as it had happened, Bosley Crowther giving a dramatic reading of his tirades against *Bonnie and Clyde,* Andy Warhol turning his camera on whatever was there, and, perhaps most definitively, the awarding of the Oscar for Best Picture of 1969 to an X-rated title, John Schlesinger's *Midnight Cowboy.*

The X rating, one must remember, was universally perceived as a denotation of sleaze. The X referred not to content as much as to quality. X movies were supposed to be low-budget, pure-blooded exploitation rip-offs. Well-made movies, much less major ones, were not rated X. True, the MPAA did not judge quality but content, and by its guidelines certain Anglo-Saxon expletives and uses of nudity meant an automatic X, and *Midnight Cowboy* qualified. Still, United Artists did not release X-rated movies. John Schlesinger, who had directed *Billy Liar, Darling,* and *Far From the Madding Crowd,* did not make X-rated movies. Dustin Hoffman, fresh from *The Graduate,* did not star in X-rated movies. And the Academy of Motion Picture Arts and Sciences did not honor X-rated movies. It's a simple matter of prestige, no?*

In fact, *Midnight Cowboy* copped seven nominations, winning not only Best Picture but Best Director and Best Screenplay (by Waldo Salt). This is Heavy Oscar Treatment. This is Industry Imprimatur. The year's far more successful and undeniably more beloved *Butch Cassidy and the Sundance Kid* also took seven nominations, but less crucial ones—Sound and Song, for instance, where *Cowboy* earned two Best Actor nominations and a Best Supporting Actress. *Butch* won five awards to *Cowboy*'s three, but *Cowboy* walked out of there *hot stuff* and everyone knew it. This was

---

*The very citation of *Midnight Cowboy* as Best Picture forced the MPAA to revise its X rating to an R, as if saying that any movie that nabs the Oscar cannot be an X by rules of status. The film had to be rehabilitated to spare the Oscar embarrassment.

quite a haul for another of those depressing sixties movies—not just depressing but a sort of East Village *Misfits* refitted for tragedy.

Two bus trips frame the film, from James Leo Herlihy's novel. First, Joe Buck rides to New York from Texas to hit it big by playing stud to Manhattan women, presumably desperate for an antidote to the effete Manhattan male. The fantasy suffers degradation, and Joe ends up hustling gays off the street; but he has meanwhile struck up an absurd relationship with the disgusting Ratso Rizzo, a small-time con artist. Ratso, too, has a fantasy—to make Miami Beach and con the rich Jewish queens. Bingo at the Fontainebleau. Joe and Ratso take the second and final bus trip, near the end of which Ratso dies.

There was a lot of discussion—again the critics brokered a dialogue for the nation's intelligentsia. Was the shattering of these two losers' pathetic dreams a matter of personal tragedy or of a corrupt culture? Was Schlesinger discussing the vulnerability of two spectacularly common men or holding American nationhood responsible for them? Was their friendship crypto-homosexual or merely an alliance of convenience? ("One could accept mutually exploitative, explicitly stated faggery," explained Richard Schickel, always sensitive to the issues.) Why do the two, even after more or less accepting the tact of their union, keep assaulting each other verbally? Why didn't Joe just get a job when his bankroll ran out? He's dumb, but he's healthy and attractive; *someone* would hire him.

Midnight Cowboy is both personal and national, vignette and epic. The two men's friendship is friendship; they need support so *needfully* that Joe's distaste for Ratso's condemned-building life-style and Ratso's contempt for Joe's hick stupidity don't matter as much as the possibility that these two could forge something unselfish out of their loony, mismatched fantasies. Sure, they both hope to entertain women—Joe sexually and Ratso recreationally. Joe will screw them and Ratso will game them. Or is that the same fantasy? And why do the two assault each other? Because that's how certain frustrated personalities remind each other that they're alive. And why didn't Joe get a job? Because American culture taught him that he had a cinch to tie up as a hooray-for-me stud, and, like most obsessed creatures, he would rather drag the dream into its own dregs than give it up. Hustling gays is a debased form of having sex for a living (especially the grotesque gays Joe meets up with—a terrified teenager who throws up and has no money, and an old man who masochistically edges Joe into beating him). But hustling is nevertheless a form of having sex for a living; it connects Joe to the dream of being what America most prizes, a star. To take a day job—washing dishes, say, as he does when we first see him—would be to blast the dream, to become just another figure in a crowd scene. To give oneself up.

Joe's dream is no different from that of millions of working-class males, who think that all it takes is cock and guts. What makes Joe's dream outstanding is that he is not only too stupid but too nice to accomplish it, and what makes his story touching is that he is willing to trade his dream in to support Ratso's. So, having taken the movie's opening bus ride along a yellow brick road of self-realization, Joe puts his friend on the movie's closing bus ride, to try to give Ratso what Joe himself had wanted.

Schlesinger makes it clear, in countless aural and visual references to American culture, that it is the national worldview that has corrupted Joe, its ruthless determinations of winner and loser and its obsession with fame that inspired his dream. In Schlesinger's America, television and radio beam messages at you like mind-control apparatus in some futuristic sci-fi adventure, and the social structures throb with manipulative schemes. Joe is Candide; nearly everyone else is greedy, reckless, and vulgar. Schlesinger's Southern good ole boys are vicious louts hot to rape, his New Yorkers are mostly freaks (including the most loathsome poodle in the history of film), and the fantasy views of Ratso amid the Miami Beach matrons lavish a savage hatred upon these leisure-class biddies. Gliding in their wheelchairs and sunning in their hats and nose guards, they are made to look like some newly discovered order of reptile.

Joe crosses paths with a few attractive people—the bridge-club type of whom Joe asks, in the middle of Park Avenue, for directions to the Statue of Liberty (his idea of a come-on) and who is too polite not to take him at his word (at first, anyway), or the coolly vicious Brenda Vaccaro, whose paid date with Joe provides the film's sole instance in which sex is not a metaphorical transaction or an act of violence but an emotional communication.

Still, the people who make the strongest impression tend to feed Schlesinger's horror of Americans—John McGiver's droning religious zealot; or Sylvia Miles's self-absorbed, grasping New York Woman, the first gig of Joe's career as a stud-for-hire, who bursts into tears when he asks for money and ends up carving off a sizable chunk of his bankroll;

or Viva, as an arty downtown type (note the testamentary value of the Warhol underground, so associated with The Scene that its members authenticate underworld art by their very presence), who gets up a party by photographing street people, then handing them invitations. And there's Ratso himself, utter scum, so given to cheating that at Viva's banquet table he's furtively stuffing food into his pockets: even when something is free, he finds a way to steal it.

This is Schlesinger's America, swindlers, show-offs, bullies, and self-righteous lunatics. Only in the late 1960s would such a stern indictment of America—made, moreover, by an Englishman—be tolerated, not to say rewarded. But by 1969 we were deep in the crisis of national identity brought on by a decade of political turmoil that culminated in a widespread alienation from belief in our power and wisdom and fairness. This belief had informed American cinema almost from its inception, and had led us into Vietnam. By the summer of 1969, when *Midnight Cowboy* was released, we didn't see ourselves as the world's savior but as a Mrs. Bates, hacking away at the Far East as if the way to save a country from Communism were to destroy the country.

So Schlesinger's view of America was welcome, part of the shriving process—the "guilt trip," as the local terminology phrased it. This is a political film. Yet its force to move lies not in its caricature of American life but in this bizarre friendship of the innocent and the cynic, the fool and the miscreant, the angel and the gremlin—and the solid interlock of Jon Voight's cheerful haplessness and Dustin Hoffman's numb pluck. Hoffman is the brains of the outfit, Voight the muscle, in the classic American buddy coupling, from *Moby-Dick* and *Huckleberry Finn* to *Of Mice and Men.* Together, the two losers derive something that neither has alone, a sad yet hopeful softness. It is *Midnight Cowboy*'s softness that gave it greatness, the feelings we hear in the sorry music of its theme song, Fred Neil's "Everybody's Talkin'" (sung on the sound track by Harry Nilsson). This is, no doubt, what disturbed critics like Schickel—softness in a film whose love story connects two men. Gable and Tracy would never have let softness vex *their* buddy films.

But then Gable and Tracy were members of a stylish and stylized world, and a carefully limited one. A lot of truths and curiosities that narrow minds cannot handle were deleted in their day, on the theory that the adventures of degraded people were uninspiring. Even if the adventures themselves made up a good story, they wouldn't make what would have

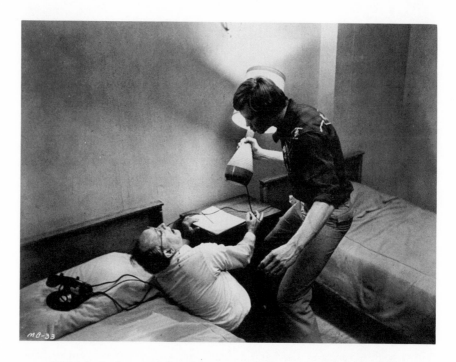

Midnight Cowboy, real-life and fantasto. Above, Jon Voight menaces Barnard Hughes, though this is exactly what Hughes needs; below, Dustin Hoffman, in a dream vision, banks a crap game for the ladies of Miami.

been thought a worthy movie. This is why the movies of the Studio Age seem debonair compared with those of the 1960s, and why those of the 1960s seem so dark and despairing compared with those of the Studio Age. Speaking very roughly, there are three eras of American film: first, the silent period; second, the Studio Age; and last, the modern age (c. 1960–), and one of the defining characteristics of the modern is its ability to find humanity everywhere humanity is, not just where Gable and Tracy would have felt appropriate. Humanity is larger than Hollywood's traditional catalogue of types allows, and the star system—and the list of roles stars would consider—had to expand to fulfill the movies' survey of what life is. This is something even the underground couldn't manage. But the movies have been handling it since the late 1960s, as if somewhere in Hollywood someone had laid down a guideline that says, more or less: *All good stories are equal, even if the setting is lurid and the main characters are losers.*

What life is: this is the subject of the new American cinema that rose up in the 1960s. Even among middle-class characters, the college-educated, the people with mailing addresses and Thanksgiving Days, the view can be grim. In *The Rain People,* one of the less celebrated films of 1969, writer and director Francis Ford Coppola traces a voyage of self-realization very unlike Joe Buck's, yet, in the end, not unlike. Shirley Knight makes a collect call to her husband from a pay phone on the Pennsylvania Turnpike. What we hear and see is astonishingly naturalized even for the late 1960s, photographed and recorded in a kind of near-underground vérité: Knight's hesitant explanation, her husband's irritated insistence, and the remote operator—no more remote than the husband, really, just less involved—collaborating in a scene so deftly made of blank spaces and colloquial incoherence that we wonder if Coppola actually "made" it at all. Could he have simply given his players a rough idea of what's happening and let them improvise it? It's a very long, very still sequence, all talking yet spellbinding. In fact, there's far more to see than hear in *The Rain People,* more atmosphere and thoughtful long shots and waiting and watching than outright dialogue. Coppola's camera is constantly considering its subjects—the ambivalent, self-absorbed Knight; the calmly incomplete James Caan, a college football hero with a brain disability; and cop Robert Duvall, a murderously cool number.

What people are is the theme. Knight claims to be confused and out of control, but she seems well in command of every situation. She even, reluctantly, takes care of Caan. Knight is contemplating having an abortion, yet she in effect "has" a child—Caan. And Duvall, who as a lawman should be a protector, an officer of justice, is a creep. What people *really* are. It's a tormenting film, because its realism is so helter-skelter real that its pathos is even more affecting than that of *Midnight Cowboy*. Coppola's confidential tale won't allow the front-burner portrayals of a Hoffman or a Voight; Knight, Caan, and Duvall can't do anything they couldn't get away with in a backyard or on the street. So Knight doesn't give us a study in early-middle feminist quandary. Caan doesn't style his pathetic idiot. Duvall moves in real slow. They appear as ordinary as Coppola's turnpike, motel room, green hills. But if this is ordinary, is *everybody* hurting? *The Rain People* is a terribly sad and touching film, grim poetry, all the more so because we know that only a few years earlier, it would have ended not in the death and despair it honestly leads up to but hopefully, the menacing Duvall disarmed and Knight and Caan some-how planning a life together. "The rain people are people made of rain," Caan tells Knight. "And when they cry they disappear altogether." So another guideline is: *Tragedy is allowed. It may even be essential.*

This does not mean that the Old Cinema of happy endings and justice for all is utterly gone. But it has become somewhat exceptional. I take *True Grit* not as an aberrant release for 1969 but as a report from a minority stockholder, someone who has no great say in how matters will proceed but who keeps showing up at meetings and always gets noticed. The film's star, John Wayne, got noticed with his first Best Actor award on Oscar night, proving how protective Hollywood felt not just about its icons but about the heroic mythology they embodied, the Old Cinema that loves life.

Citing Wayne as Best Actor was partly out of sentiment, sheer industry pride in this last of the big male action stars. But it also expressed Hollywood's approach-avoidance conflict over what it had become. It was a defiant gesture—defiant most directly of Dustin Hoffman and Jon Voight, whose outstanding performances in the year's Best Picture were two of the reasons why it won in the first place. Wayne gave an outstand-ing demonstration of survival, no more. Unlike Clark Gable, Gary Cooper, Victor McLaglen, Joel McCrea, Robert Mitchum, and other men who were not natural-born thespians but who picked up the rudiments, then the refinements, as they went along, Wayne never learned to play character. He couldn't even play Wayne. He just *was* Wayne; and his successful movies (*after* John Ford's *Stagecoach* in 1939) tend to build up around him the way a medieval saga follows its hero. Giving Wayne an acting award over Hoffman and Voight—not to mention Richard Burton (for *Anne of the Thousand Days*) and Peter O'Toole (for *Goodbye, Mr. Chips*), both superb—marked the distaste many felt for the kind of characters Hoffman and Voight portrayed, for the kind of movie *Midnight Cowboy* was.

True Grit was seen as a kind of antidote—an old-fashioned western about the good guys going after the bad guy. The project seems to have been conceived precisely as a retro entry in the history books, a one-film resistance movement, produced by old-timer Hal Wallis (who had been in Hollywood since 1922), directed by Henry Hathaway (who got his start playing tykes for Allan Dwan in 1910 or 1911), and of course designed to make the most of what Wayne by then represented: the invincible cowboy of righteousness, kind (if patronizing) to the nice and weak and certain death to the villainous—not only two-fisted but two-gunned, when, in a climactic confrontation, he clamps his horse's reins between his teeth and fires away with both hands. There was an air of the fine old ways of Hollywood everywhere: in the quaintly stylized dialogue (taken right off the pages of Charles Portis's novel); in the sweet, slightly quirky sound-track score, rather antebellum after what we had heard from Ennio Morricone in Sergio Leone's westerns; in the use of clean-cut kids Kim Darby and Glen Campbell, who kick the plot into gear by enlisting Wayne's help in taking revenge on killer Jeff Corey. Actually, it's Darby who hires Wayne, for Corey has murdered her father and she wants to murder Corey. Wayne has been recommended to her as an odd-job paladin. "I hear you're a man with true grit," she tells him.

True Grit did blend touches of the New into its nostalgia, its very nearly fifties simplicity of style and philosophy. Robert Duvall, in a smallish role, cuts the hard edge of the sixties villain-hero, and that ultra-contemporary figure, Dennis Hopper, is on hand as well.* Moreover, Glen Campbell, Kim Darby's how-I-hate-to-love-you vis-à-vis, is killed near the film's end, a rather daring surprise for the kind of film that wants its public to come out feeling ten feet tall.

*Casting Hopper must have been Hathaway's ironic joke, for back in 1958 Hopper fought Hathaway on the set of *From Hell to Texas* because Hopper wanted to maximize his portrayal through Method realism and Hathaway wanted him to stand there and just do it. When the film was finished, Hathaway told Hopper he'd never work in Hollywood again, but God wasn't listening.

Still in all, *True Grit* fulfilled its intention to reinstate the life-loving, traditionally moralistic movie that believes in heroes who keep the world whole. To conservative taste, it's a virtuous film in the way *Dr. Strangelove, Bonnie and Clyde,* and *Easy Rider* are not. They challenge; *True Grit* sanctifies. All four of these films are about America, but the first three, in varying ways, denounce America's self-image as the delusion of a murderous idiot who thinks he's Prince Valiant. *True Grit* says the 1960s are the delusion: Prince Valiant's still in there somewhere, obscured by a bad press and perhaps a few race riots.

The Prince is old now, sagging in the saddle, his face lined and his hearing bad, but if he can't bring Kim Darby's murdered father back to life he can still knock off guilty Jeff Corey and put society back in order. Those who were made uncomfortable when General Jack D. Ripper blew up the world, or when Bonnie and Clyde were lovingly riddled with invisible bullets in slow motion, or when Southern rednecks shot the easy riders off the road must have felt exhilarated by *True Grit's* fade-out. Wayne bids So long to Darby at her father's grave—most fitting, for Wayne has in a way become her new father. As his horse rears up, he shouts, "Well, come see a fat old man sometime!" and rides away. Clearly, *Old Cinema will survive, even in (more or less) its old form.* Movies can't all be bad dreams, and even a public attracted by *Dr. Strangelove's* voodoo or *Bonnie and Clyde's* farcical thriller romance or *Easy Rider's* freak-show tragedy is going to need, every so often, what is known as a break.

Of all the breaks Hollywood traditionally provided—the purely escapist fare—the most dependable was the musical, precisely because it is utter fantasy, made of fun and never dangerous. No one ever dies in a musical. (Well, hardly ever.)* But the musical didn't make it past the next decade. The drastically enhanced budgets of the big Broadway adap-

---

*Once you start looking, you find a surprising amount of death in movie musicals—Helen Morgan, the heroine of one of the first musicals, *Applause,* takes poison, and even Fred Astaire dies in an aviation accident in *The Story of Vernon and Irene Castle.* However, death is generally ignored in the movie musical, something that not only doesn't but couldn't happen, or happens only to old people (Helen Westley in *Roberta*), villains (Margaret Hamilton in *The Wizard of Oz*), minor characters (Judy Garland's younger brother Richard Quine in *For Me and My Gal*), or people who shouldn't have been in a musical in the first place (James Mason in *A Star Is Born*). The emphasis on transcriptions from Broadway made death a little more common, especially in *Carousel* and *West Side Story*; and *The Sound of Music* is so dangerous it has Nazis, though some viewers find the nuns even scarier.

tations and dwindling audience response ran the form so deeply into the red that, after seventies bombs like *On a Clear Day You Can See Forever, Song of Norway, Darling Lili, The Great Waltz, Man of La Mancha, Lost Horizon, Mame, At Long Last Love, The Little Prince, A Little Night Music, New York, New York,* and *Hair,* the musical as such was less than moribund. *Fiddler on the Roof, Cabaret, Grease, Funny Lady,* and *A Star Is Born* were successful, but the form had become terribly risky. Sporadic attempts to reinstate it, in *Pennies From Heaven, Annie,* and *A Chorus Line,* were failures, though the adaptation of the off-Broadway version of Roger Corman's *The Little Shop of Horrors* came off nicely.

So the musical turned into other things—the rock-concert souvenir (like *The Last Waltz*); or the jukebox-sound-track drama, in which songs are laid over the action of a non-musical film as if the public were watching a movie and playing records at once (like *Paper Moon* or *FM* or *American Graffiti*); or the two-disc sound-track-album movie, in which you scarcely notice the music at all while the film is on and then discover that four sides' worth of numbers have suddenly materialized (like *Saturday Night Fever*); or the one-person musical (like *The Buddy Holly Story* and *The Rose*). Still, these aren't musicals in the sense that *Whoopee!, Swing Time, Meet Me in St. Louis,* and *Gigi* are musicals: song and dance invigoratingly threaded into a story.

Oddly, one of the best musicals of the late 1960s wasn't a musical in this sense, either. Herbert Ross's *Goodbye, Mr. Chips,* a road-show spectacular of late 1969, was barely a musical in any sense. There is but one full-out song-and-dance number, "London Is London," establishing Petula Clark as a "soubrette" (her word) of the West End stage, a tour of the city from modest Fulham to Park Lane and Buckingham Palace, with a full change of set and costumes for each locale. It's a bit lavish but a reasonable re-creation of twenties musical comedy—and, as director Ross is also a choreographer, we know that, for once in a modern musical, the film's auteur is truly in charge of a sequence instead of just looking on. Much later in the film, after the supposedly raffish Clark has married Peter O'Toole (the supposedly dreary Brookfield master Chipping), she performs a canes-and-boaters bit with some Brookfield boys, hardly a great moment in the history of movie musicals, hardly meant to be.

But then with Clark and O'Toole in the leads we cannot expect the kind of score Chevalier and MacDonald or Astaire and Rogers or Rooney and Garland handled, because O'Toole can't sing or dance, and to give a brace of numbers only to Clark would sabotage the rapport of their union. For *Goodbye, Mr. Chips* is above all a romance, a valentine to what love can do for a solitary and unadventurous man whose life is set, all over but the playout, by the time he's twenty-five. So O'Toole *must* at least sing, must give us some sense of how he feels before meeting Clark and how after.

Ross is sage: he *sneaks* O'Toole into the music. "Where Did My Childhood Go?" starts *inside* him as an interior monologue, in tape-over, drops out as the scene continues in dialogue, returns, and finally comes literally out of his mouth, allowing O'Toole to evade the all-out shaping and presentation of a musical number—the surest thing, more than voice, that separates the incompetent outsider from the veteran pro.

Clark, too, sings in voice-over, to blend the approach stylistically into the whole. In fact, not till forty-five minutes on do we get anything like a regular movie-musical story number, "When I'm Older," which follows the Brookfield students back from vacation, dreading school and looking forward to the independence of maturity. This is all mouth-to-mouth singing—that is, we see the kids sing the words we're hearing—but it moves from "real" time into a montage of the boys in class, at recreation, and so on. So even this number isn't "regular." Like O'Toole's and Clark's voice-overs, the song helps provision a new kind of musical, perhaps one better suited than Big Broadway for an era increasingly bored by retreads of stage shows and bedeviled by non-musical performers.

Goodbye, Mr. Chips is of course a retread of an earlier adaptation of James Hilton's novel, another classic from that *annus mirabilus* 1939, with Robert Donat and Greer Garson. No one but me seems to think so, but the musical is a vast improvement on its predecessor. Granted, Leslie Bricusse's score is dull, but everything else gives delight: Terence Rattigan's literate screenplay; the versatile cinematography that uses the "London Is London" theatre perspective, the verdant, sun-basted Pompeii sequence (in which O'Toole meets Clark), a claustrophobic London flat in the full cry of a mildly bohemian party to break up the vistas and heights and breadths of the Brookfield campus; and particularly the performances. Rattigan prudently included another in his peculiar series of Dizzy Dames, a high-fashion friend of Clark's, the flamboyant-to-die Siân Phillips, who arrives at a Brookfield festival in a car that runs right onto the cricket pitch in the middle of a match. "Parents' Day!" cries Phillips to all and sundry. "What could be more riveting?" A master offers to show Phillips

The once-and-future Siân Phillips disrupts Parents Day at Brookfield School in *Goodbye, Mr. Chips.*

the bell tower. "I hope you like early English perpendicular," he says. "Darling," she replies as she takes his arm, "I *revel* in early English perpendicular."

O'Toole and Clark make a perfect misalliance. One of the earlier film's defects is the utter lack of challenge in the mating of Donat and Garson. They're ideal; they're suited; so what? O'Toole is a plop and Clark is "unsuitable." *That's* a story. O'Toole manages to show not only the character's awkwardness but his gallantry, the hero inside the nerd that romance calls into being, and O'Toole was praised. But Clark won no honor for her charming presentation of a woman cut squarely between the extremes of the glamorous, like Phillips, and the dowdy (like the headmaster's wife). Clark is as basic as a headmaster's wife but in a glamorous way. She's the Siân Phillips of Brookfield.

The film in general won no honor, and today's video guides routinely put it down as underpowered. I profoundly disagree. What is more moving than the tale of a man who had come to see himself as a nobody, who finds himself turning impressive because a soubrette sees something in him, and loses her in the moment of triumph? For just as Chips is promoted to headmaster of Brookfield, his wife is killed in an air raid. In a scene common to novel, to 1939, and to 1969, an unknowing class baits him with jokes moments after the annunciation of death, and O'Toole's stunned reception, inanely struggling to carry on and make sense of what he has heard and what is happening, is one of the acting tours de force of the decade.

Perhaps *Goodbye, Mr. Chips* was too touching, too sentimental for the day. It capped a decade in which glamorous people of all kinds—the two Kennedys, Marilyn Monroe, Martin Luther King, Jr.—were being killed off. By *whom?* Touching wasn't a pertinent affect in 1969. Many critics resent films that deeply touch us, and by this time critics were disgusted by the musical as a form—they fell upon the expert *Hello, Dolly!* like the fold on the wolf. This is an age that likes its film hard-grained, musicals included—*Tommy,* in the mid-1970s, is just right. So: *The musical will have to realign itself with the energies of the times before it can come back.*

Ironically, an even older Hollywood form—the oldest form, really—was on the verge of retirement by 1969: the western. Film historians chart the rise of narrative cinema in America from Edwin S. Porter's *The Great Train Robbery* (1903), a western, and the genre steadily grew as the nation's ethical storybook, its illustrations of how good and evil functioned, why societies formed, what heroism contained. But by the late 1960s, the American screen no longer had the moral authority to depict ethical values—which no doubt explains the outstanding popularity of the Italian westerns of Sergio Leone, a series of requiems for America's lost innocence by an outside, an uncompromised, observer. The pop action thriller, from James Bond on to Indiana Jones, took over the western's mandate as the undisputed vessel of good-versus-evil adventure—but Leone had not yet shot his bolt in the western, and decided to make a kind of "last" western, an epic, more traditional than the *Dollars* trilogy, something without the *Dollars* satire, perhaps something like the western an American might have made if Americans saw the western—or, rather, America—as Leone did. *Once Upon a Time in the West* is indeed a kind of last western, for it opens up an entire history of the westward movement and closes upon the moment when the old West could foresee its end as a culture, when the rest of the American nation will soon have claimed, settled, and declared it finished.

Leone was so determined that *Once Upon a Time in the West* mark a breakaway from his outlandish *Dollars* style that he planned to open the saga with a big set piece at a deserted railroad station, in which super-human good guy Charles Bronson would shoot down three hired guns— the *Dollars* boys, Clint Eastwood, Lee Van Cleef, and Eli Wallach. Considering Leone's fondness for *hommage,* it would have been telling, and Van Cleef and Wallach were game, but Eastwood declined. The scene is there,* with Leone gaming (a fly bedevils one of the gunslingers while they're waiting for Bronson's train; surely this is chance event that Leone impishly decided to lock into his romance); Leone painting (the station, a mass of weathered planks and an adobe-styled shack for the station house, is more real than reality); Leone eliciting (awaiting the train, he builds a suspense to rival Hitchcock); and Leone brilliant (the train arrives, no Bronson; the train pulls out, and suddenly Bronson is standing as still as death on the far side of the tracks, as if he had not arrived but materialized, and Leone catches this in a frame bordered by the bad guys, Bronson a tiny figure in the distant center, spellbinding).

The coming of the train is the film's central act—the coming of the railroad, actually, for Leone is catching the West just as the all-male society of loners and posses and saloons is about to cede to the civilized West of families and children and churches. All three male principals—Bronson, Henry Fonda, and Jason Robards—at various times remark or realize that the enfolding of the West into greater American society will wipe them out, and the plot hits into gear when Claudia Cardinale arrives to join her new husband and his kids (by a former marriage): to form a family.

This marks another important change from Leone's *Dollars* procedures: a leading woman. Cardinale's husband-to-be and the stepchildren have been murdered for their land, but she has the deed and holds her ground. She fights and wins, and the town that will rise on her land, at a major station point of a new railroad line, symbolizes the coming of the future. To boot, Leone endows Cardinale through thematic riffs as an earth mother and water-carrier, so that the final shot of a train steaming into the makeshift station and Cardinale pouring water from a jug for

*Jack Elam, Woody Strode, and Al Mulock play the desperadoes.

On the set with Sergio Leone. The director of *Once Upon a Time in the
West* demonstrates to Claudia Cardinale the most dramatic, intrepid, and
virtuous method of drinking from a jug. What an auteur! Every detail
just *so!* And see how Cardinale dotes upon the master's instruction.

thirsty workers—the only woman in a sea of men—is something of a
promise that wild land will be turned into a safe place, as if depicted in
a historical print entitled "The Closing of the West."

Casting Henry Fonda is essential to Leone's approach, for here, for
the first time, this Studio Age Folk Hero plays an unmitigated monster,
as if Leone were closing not only the historical West but the fabled West
of Hollywood's imaginings. If Fonda is a creep, *everything's* over. Fonda
fell in with the scheme, showing up for his first day of shooting with
special contact lenses to darken his baby-blue eyes and a melodrama villain's mustache. *"Off!"* said Leone. He wanted the familiar Fonda, the
Folk Hero, to unnerve his public's expectations. This Fonda does in his
first scene, the massacre of the family Cardinale is coming west to play
mother to. Five men in dusters and flat-brimmed hats arrive at Sweetwater
Farm, and simply mow everyone down—father, daughter, and two young
sons. Then Leone closes in on the famous Fonda face, blue eyes and all
. . . and the man is smiling.

Leone pursued his valedictory by filling the film with a museum's worth of tributes to the American movie western, including a final long ride through John Ford's beloved Monument Valley—which, significantly, Cardinale passes through upon her arrival. Unlike the European-made *Dollars* films, *Once Upon a Time in the West* was produced by Paramount and made in California, which aided the highly pictorial Leone in giving his last western a more magnificent (even arty) look than he had found for the seedy *Dollars* locales. Oddly, one element remains from the *Dollars* style, the brazen Morricone sound-track accompaniment, very slightly modified, just that much less brazen.

Once Upon a Time in the West failed in the United States when it came out in 1969. The critics didn't take to it, it disappointed *Dollars* fans, and the release print was marred by twenty-four minutes of cuts, making the principals' already highly elaborate and volatile relationships virtually incomprehensible. (Only Italy saw the full-length, 168-minute *C'era una Volta il West.*) Nevertheless, repeated viewings of the complete original convince me that this is genius film, one of those rare productions that are not only unique, enlightening, and artistically fulfilled to the utmost, but that involve us so much more deeply than even the best films that their power to enthrall becomes incomparable. Think of *Intolerance, Sunrise, Les Enfants du Paradis, The Wizard of Oz, Citizen Kane, La Strada*: experiences beyond experience. Genius film also stands above the High Maestro sweepstakes, for it doesn't necessarily explain or exalt a director's oeuvre—may not even claim an all-governing auteur. Who is the author, after all, of *The Wizard of Oz?* Victor Fleming? Surely L. Frank Baum, the Harold Arlen–E. Y. Harburg score, and MGM's design, makeup, and special-effects departments gave more to the work than director Fleming did.

I find it interesting that the titles I cite, all acknowledged classics, did poor or somewhat disappointing business when they were first released. Perhaps genius film is its own flaw: it overwhelms. Cinema is supposed to be the most immediate of the arts, yet it is also supposed to play to the widest public, and at times it outruns them. The 1960s appeared to be the first decade in which the audience took so active a part in the reception of films that the most conveniently estimable collaborator in filmmaking, the director, became the world's significant artist. Certainly, Leone—clearly the author of his films as conceiver, co-writer, and director—had his time of glory. Yet it was over in two years.

Jumping into the future, we see similar problems for Ken Russell, Brian De Palma, Robert Altman, Francis Ford Coppola, Steven Spielberg, and Michael Cimino, all of whom were reproved or even disdained almost as soon as they were hailed. High Maestro critique has already become obsolete, and the emergence of new directors will be greeted cautiously, even cynically. Apparently: *The cult of the director is over.*

After all, no one spoke of admitting George Roy Hill into the club after *Butch Cassidy and the Sundance Kid,* though it was one of the most clever and popular films of the 1960s. Hill is the kind of director who doesn't get into those encyclopedias, though he has to his credit the charmingly child's-view Peter Sellers comedy *The World of Henry Orient* (1964); an intriguing adaptation from the files of Kurt Vonnegut, *Slaughterhouse Five* (1972); and one of the most clever and popular films of the 1970s, *The Sting* (1973). True, Hill also directed *Hawaii* (1966) and *Thoroughly Modern Millie,* and all-star epics and musicals do violence to reputations. *The Bible* might be John Huston's worst film, George Stevens's fans become quite, quite still when you mention *The Greatest Story Ever Told,* and who in his right mind would direct a musical? Then, too, critics find no auteurist hook in Hill. Where are his jags, his stylistic hiccups? Versatility looks suspicious to people who can only do one thing.

But then, as a number of critics noted at the time, most of what was delightful in *Butch Cassidy* lay in William Goldman's script, which was published simultaneously with the film's release. Returning to his "Hole in the Wall Gang," Butch is challenged for supremacy by a lugubrious but monstrous thug, and Butch tells Sundance, "Listen, I'm not a sore loser or anything, but when we're done, if I'm dead, kill him." Or Butch, robbing the railroad, blows open a safe with such finesse that he is forced to cry out, "Damn it all, why is everything we're good at illegal?" Or Sundance slips into a beautiful woman's room as she is undressing for bed; she sees him and freezes. "Keep going, teacher lady," he tells her at gunpoint, and she does; and he goes over to her and this is sheer rape, and she suddenly says, "Do you know what I wish?" "What?" he asks, and she replies, "That you'd once get here on time."

Or Butch convinces Sundance and their teacher friend Etta Place to try Bolivia, but when they arrive they see nothing but "horrid low adobe huts" and "an occasional pig," and Sundance, "close to a Homeric anger," lashes out at Etta and Butch, and Butch consoles Etta with "He'll feel a lot better once we robbed a couple banks." Or finally Butch and Sundance are cornered by the Bolivian cavalry, outnumbered one hundred to two and each mortally wounded seven times over. This is it. It is certain, if shocking (even after all the death we've seen this decade, all the death of heroes—or, at any rate, of stars), that the two are about to die. So, of course:

BUTCH   I got a great idea where we should go next.

SUNDANCE   Well, I don't wanna hear it.

BUTCH   You'll change your mind once I tell you.

SUNDANCE   Shut up.

BUTCH   Okay, okay.

SUNDANCE   It was your great ideas got us here.

BUTCH   Forget about it.

SUNDANCE   I never want to hear another of your great ideas, all right?

BUTCH   All right.

SUNDANCE   Good.

BUTCH   Australia.

(*A pause as Sundance stares at Butch.*)

BUTCH   I figured secretly you wanted to know, so I told you.

Another comedy about thieves, another study in how charisma overwhelms morality. Like *Bonnie and Clyde*, *Butch Cassidy* textures its comedy with startling violence: just as we're getting used to the different members of Butch's band, two of them are killed during a robbery, and, quite late in the picture, Butch and Sundance have to shoot it out with some Bolivian *bandidos*, and Hill films the Bolivians rolling backward downhill in slow motion, to the magnified roaring voice of one man. Like *Bonnie and Clyde*, *Butch Cassidy* instructs us powerfully in the autonomous superiority of beautiful people. This is Paul Newman and Robert Redford in the roles they may well be best remembered for, merrily skimming the cream off the top of the system, here a train and there a bank.

But unlike *Bonnie and Clyde*, *Butch Cassidy* is far more a quirky buddy picture than a shoot-'em-up, and bears no brief for the moral position of Us against Them. If the Barrow gang in *Bonnie and Clyde* is supposed to represent some sort of demented freedom-fighting outfit (if only to Arthur Penn), Butch and Sundance are nothing but brigands, and they know it, and Hill and Goldman know it, and we know it. So *Butch Cassidy* provoked no controversy, other than that between those who thought it marvelous entertainment and those who thought it empty, slick, and false.

Perhaps they're both right. *Butch Cassidy* could seem marvelous yet empty because, unlike the major criminal-hero movies of the day, it isn't about crime, isn't interested in how Butch and Sundance's activities reflect their view of the world. They have no view. Bonnie and Clyde, or *In Cold Blood*'s Hickock and Smith, are thoroughly committed to crime in the way sensualists are committed to sex. They couldn't live without it. Crime isn't their means; crime is their end.

To Butch and Sundance, crime is just a living, and one has the impression they'd be just as happy doing something else if there was something else they could do. That line about everything they're good at being illegal isn't quite right; they're not all that good, just persistent. The second time Butch blows a safe, he uses so much dynamite that he destroys the entire railroad car and cash rains from heaven, and neither he nor Butch can master even rudimentary bank-job Spanish for their Bolivian expedition.

What's marvelous about the film is Butch and Sundance's friendship, crackling with affection through the mock-put-down lines and occasional grouching interludes; but what's empty about the film is that the friendship never goes anywhere. Newman and Redford are like a stand-up comic duo—like, in fact, a much wittier and more charming version of television's *Laugh-In* hosts, Dan Rowan and Dick Martin. The characters are fixed, the routines schematic. It's all transaction, no development: a movie about banter. As Hill later reported, Goldman told him, "I gave you *Shane* and you gave me *Gunga Din*"; and Hill himself thinks what they really got was "the Laurel and Hardy of Deadwood Gulch."

It's a very hip film for a western, loaded with anachronisms to make us feel that the turn of the century was a rather sixties sort of time. Burt Bacharach's sound-track score is utterly out of synch with the setting, not only in the breezily sappy "Raindrops Keep Fallin' on My Head" but strains of modernized twenties jazz and Swingle Singers imitations to accompany the Bolivian bank robberies. Goldman slips in some state-of-the-tongue slang, including "We lucked out," and the sepia-tinted silent film on the exploits of the Hole in the Wall Gang that opens *Butch Cassidy* looks like a new movie without sound, not an old silent. (The sepia look holds for the first scenes, and only cedes to color when the two leads finally get on horseback, a nice touch.) So here is another "last" western, one that acts like the latest thing in westerns, not least in its "cream and bastards rise" outlook. Of course, when Newman uttered the phrase in *Harper,* he was decrying the prevalence, the *prominence,* of crooks. In *Butch Cassidy,* he's supporting it.

Naturally, the movie expects us to love Butch and Sundance and resent their enemies. "There was a general sense of approval in the liberal community for defense lawyers, and a corresponding loathing for prosecutors," Lawrence Wright recalls in his memoir *In the New World: Growing Up with America, 1960–1984.* "Punishment was seen as repression. It was the same mentality that encouraged shoplifting, looting, and telephone fraud as a means of striking back at the Establishment, of 'ripping off the system.'" Well, Bosley Crowther warned us. In Bolivia, would-be depositors Newman and Redford have a bank manager show off his impenetrable vault, and the poor guy opens it and turns proudly to Redford only to face his gun. The stunt turns on the mortification of a fat cat's vanity, and we're supposed to laugh. I feel sorry for the bank's depositors.

Bonnie and Clyde ridiculed the pursuing adversary figure, Texas Ranger Frank Hamer—"some hidden evil sometimes shows in his face," the screenplay warns. He is a monster who destroys beauty. *Butch Cassidy* goes further, dehumanizing the posse that trails Newman and Redford. They are distant figures, without character motivation (unlike *Bonnie and Clyde*'s Ranger, who has been personally humiliated by the Barrow gang) and unnaturally tireless and efficient. "Who are those guys?" Butch asks. They're goblins. Only a vindictive horror like railroad magnate E. H. Harriman could dream up this superposse that never rests and never errs and follows you until it catches you. They're like the ghastly ring wraiths in J. R. R. Tolkien's *The Lord of the Rings* (one of the most popular titles in sixties fiction), and Harriman is the Dark Lord. Let's not waste any pity on one of the nineteenth century's great robber barons—but all the guy wants to do is stop Butch and Sundance from robbing his trains. As Harriman's posse tracks Newman and Redford in an extended sequence of comic suspense, we are meant to share the stars' growing fear that these ghouls of justice cannot be shaken. The two veil their fear in wry pleasantries, which makes them all the more likable. "Who *are* those guys?" Newman asks again and again, punctuating the sequence's episodes with a mingled respect and horror. Newman outwits and Redford outshoots everyone, but at last they have been overmatched. They are about to become extinct. This isn't just our last western. It's theirs.

Like the other nine films discussed in this chapter, *Butch Cassidy and the Sundance Kid* came out in 1969, and it feels very strongly like an end-of-an-era piece—in the incongruity of an "old West" rob-and-run gang happening late enough in history to see itself in a movie;* in the introduction of the bicycle that a salesman predicts as the miracle of the future; in a friendly sheriff's warning to the two leads, "You want to hide out till it's old times again, but it's over. . . . It's over and you're both gonna die bloody, and all you can do is choose where"; and particularly in Katharine Ross's big aria, technically a solemnization of the incipient end of her relationship with the two men, but, by implication, a eulogy in advance for all that was wonderful that now must end:

> ETTA   I'm twenty-six, and I'm single, and I'm a school-
> teacher, and that's the bottom of the pit. And the
> only excitement I've ever known is here with me
> right now. So I'll go with you [to Bolivia], and I
> won't whine, and I'll sew your socks and stitch you
> when you're wounded, and anything you ask of me
> I'll do, except one thing: I won't watch you die.
> I'll miss that scene if you don't mind.

But this is an end-of-an-era picture that cares more about the stars than the era. Social order is restored at the film's end, when Newman and Redford echo forth to certain death, guns ablaze, and Hill slips back into sepia in his closing freeze-frame to round it all out. It's a heavy price to pay for peace, no doubt, but then these two *were* outlaws—just as, perhaps, making Richard Nixon President is an atrocious task, but the

---

*In Goldman's original screenplay, Butch, Sundance, and Etta saw the movie at a Bolivian theatre, the two men arguing aloud at the liberties taken with the truth, then quiet in a sea of cheering moviegoers as they watch the superposse shoot them to death. Hill moved a sweeter and inconclusive version of the film-within-the-film up front, adding in the jauntily pompous warning, "Most of what follows is true." Still, the air of over-the-hill, of the last dying gasp, is tensely felt.

nation wants the 1960s to be over, and Nixon's opponent, the concessively liberal Hubert Humphrey, might have let the era run on indefinitely.

It was a disastrous bargain. Nixon's paranoia, through Watergate, gave us Carter. Carter's backwoods ineptness gave us Reagan, whom history will remember as the President who unleashed drugs and AIDS upon the United States. But after so much disorder, so much trashing of the values Americans had been taking for granted for generations, so much divisiveness for what appeared to be the fun of it, the 1960s, as a concept (better, as a transformational agent; best, as a catalogue of unattractive and somewhat nasty and often downright destructive emotions) had to end or the center would not hold.

What the decade gave to American film will most influentially inform the next twenty years of American moviemaking, whether technical, artistic, or intellectual. But the *feelings* of the day—the sense that so many sixties movies gave that revolution was in the making, that something awesome could happen very suddenly, that someone who hated life and your face was going to be totally in charge of you starting next Thursday—all this will, for the most part, give way to an anti-1960s reaction, a healing of the factionalism, a yearning for harmony, and a revulsion against the lawless, the bizarre, the corrupt: *Gimme Shelter, Joe, Love Story, Patton, Straw Dogs, Billy Jack, Dirty Harry, Magnum Force, Murder on the Orient Express, The Exorcist, High Plains Drifter, Oh God!, Death Wish, Annie Hall, Superman, Rocky, Dog Day Afternoon* (another based-on-life crime thriller but, unlike *Bonnie and Clyde* and *In Cold Blood,* one without glamorized criminals; in fact, one in which the narrative energies are bent toward a sense of relief when the criminals are destroyed), *American Graffiti* and *Grease* (marking a return to Kid Film, in which the kids are playful rather than disturbed or, God forbid, political), *That's Entertainment* and *Movie Movie* (both uttering a nostalgia for the kind of world Hollywood used to describe), and *The First Deadly Sin* (in which Frank Sinatra, unable legally to nab the man we know is killing New Yorkers at random with a mountain climber's ice hammer, simply breaks into his apartment and shoots him). Most notably, when Butch and Sundance return, in *The Sting,* we remark that while they are still con men, it is a fellow criminal they cheat, not the public. In short: *The 1960s are coming to an end.*

One sixties theme the 1970s was happy to retain was the so-called sexual revolution, though commentators couldn't settle on the true nature of Paul Mazursky's satire *Bob & Carol & Ted & Alice.* Some thought it prurient and vulgar, smut disguised as sensitivity, a series of cheap shots without a conclusion; others found it a legitimate crisis piece, confronting sexual mores with a tensely eliciting honesty. The film arrived in the fall of 1969, and is, indeed, a somewhat autumnal work, for all its California vitality. It is not about the sex that all the kids were supposedly having, but about the sex that married grown-ups felt cut off from—particularly grown-ups Bob (Robert Culp), who is attractive and travels and thus has plenty of opportunity for but mixed feelings about extramarital escapades; and Ted (Elliott Gould), who keeps hearing about wife-swapping and orgies but can't seem to find them.

Mazursky and co-writer Larry Tucker have rich terrain to mine, from awareness-encounter institutes (they open in one, possibly modeled on Esalen) through suburbia's pot parties to the next-to-closing foursome, the title characters ranged in a single bed. *Bob & Carol* is a very funny film, but descriptive rather than witty. One laughs not at the cleverness of the lines but at the familiarity and irony of the situations: Culp and his wife Carol (Natalie Wood, in one of her best roles), liberating their feelings at the institute by hugging and weeping with strangers; Culp liberating his guilt by telling Wood about a recent fling as the two then struggle to Be Open, Have Insight, and Admit Hostilities; Gould trying to get some nitty-gritty hard-core report out of Culp in a swimming pool while Gould's little boy keeps paddling over for attention and Gould keeps pushing him away; Culp, coming back from a trip to find Carol eager to be open about *her* extramarital escapade—and her partner, a German tennis instructor, is upstairs, locked in a bedroom, as we speak; Culp manfully talking the tennis pro into unlocking the door so they can have a drink over it, in the new "now" manner ("You are one hell of a guy," Horst Ebersberg tells Culp as they clink glasses. "You've got a lot of class." To which Culp, radiantly humble, replies, "Thank you"); Ted's wife, Alice (Dyan Cannon), in session with her psychiatrist, running on distractedly after her time is up and the doctor tries, in High Middle Nerd, to shoo her out of the office.

Cannon is the public's surrogate, the one of the four who's leery of all this now behavior. How far, she seems to ask, is the 1960s going to go? She doesn't like pot smoking or Being Open. She is disgusted when Wood glowingly tells her how her fling with the tennis pro brought her closer to Culp. "I am a *very happy person* most of the time," Cannon insists. Yet she spends much of the film being disgusted. When she tells the psychiatrist how her little boy asked her why she has a "titi"—his term for "vagina"—the doctor has to ask what a titi is. What *else* could it be? his patient's face reads. All right: "What name do you use with your children?" Cannon asks. "Vagina," says the doctor calmly, as if explaining that two plus two equals four. And Cannon is *supremely* disgusted.

Mazursky and Tucker are careful to air the subject of sex from the woman's as well as the man's viewpoint, which strengthens the four stars' team playing. Just as well, for they are the movie. Every other role—the tennis gigolo, Culp's fling partner, the two couples' children—are little more than sketch players, feeding ideas to the principals so we can learn how they feel. Interestingly, the men don't simply want more sex; they want to *think* they do, because sex is what's happening. Besides, men are bombarded by appetizing visuals—on the street, on television, and, of course (particularly in the 1960s), at the movies. A guy is going to feel guilty for wanting it whether he goes after it or not, and, as Culp puts it, "Why waste the guilt?" Do it.

The women in this film are bound by reasonable expectations. The culture can't overwhelm their sense of proportion the way it can the men's. Do it, for the women, has to remain within the bounds of family life and their personal desires. If they do it, it will be because they want to, not because do it is a now act. Thus, when Culp is presented with an opportunity for sensual gratification outside the home orbit, he is torn between the need to grab it and the desire to be loyal to his family, while Wood takes on the tennis pro because she feels the experience will stimulate both her *and* Culp to develop emotionally. Similarly, Gould cuts a ridiculous figure drooling over all the sex he can't get, while Cannon never loses her dignity. The men want to be true to the age. The women want to be true to themselves.

Thus, the film moves inescapably toward an orgy for four. Now playing: the stag movie you long for yet fear, comical yet unnerving, *Bob & Carol & Ted & Alice Doing It*. Naturally it is Cannon who suggests it—not because her volcanic desire has at last exploded, but because she is defying the now mentality. She wants to show how useless, how stupid it is. This is her act of rebellion, not against repressiveness but against permissiveness.

So nothing happens. You've seen the still of the two title couples grinning in style, in the nude, in bed. It's here and it's now. But the four get dressed and leave their hotel to join in an *8½*-like procession of strangers of all kinds, a reprise of the opening encounter session—a mass orgy that is all feelings, no sex.

This is the "cop-out" ending that so many critics derided, the failure to fulfill the "sniggery" vignettes. *Bob & Carol* got some of the worst notices a hit film received in the 1960s, worse than *Butch Cassidy,* worse even than *The Green Berets.* But *The Green Berets* was a dismal irritation, not a revelation of public secrets. Neighborhood adultery is no laughing matter; it's a horror show, because everyone knows it happens and everyone has something to lose if it gets out. Most people like living in some form of authoritarian tribal containment, observing tradition and taboo. Mediocrities don't like freedom; they like containment with a little hypocrisy on the side. *Bob & Carol* dishonored tradition and tickled taboo. Like it or not, the approach turned out to be seminal, surviving the now. Whether one views *Bob & Carol* ultimately as repressive or permissive, it was to leave its mark on many a film that followed, in a more honest yet at the same time more casual report on what men and women do when no one but the audience is looking. The 1960s may be over, but *Sex is here to stay.*

Bob & Carol is one of the most determinedly contemporary films of the 1960s, wired into what's happening and fluent in hipspeak. Sydney Pollack's *They Shoot Horses, Don't They?* was an antique, much more carefully scaled back into period than *True Grit* or *Once Upon a Time in the West.* The period is hard times and the setting a dance hall, where the persons in the drama form a microcosm of life's losers, victims of an unequal society. The screenplay, by James Poe and Robert E. Thompson from Horace McCoy's novel, avoids all possible references to today, and Pollack fills his camera with keen reconstructions of the 1930s: movie posters and a soap endorsement by Barbara Stanwyck; "Brother, Can You Spare a Dime?" and the pathetic singing of the late-twenties hit "The Best Things in Life Are Free," an ironic classic by the early 1930s; the "Yowsah, yowsah, yowsah" of Gig Young (who won one of the most undisputed awards in Oscar history, Best Supporting Actor for his amiably exhausted marathon manager). Yet the overall feeling is that of an immense political statement, and politics is always about now. *They Shoot Horses* is the last *cri du coeur* of sixties conscience, not about the sixties things—war, racism, Bad Fathers—but about the torment of people at the bottom: the wide-eyed, rootless farmboy (Michael Sarrazin); the demented imitation Jean Harlow who thinks a producer will discover her on the marathon floor (Susannah York); the beached old sailor who dies during a special event of the "dance contest," the elimination race (Red Buttons); the dust-bowl orc and his pregnant wife (Bruce Dern and Bonnie Bedelia); and, mainly, Jane Fonda, the only one of the team who appears to have the wit and strength to survive, even win, a grueling contest for physical and emotional endurance—in other words, the Depression.

This is Fonda's first important performance in an important film, and marked her rise as a major movie star. Her political connections would suggest that she was a reigning sixties figure, but it was only in the 1970s, in such films as *Klute, Julia, Coming Home, California Suite,* and *The China Syndrome,* that Fonda won genuine prominence. Her sixties work comprised potboilers like *Barefoot in the Park* and *Cat Ballou,* politically appetitive but artistically savorless films like Arthur Penn's *The Chase* (1966) and Otto Preminger's *Hurry Sundown* (1967), and the dismaying French interlude with Fonda's husband Roger Vadim, Barbarella psychedella.

Though Fonda was an Oscar nominee for *They Shoot Horses* (losing to Maggie Smith for *The Prime of Miss Jean Brodie,* probably because of Fonda's political interests), Fonda was criticized for being too resourceful a figure to have sunk to the level of the doomed. She has the power to outlast everybody and win the marathon. So when Young reveals that the contest is a fake, that his expenses will be deducted from the $1,500 prize money she expected, would she really decide to kill herself—and, on top of that, lack the strength to pull the trigger and hand the gun to Sarrazin, imploring him to do it for her?*

But isn't it the very point of this work that an economic system of such asymmetrical breadth that some have more than enough and some have nothing oppresses the nothings so fiercely that even the most valiant spirit will shatter? It is Bonnie Bedelia who shyly toots her way through "The Best Things in Life Are Free," then dives for the pennies the

---

*The murder episode, connecting the young Sarrazin's witnessing the shooting of a horse to his mercy killing of Fonda and following his arrest and trial, was filmed in a gauzy, soft-tech, fantasy look at odds with Pollack's grimy naturalism and the harshly bright lighting and whirling camera of his cinematographer, Philip A. Lathrop. Apparently these scenes were shot and inserted into the movie after preview audiences found the climactic shooting farfetched and laughable.

audience tosses. That's one picture. That's sympathetic, pitiable. But Fonda, ice and fire that she is, begging Sarrazin to kill her because the misery is unbearable is another picture. That's terrifying.

The emcee assures his public, "There can be only one winner, folks, but isn't that the American way?" This is Studio Age thinking, the philosophy behind the movies of the 1930s: there *need* be only one hero because he redeems us by proxy, draws us up with him. But in *They Shoot Horses* there is no hero, not even the one winner Young has promised us. Life is too tough, too hateful, for anyone to win except in the movies. McCoy's novel is so bleak that though it was sold to Hollywood in the 1930s, it couldn't be filmed, even by street-mean, forgotten-man Warner Brothers. Anyway, we've seen the shattering of some valiant spirits in these pages: Cool Hand Luke, for instance, titanic and resolute—yet, in the end, broken.

Tragedy, once reserved for special occasions in Hollywood, became almost commonplace in the 1960s. Of the ten films of 1969 discussed in this chapter, only three have what could be called happy endings— *Bob & Carol & Ted & Alice, True Grit,* and *Once Upon a Time in the West.* (At that, likable principals are killed off in two of them.) For, in giving up the Studio Age belief in feelgood cinema for an outlook that observes life rather than gilds it, the movies of the 1960s had to reflect the many sorrows and disasters that even the most unadventurous of us must endure. An ultimately tragic view of life will surely never subsume the bulk of Hollywood's output, the *Rocky, E.T.,* or *Field of Dreams* line of wish-fulfillment exhilaration. Even essentially unhappy films like *The Last Picture Show* and *The Big Chill* do not describe the world as darkly as *They Shoot Horses* does. Still: *The I Hate Life syndrome will to some extent inform the movies from now on.*

Luchino Visconti's *The Damned* is something like *They Shoot Horses'* opposite. Just as Sydney Pollack uses the dance marathon microcosmically, Visconti pictures the collapse of an entire society through the downfall of a single family, the von Essenbecks. But the marathoners in *They Shoot Horses* are innocents, the exploited class. The von Essenbecks are the corrupt, the exploiters, a highly placed clan who align their steelworks and political weight with the Hitler of 1933–34, from the Reichstag fire to the Night of Long Knives, when the SA was purged and the SS became Hitler's supervising police apparatus.

Why make an epic about Nazis when Visconti had his own country's Fascist past to draw on? "As the perfect archetype of criminality," Visconti explained, "Nazism seemed to me more exemplary, because it was a tragedy that, like a hideous bloodstain, seeped over the whole world." Besides, "I'm very German. I like German culture, German music, German philosophy; and the origins of the Visconti family are in Germany." True, this great Milanese family rose to power during one of the barbarian invasions, though after some seven centuries of residence in Lombardy, thinking oneself German is something of a reach. Visconti gave the film a German title, *Götterdämmerung* (literally, Twilight of the Gods, after the closing work of Wagner's *Ring*), though in Italy it was released as *La Caduta degli Dei*, The Fall of the Gods.*

Many thought Visconti chose his subject out of a longing to make the most decadent movie ever seen, a kind of operatic cinema in praise of the most depraved aspects of the many liberations and revolutions of the 1960s. "If the picture were speeded up a trifle," Pauline Kael suggested, "it could be a camp horror film." *The Damned* has transvestism, child molestation, incest, rape, a gay orgy, and plenty of murder, filmed in shades of runny-mascara black and full-moon yellow and kept obscure, opaque, in menorah lighting that turns the cast into ghosts. Ingrid Thulin is frequently filmed nude in bed, her skin like chalk and her eyes like rutting Easter eggs. Dirk Bogarde, her adulterous lover, moves like someone at the bottom of a swimming pool filled with peanut butter (extra crunchy, the health kind where the oil flows to the top). And Helmut Berger, Thulin's loving-hating son, is a new comic-book hero, Wormboy the Nazi. Everyone looks repulsive till the climactic massacre of the SA at the resort of Bad Wiessee, where lean young warriors party in drag with dissipated veterans, and the focus suddenly runs from the high-resolution colors of the von Essenbecks to soft-tech photography. The "Visconti waiter" figure had haunted the edges of his cinema almost from the beginning: handsome, quiet, butch-suave, an extra whom Visconti had beckoned out of the crowd for a moment, unimportant but something to see. In a kind of pun on his "Twilight of the Gods" theme, Visconti now kills off a troop of them; and there is an awful, beautiful scene, on

---

*For some reason, Visconti avoided using the traditional (and literal) Italian translation of Wagner's title, *Il Crepusculo degli Dei*. The renovated title, so near yet so far, makes for a lousy symmetry.

a terrace overlooking a lake, where two of these figures idle in the moonlight and stand, and hear, steadily growing, the sound of the motorboats drawing the SS to the hotel to ban the SA from further history.

A kind of sex nausea, a disgusted adoration of sensuality, troubles all of Visconti's final films, this one especially. In Visconti's art, decadence is used as a symptom of collapse. The best people are ascetic, limited. The worst people do everything. "Private morality is dead," says one of the damned. "We are an elite society to whom everything is permitted."* Apocalypse now. This is the decade's most intense Bad Father film, the most expansive condemnation of the older men who make wars that younger men fight, for where American films like *Splendor in the Grass* and *The Manchurian Candidate* concentrated on authoritarian individuals, *The Damned* reviles an authoritarian system. It is a culminating work, then, less the majestic freak show that it was thought to be than an implied call to revolution. From the anti-Studio rebellion of Hollywood's self-liberating artisans we arrive at a massive, historicistic rebellion, mannered and lurid, fascinated by its own repulsion—yet rebellious all the same.

The Damned was a tremendous success, the one genuine commercial blockbuster of Visconti's career. He had always been thought of as one of the least popular of the great European directors, complicating *Ossessione* (his version of James M. Caine's *The Postman Always Rings Twice*) with homosexuality, filming *La Terra Trema* in an unfathomable Sicilian dialect, drawing even the brilliant *Rocco and His Brothers* out to such lengths that the original, nearly three hours long, was slashed to little more than half that and still has its longueurs. But then the 1960s saw a breakdown in American resistance to the foreignness of foreign film—the language barrier, the snob cachet, the puzzling mores, the heavy class-consciousness. In 1960, the only way *Seven Samurai* could go over big here was in its Americanized remake as *The Magnificent Seven*. But the flash success of

---

*The line anticipates a very similar one in Pier Paolo Pasolini's *Salò* (1975), which treats sexual sadism rather as Visconti did, as a metaphor for totalitarianism. Where Visconti follows the moral meltdown of a family, Pasolini looks in on four Fascist chieftains who kidnap two dozen children to test the limits of savagery by improvising torments and terrible deaths for them. Both directors agree that where power is absolute, savagery has no limits, though, except for the SA purge, Visconti's decadence is all bedrooms and parties and the loving, almost hypnotized filming of the setting down of place cards for a birthday banquet, while Pasolini's is the most punishing terror ever put on screen.

Helmut Berger in *The Damned*. What a redolent sixties image! Consider the history-is-show-biz aspect (louche cabaret directly leads to operas by Hindemith, then apocalypse). Consider the current-events correspondence (end of Nazi era directly relates to end of sixties era). Or consider my Aunt Agnes's theory ("What would Marlene Dietrich say about that transvesto in the chair?").

films like *La Dolce Vita, Tom Jones, A Man and a Woman,* and *A Fistful of Dollars*; the polyglot casts of the big epics like *The Fall of the Roman Empire* and *The Longest Day*; and especially the rise of the big British stars and big British pictures like *Lawrence of Arabia* all acculturated foreign film.

In fact, by the late 1960s, foreign film was no longer entirely foreign, for the decade had introduced the international co-production—*The Damned,* for example, was produced by Italnoleggio and Warner Brothers, and came out here not a year or two after the Italian premiere (as would have been usual in the 1950s and early 1960s) but within a month of it. So: *Foreign film has been emplanted on the all-American moviegoing scene*—even foreign film that does those foreign things like guys dressing in women's clothes and raping their mothers.

Of course, the main reason why foreign film became better acculturated in the United States was its sophistication, the worldly outlook and technical daring. In the mid-1950s, a comparison of the standard

Hollywood product and anything by Visconti, Bergman, or Buñuel would
have exposed American naïveté and hypocrisy, not to mention the quack
feeling of the doctored studio "reality"—those absurdly neat streets and
avid meadows and sublime parlors. New Cinema made Hollywood contemporary, competitive, state-of-the-art. In the Studio Age, you usually
knew what to expect from a movie by its stars, (sometimes) its director,
its studio, and perhaps a line or two of PR rhapsody ("Waiting—always
waiting—in the shadows of the back streets . . . longing for the man
she loves . . . asking nothing, receiving nothing—yet content to sacrifice
all for him. WHY?")* In the 1960s, most of the important films defy the
clichés and cautions. Who was ready for *Psycho,* Hitchcock experts included? Who could have foretold what *Dr. Strangelove* would be like, given
Stanley Kubrick's unpredictability, the polymorphous casting (Peter Sellers
and George C. Scott in the same work?), and the oxymoronic production
of a comedy about apocalypse? Look how unprepared even professional
moviegoers were for *Bonnie and Clyde,* the exploitation film as art.

So Sam Peckinpah's *The Wild Bunch* is, in its way, and even today,
twenty years after its release, a most surprising film. It shouldn't be,
perhaps: Peckinpah is known for westerns, and carnage uncurbed, and an
honor-among-thieves philosophy, and all this *The Wild Bunch* embodies.
Its cast is expectable: William Holden, Ernest Borgnine, Warren Oates,
and Ben Johnson as the leaders of the outlaw Bunch, Jaime Sanchez as a
Mexican freedom-fighter who rides with them, Robert Ryan as the pursuing adversary, and Emilio Fernandez as a Mexican general hunting Pan-
cho Villa. The heist-and-chase plot frame is generical. It's all desperadoes,
horses, guns, dynamite, and local color, from the hymn-singing Temperance League north of the Texas-Mexico border to the bordello señoritas
south of it.

Yet *The Wild Bunch* is an astonishingly unique film virtually frame
by frame, Peckinpah's masterpiece and, as aficionados are gradually learning, one of the masterpieces of American cinema. It's controversial, divisive in the sixties manner. Men like it, but few women do. Youngsters
delight in it, and oldsters shudder. Conservatives don't understand it;
freethinking liberals enjoy it guiltily. Western buffs resent it for forcing
the traditions inside out, while people who don't like westerns are in-

---

*Especially when the man she loves to long for is John Boles, though the
posters identify him as the "leading man of *Seed*"; I didn't think he had it in him.
She is Irene Dunne, in *Back Street.*

trigued. And of course there's the violence, far more than the roughest movies present, a more elated violence than even *Point Blank,* a more lyrical violence than the death of Bonnie and Clyde, a festival of violence. In other westerns, people get shot and fall down. In *The Wild Bunch,* people get shot and blood glops out of them and they scream. They don't just die; they get destroyed.

As early as in the titles, just before Peckinpah's name appears, Wild Bunch leader Holden, about to launch a bank robbery, tells his men, "If they move, *kill* 'em!" It could be the movie's motto. Under the rolling credits we have seen Peckinpah marshaling his forces for an opening set piece of unparalleled mayhem: a group of children setting two scorpions onto a horde of red ants and giggling at the scorpions' torment; the Bunch taking position, their characters ranging from the grimly ruthless to the downright psychotic; Ryan's gang of bounty hunters, their characters no better than those of the Bunch, except Holden's men for the most part seem to know what they're doing; and the band of Temperance agitators, whom Peckinpah gleefully sends right into the middle of the killing zone, singing, "We Shall Gather at the River."

It's the River Styx, for immediately guns go off everywhere and everybody's shooting at everybody else, and the Temperance folk are caught in the center of it, and the blood is flying like pop-bottle tops after a good shaking, and Peckinpah takes his time getting it all in, something like a hundred camera setups. Like scorpions to wanton boys are we to Peckinpah. If they move, *kill* em!

There is no question that it was the 1960s, from *Psycho* to *The Wild Bunch,* that developed realism of murder. Maybe its time had simply come, as with sound in the late 1920s or three-strip Technicolor in the early 1930s. Maybe it was another example of New Cinema's push toward authenticity of representation. But the 1960s was a violent age generally, not only an age of assassinations but a time when television began presenting real-life death, from Jack Ruby's shooting of Lee Harvey Oswald through Vietnam battle casualties to Brigadier General Nguyen Ngoc Loan's summary execution of a Vietcong man on the streets of Saigon. With so much killing on view, the movies had to work harder to compete, to stay larger than life.

So Peckinpah doesn't film mere shootouts; he holds massacres. But then, like so many sixties movies dealing with lawlessness, *The Wild Bunch* refuses to give us clarity of righteousness. Like *One-Eyed Jacks,* this

The Wild Bunch: one of Peckinpah's more tender moments. The villainous
Mexican general (Emilio Fernandez, standing in car) has been dragging
Jaime Sanchez behind the automobile. We've caught them on break.
The car, novel technology in 1913 Mexico, underlines the theme of
timechange, of epochal evolution, that haunts sixties cinema. The era
is giving out . . . as we look on.

is a western about the bad guys.. Of course, casting William Holden as
their chief gives us a clarity of glamour. And counting idealistic little
Jaime Sanchez among their members gives us a clarity of politics: if the
Bunch is bad, at least it is indirectly aiding a good cause.

And there is clarity of expertise, for one thing that Peckinpah admires is a man who can do his job, quick, trim, and true. This distin-
guishes the Bunch from Ryan's jokers, as immoral as the Bunch (if
temporarily on the side of the law) but at best ineffective and at times
mindlessly destructive. As Ryan's men catch up with the Bunch at the
bridge to Mexico and freedom, American law forces ride up to assist
Ryan—and, in a very Peckinpavian sequence, Ryan's idiots unthinkingly
turn and fire at them. If they move, *kill* 'em! Or, as Ryan puts it, "We're
after *men*—and I wish to God I was with them!"

So we do have a side to root for—at least, a side to prefer to other sides. But when the Bunch has finally outrun Ryan's gang and discovered that the bank haul is nothing but bags of slugs, the Bunch agrees to hijack an American arms shipment for the vile, oppressive Mapache, Jaime Sanchez's mortal enemy. Hiding out in Sanchez's village, the Bunch find devastation and despair, for Mapache's men have overrun the place, killing the men and stealing food and horses. Holden asks the villagers why the federal troops didn't protect them, and an old man replies, "Those *were* federal troops!"

Now we have lost our clarity. Robbing a bank is bad enough, but provisioning a warlord is the nth of corruption. In an age that has learned that there are different kinds of history to be made, this is contributing to evil history. Peckinpah even drags in a few pre-Nazi Germans on Mapache's side to emphasize the moral coloring of the people the Bunch is now working for. At least our villain heroes are aware of the ethical choice they are making. When Ernest Borgnine expresses disgust for Ryan—formerly a member of the Bunch—Holden sees the other side of things:

> HOLDEN   He gave his word.
>
> BORGNINE
> (*contemptuously*)   To a railroad!
>
> HOLDEN   It's still his *word!*
>
> BORGNINE   That ain't what counts! It's *who* you give it *to!**

Even among the lawless, one observes a concept of the honorable and the disgraceful alliance. This conflict sets up the tragedy—for *The Wild Bunch,* though too lively and colorful to be Another of Those Depressing Sixties Movies, is certainly another one that closes sadly. The Bunch has given its word to Mapache—not only a vicious oppressor but a jerk, which we learn when he greets the arrival of his new Gatling gun by personally testing it in a town square, sending a hail of bullets all over the place as the population dives for cover. Peckinpah doesn't like vicious oppressors but he *loathes* jerks. This is the creature the Bunch has bargained with? It can only redeem itself through heroism to the death.

---

*Peckinpah is never mentioned as an actor's director, but the usually ridiculous Borgnine is, frankly, magnificent throughout the film, and the other leads are similarly at their best. Students: Any takers on a monograph?

Mapache had taken Sanchez prisoner for appropriating one crate of the hijacked rifles for his beleaguered village, and now the central quartet of the Bunch—Holden, Borgnine, Warren Oates, and Ben Johnson—offers to buy Sanchez from Mapache. The monster general, who has been torturing Sanchez, agrees. As he hands the boy over, Mapache slits his throat.

Now, consider. The four Americans are in a Mexican town, surrounded by hundreds of hostile townspeople and Mapache's army. The four are going to kill Mapache, but then everyone else will kill them. There's a wonderful Peckinpavian *Luftpause* just then—not because our boys have any doubts about what they're going to do, but because timing is style and they want to get it just right. And the right time comes, and they move.

The battle that follows is ultimate sixties—politically, in the Bunch's defiance of unentitled authority; personally, because Peckinpah has brought us over to admiring felons, seeing them on their terms, as heroes; technically, in the devastating realism Peckinpah exploits, as when a woman shoots Holden in the back and he whirls, shouts "Bitch!" and kills her. Like *Cool Hand Luke*, the movie tries to back up on the death of people we like by flashing shots of each member of the Bunch, grinning and chuckling in happier days (the result, one presumes, of resentful advance-screening reactions), but the film is tragic and the Bunch is killed. They moved.

Despite the helpful publicity of a controversy, based on some critics' revulsion at the heavy body count and the use of women exclusively as whores, *The Wild Bunch* was not generally regarded as one of the era's climactic (or even important) films. Of immediately coeval titles, *Easy Rider* seemed more accessibly epochal, *Alice's Restaurant* more chummily countercultural, *Medium Cool* bolder, *They Shoot Horses, Don't They?* more responsible, and *Midnight Cowboy* more artistic. Unfortunately, *The Wild Bunch* was crippled by sixteen minutes of cuts, deducting some of the violence and much of the flashback sequences that explain who the Bunch are and how former Buncher Ryan has come to be playing on the other side of the table from them. Sixteen minutes may seem less than crucial in a two-and-a-half-hour movie, but Peckinpah's final cut was already stripped to the bone, so the battles lose their rhythmic elegance and the relationships their logic.*

*The video print now available restores the missing scenes.

Was the film scissored to tone it down or to make it less expansive, more immediately intelligible?—for it is a complex piece, based more on how the principals regard each other than on what they actually do. The 1960s, especially the late 1960s, had come to delight in the playfulness of film, the confounding intellectualism of the visual, the high-concept elaboration of the movies' technical resources—the sheer prowess of a High Maestro at work, not just telling his story but showing it. By 1969, the audience, or perhaps just conservative elements in the industry, seemed to be pulling back—and by the early 1970s, as we've noticed, the High Maestro approach was in decline. "Too much sixties and not enough story" was how Andy Warhol described films of this kind; they were, above all, contemporary, but they weren't universally enjoyable the way *It Happened One Night* and *Casablanca* and *All About Eve,* equally contemporary in other times, were enjoyable. From now on: *There must be less "direction" and more narrative,* because the 1960s has peaked. The big films of the following decades will have less seventies or eighties in them but lots of story: *The Godfather, Klute, Chinatown, Jaws, The Exorcist, All the President's Men, Close Encounters of the Third Kind, Alien, Ragtime, Reds*; the *Star Wars, Superman,* and *Indiana Jones* series. The outstanding exception, *The Big Chill*—conversational rather than narrative and distinctly contemporary— is, typically, about looking back to the 1960s.

In fact, the 1960s seems to have been working toward its own apocalypse all along, in many a film about the passing of an age, the end of a type, the death of valuable attitudes. *The Wild Bunch* is the fourth western in this chapter, fourth of major westerns in a single year—yet this was virtually the last year of the western as a viable Hollywood form. From *Ride the High Country, The Misfits,* and *What Ever Happened to Baby Jane?* on to *Camelot, Butch Cassidy,* and *The Damned,* we keep learning that time is outlawing tradition. The age has scarcely implanted itself before it's over. What a long journey it was from *Psycho*'s Phoenix hotel room to *The Wild Bunch*'s last stand: from anti-Studio revolt to anti-authoritarian politics, from genres in black and white to a most colorful elaboration, from heroes to monsters. Yet it ends suddenly. "That's what I can't get used to," said Marilyn Monroe. "Everything keeps changing." *Blink!* and the era is over.

INDEX

A

Adams, Nick, illus. 96
Adler, Renata, 184, 202–3, 211, 243
Advise and Consent, 38–9, 43, 115, 216
Agee, James, 176
Alamo, The, 109, 112
Albee, Edward, 43
Aldrich, Robert, 88, 90
Alice's Restaurant, 286
Allen, Dede, 188
Allen, Woody, 153
All Fall Down, 56, 81, 126, 127
All the Way Home, 132
Alpert, Hollis, 184
Amarcord, 193
America, America, 115
America, Paul, 245, 246
Americanization of Emily, The, 41–2, illus. 42, 115
Anderson, Lindsay, 162–3
Andrews, Dana, 127 *n.*
Andrews, Julie, 41–2, 205, 206
Angels Die Hard!, illus. 230
Anger, Kenneth, 242, 243
Anne of the Thousand Days, 259
Ann-Margret, illus. 16, 101, 102, 104, 106, 126–7, 252
Antonioni, Michelangelo, 181
Apartment, The, 45, 55, 58, 71–2, 92, 115, 172

Arkin, Alan, 168
Arkoff, Samuel Z., 222
Arnold, Edward, 60, 66, 122
Around the World in Eighty Days, 109, 111
Arthur, Jean, 31, 129
Asher, William, 104
Ashley, Elizabeth, 120
Astaire, Fred, 69, 104–5, 106, 181, 202, 203, 204, 260 *n.*, 261
Astor, Mary, 90
Attenborough, Richard, 64
Aulin, Ewa, 214
Avalon, Frankie, 104–5
Axelrod, George, 21–2, 23, 26, 153, 169, 186
Ayres, Lew, 39
Aznavour, Charles, 214

B

Baby Doll, 23, 33
Bacall, Lauren, 99
Bacharach, Burt, 270
Baker, Carroll, 111
Ballad of a Soldier, 34
Bancroft, Anne, 180, illus. 183, 251
Bara, Theda, 55
Barbarella, 154–5, 237
Barefoot in the Park, 55, 56, 148, 277

N

A NOTE ON THE TYPE

This book was set in a digitized version of a typeface called Garamond. Jean Janson has been identified as the designer of this face, which is based on Garamond's original models but is much lighter and more open. The italic is taken from a font of Granjon, which appeared in the repertory of the Imprimerie Royale and was probably cut in the middle of the sixteenth century.

Composed by the Brevis Press, Bethany, Connecticut

Printed and bound by Halliday Lithographers,
West Hanover, Massachusetts

Designed by Anthea Lingeman